Finding the Fountain of Youth Inside Yourself

Shad Helmstetter

POCKET BOOKS

New York   London   Toronto   Sydney   Tokyo   Singapore

POCKET BOOKS, a division of Simon & Schuster Inc.
1230 Avenue of the Americas, New York, NY 10020

ISBN: 0-671-74620-0

First Pocket Books paperback printing December 1991

10 9 8 7 6 5 4 3 2 1

POCKET and colophon are registered trademarks of
Simon & Schuster Inc.

DESIGN: Stanley S. Drate/Folio Graphics Co. Inc.

Front cover design by Andrew Newman

Printed in the U.S.A.

*This book is dedicated with love and affection
to my parents, my children and
my grandchildren*

CONTENTS

CONTENTS

PART

III

A TREASURE MAP TO THE FOUNTAIN OF YOUTH

PART

I

THE

MAGIC

GLASSES

1

•

THE BOY WHO FOUND THE
MAGIC GLASSES

•

"May you find your INNER YOUTH,
and may you let it live
every magic moment you have
in the future that awaits you.

If you want to live while you are here
then go ahead. Live."

Clyde William was nine years old when his parents
moved to the old house in the country. The new home
was within commuting distance of the city, but the
home itself and everything around it was in the country. Clyde had never lived in a house like this before.
It was an old two-story Victorian house with an attic.
For the first time in his life, Clyde had room to play,
room to run, and places to explore.

Clyde and his family moved into the big old house
on a Saturday. Left to his own resources while his

parents busily opened the cardboard boxes that the movers had stacked in neat rows in the rooms down below, Clyde decided to explore the upper stories of the old house and find for himself any secrets it might hold.

In all his nine years, he had never found anything as compelling and as adventuresome as the mysterious attic of his new home, so he naturally decided to begin his adventure by exploring that attic.

The door to the attic stood silently at the top of a narrow, steep stairway at the end of the second-floor hallway. The rest of the house had been cleaned and scrubbed, but the top of the stairway was covered with dust and cobwebs. Clyde could tell that the attic door had not been opened for years.

When he first opened the door at the top of the stairs, it was too dark for Clyde to see much of anything at all. But as his eyes slowly adjusted to the small amount of light that came through the windows on either end of the attic, he was able to see a vast expanse of dust-covered clutter.

There were pieces of old furniture, old chests of drawers, and boxes and containers filled with long-forgotten toys and books. There were other boxes filled with accounting ledgers and boxes that held hammers and saws and gardening tools. There were old iron coat racks of clothing, faded and dust-covered, from an era long since past.

Stepping into that attic on that Saturday afternoon, it was as though Clyde were stepping into a different time—as though he were stepping into the twilight of a distant past. At the time he could never have imagined that what he would find in that attic would change his life forever.

The waning sun filtering through the attic windows gave off just enough light to make everything seem different. The faint rays of sunlight were filled with motes of dust that made the room feel ancient, as though it had been locked away in a time capsule, unchanged over the years.

And to the mind of this adventurous nine-year-old, that attic held the promise of untold treasures waiting to be found.

As his eyes surveyed the opportunities in front of him, his attention was caught by an old rolltop desk tucked away in a corner at the far end of the attic next to one of the small windows. Its tambour cover was closed and covered with dust. It was that old desk that drew his attention the most. And it was that desk which held the secret.

Carefully stepping over the boxes and clutter, Clyde found himself standing in front of the desk. When he nudged the roll top that covered the writing portion of the desk, it resisted at first and then gave way, rolling up on its tracks and flinging a snow of dust into the air.

There in front of him were revealed several cubbyholes, a tattered leather pad for writing on, a worn receptacle for a bottle of ink, and small drawers, their contents unknown. In the cubbyholes and on the desk were old papers, letters, and documents.

The old yellowed papers that had most certainly been important at one time now lay forgotten and unimportant. There were letters in trays stamped with dates from years long in the past. There was even a recipe book that stood among the papers; its recipes could not have been used for at least a generation or two. It was as though for whoever had lived there in the past, their lives at some moment had been stopped in time.

Everything Clyde saw was old. Everything he saw

was from a different time than his own. He was curious enough to want to look at everything at once.

But of the greatest curiosity to young Clyde was one letter-size drawer with a brass keyhole in the middle of it. Try as he might, Clyde could not get the drawer to open; it was locked. And just as he began to look for the key that would open the small drawer, he heard his mother calling, "Clyde William! You come on down now and unpack your things!"

It was not until the following Monday afternoon that Clyde was able once again to venture up the steps into the attic. This time he was armed with a flashlight to search for the key that would open the drawer in the old rolltop desk.

He searched everywhere—in every cubbyhole, every drawer, and every space he could find. Ignoring the importance of the antiquity of the desk itself, Clyde even tried using a screwdriver to pry the drawer open—but he was unsuccessful.

It was almost without hope that Clyde finally ran his hand along the top of the dust-covered rafter above the desk, straining up onto his toes to be able to reach it. But it was there on the rafter that he found the small brass key he had searched for so diligently.

With a pounding heart he fit the key into the lock of the small drawer, thinking that it must certainly hold something very special.

Although Clyde was only nine years old when he opened the locked drawer in the rolltop desk, he would never forget what happened next. It was as though all of the sunlight that had filtered into the attic somehow streamed out in brilliant rays from the drawer itself. Just for a moment, when he turned the key in the lock and opened the drawer, Clyde was blinded by the brightest light he had ever seen!

It was such a dazzling light that it startled him,

and he jumped back. He closed and opened his eyes to make sure that he could actually believe what he was seeing. And when the light faded, he saw for the first time what the drawer contained.

When Clyde first looked at what he saw in the drawer, it appeared to be nothing important at all. Even though part of him knew that only moments earlier the drawer had been filled with shimmering white light, what he saw in front of him now was nothing more than an old pair of wire-framed glasses and a thin leather-bound book covered with the dust of time.

He had, of course, no idea of the importance of what he had found. And he had absolutely no idea of the effect his discovery was about to have on his life. But as any boy of nine would do, he picked the glasses up, softly blew the thin layer of dust off them, and put them on.

There was no way he could have been prepared for what he would see when he put the glasses on. In the moment he put them on, *everything changed!* Everything looked different. Colors, sizes, shapes, meanings, perspectives—everything changed in an instant when he looked through the glasses for the first time. And in almost the same instant, Clyde tore the glasses off.

When he took them off, everything once again returned to normal. The second time he put the glasses on, he put them on slowly, more carefully. And once again, in an instant, everything changed. Nothing was the way it had appeared before he put them on. And once again Clyde quickly pulled them off.

It was at that moment that he heard his mother call him downstairs for dinner. So he placed the glasses safely in his shirt pocket, closed the drawer which still held the old leather-bound book, turned the key in the lock, tucked the key in the pocket of his jeans, slid the dusty top of the desk back into its closed position, and left the attic.

He had had enough adventure for the moment, but he would be back. He had the glasses with him, but he could not wait to learn what secrets the dusty old book might hold.

What could have gone from idle interest to a forgotten afternoon adventure changed forever when Clyde was sitting at the dinner table with his family that night. His seven-year-old brother Vern was pretending to be Abraham Lincoln from a play that his second-grade class was doing at school, when Clyde interrupted his brother and said, "Well, you may be Abraham Lincoln, but *I'm* Teddy Roosevelt!" And saying that, Clyde pulled the old wire-framed glasses from his pocket and put them on.

If not for everyone else, for Clyde the whole world changed in an instant. What had been the family he knew was replaced by a family he had never before seen or known. When he looked at his father, whom Clyde knew to be a very successful mechanical engineer, he saw at the head of the table a boy of about his own age, who was pretending to be big and strong but who was instead small and worried.

When Clyde turned to look at his mother, who was a confident vice president of a marketing company, he saw instead a girl of about eighteen, who looked worried and upset by the events of the day she had just gone through at the office. She didn't look anything like his mother at all!

Clyde's reaction was to grab the glasses and almost throw them off. He heard his mother saying, "Clyde William, are you all right?" And before anyone could notice, he stuffed the glasses back into his pocket. There was something very strange about these

8

glasses! Every time he put them on, Clyde's whole world looked completely different.

It was later that same night that he made his way once more up the steep attic steps. By now he had decided that he absolutely *must* examine the old, tattered book that rested in the small drawer where he had found the strange glasses that made everything look different.

By the light of his small flashlight, Clyde opened the desk, unlocked the drawer, and carefully removed the book. Printed in faded gilt letters on its cover was its title: *The Fountain of Youth*. Opening the cover, Clyde could see that it must have been written by an older, wiser person than anyone he knew, for the words in the book were very wise—and written in an elegant copperplate script that was not taught in school.

On the first page of the book were written these words:

> If you have found this book, you have also discovered a pair of spectacles. You may have even put them on already. Before you wear them again, there are some things you need to know about these spectacles.
>
> These are magic glasses. They are unique and special. Through these glasses you will see life and everything in it differently. This is why: *Through these glasses you can see only the truth.*

What followed were instructions for wearing the magic glasses:

> 1. Through these glasses you will see only the truth. You will not be able to see opinions, prejudices, or beliefs; you will see only the truth.

2. Of all those who might like to see the truths of life, there are only a few who are prepared to accept the truth when they see it.

3. Before you put these glasses on, know this: Almost *nothing* will be as you thought it to be.

4. When you wear these glasses, because you will see all truth, be tolerant of others. Be understanding. Most of the people you will meet are neither ready nor willing to see the truths that these glasses will show you.

5. If you decide now to wear these magic glasses, you will never again, even if you try, see things as you used to see them. What you see will always be a part of you. If, knowing this, you want to see truth, always remember these words: Truth is not an armor that is easily worn.

6. When you are finished with the magic glasses, return them here.

Fascinated, Clyde turned to the next page of the old book and read again the title, *The Fountain of Youth,* followed by the words: *A Handbook of Lessons for Living, Written by One Who Wore the Magic Glasses for a Lifetime.*

Clyde William held in his hands what he knew, even at his young age, could be the secret to *life!* "What if I could know the truth about everything?" he thought. "What if I could see everything the way it really is? Wow!" It was an exciting concept. And so, as days and weeks and months went by, Clyde began to wear the magic glasses.

What a different world he saw when he put the glasses on! He would watch the evening news without glasses, then put them on—and what he saw the second time was nearly always different. Everything from a presidential address to a local news report changed somehow. And the words spoken in an election campaign were dramatically altered.

Clyde also took the magic glasses with him to school. When he put them on in the classroom, he learned that everything he was being taught was not quite the way it was when he put the glasses on.

Most of what his teachers were teaching him as "truth" was partially true—but only *partially* true. One day in class Clyde read a chapter out of his history book and then read the same chapter again with the magic glasses on. It was not the same chapter at all. The magic glasses of truth changed even the truth of history he had so long been taught to believe.

In the supermarket the woman who yelled at her little son and told him he was stupid didn't look the same at all when Clyde looked at the same woman through the glasses. Instead of seeing her as being callous and hurtful, he now saw the woman in the supermarket as being frightened and insecure.

Clyde began to notice how people around him saw things the way they thought them to be. But looking through the magic glasses of truth, Clyde saw everything as it really was.

It may have been the glasses that helped Clyde see the world differently, but it was the old book called *The Fountain of Youth* that helped him figure it out. For during the same days and weeks and months he wore the glasses, he also read and reread and thought about the lessons he found between the book's tattered covers.

Even as he was reading the words, Clyde recognized that he had never read a book anything like this one. Although it was a thin book, its pages were filled with wonderment, profound ideas, and lessons for living. Everything he read in that old book made him think; the book was filled with questions, and with remarkably inspirational answers. In the pages Clyde read were revealed the myths that people live by, and the truths that could set them free.

As Clyde turned the thin, yellowed pages, what unfolded in front of him was a series of enlightening discoveries; each discovery was important by itself, but together they made a new kind of sense. Together they created a picture of the most abundant life that anyone could ever live. The kind of life he read about in the book was a lot different from the kind of lives that Clyde knew anything about.

It was later that he would recognize that the words in the book were so simple, and the truths it taught were so clear, they could be understood and used by a boy of nine or a man of ninety. And it was the words that were written in that old book that he would remember and live by for the rest of his life.

Wearing the Magic Glasses for Yourself

In the chapters that follow, you will find some of the words Clyde read in the old book, and the lessons he learned from reading the words. They are not fiction. They are a practical and realistic look at our lives. They will take us a step away from the day-to-day and give us a chance to see our lives a little differently.

As you read the following pages, you will have the opportunity (as Clyde did) to wear the magic glasses of truth for yourself—because the author of the book was wearing them when he wrote it. And all the truths written in the old book are included here in one form or another.

The most memorable lessons have been reproduced in this book in their original, beautifully written words. The first of these lessons is one that Clyde would never forget. It reads as follows:

If you seek the truth, you will find it.

When you find that truth, you give yourself a second chance at *living*.

2

•

GIVING YOURSELF A SECOND CHANCE

•

*"If you could do it over again,
and live your life differently,
what would you do?"*

What a different world we would see if we could only put those magic glasses on for ourselves! Imagine the differences you might find in what you saw. Would things really be as they had seemed to be? I doubt that much of anything would be the same at all.

In the story, Clyde took the magic glasses off at first because what he saw through them was over-whelming. He literally saw everything at once in a whole new way. That would be too much for anyone! But in our journey now, as we put the glasses on for ourselves, we are able to be more selective. We can look at just those things we want to see, and we can put the glasses on and take them off again any time we choose.

Just for a moment, put on the magic glasses and take a look at your life. If you could do it all over again, if you could live your life differently, what would you do? Or if you could live just the last ten years, or even the last five over again, would you do anything differently this time around?

I suppose there are some people who, if they had their lives to live again, would plan to do nothing differently at all. But if those people do exist, I haven't met them yet. Most of us, if we could—if we were given another chance to live a lifetime, or ten years, or five—would do things differently.

If we had that second chance, is there any reason to believe we would get it right this time? What assurance would we have that things would go any better for us if we had a second chance, or a *new* chance, to do things differently? After all, we are still the same individuals now that we were yesterday. We still do things the same way, think the same way, and we still see the world pretty much the same way today as we saw the world yesterday.

Would you do things differently, act differently, handle problems differently tomorrow if you were suddenly given a second chance for a better life? If you said to yourself right now, "Tomorrow things are going to be different. Beginning tomorrow, things are going to be better for me," would you be able to believe that beginning tomorrow, things really *would* be better?

Most of us, if we were given that chance, would make just as many mistakes the second time around as the first. Why do I say that? Because if, five years from now, we were to ask ourselves the question, "If I had the last five years to do over again, would I do things differently?" the answer to the question would be the same then as it is today. Five years from now we would still like to go back and do things differently.

That means that unless something changes *within* us—how we view life, and thereby how we do things—we will probably live out the *next* five years, or ten, or more, in much the same way as we have lived out the years that have already passed.

It seems the problem, then, is not whether or not we get that second chance (if we're still here, we've still got second chances left)—the real problem lies in what we will do with the second chances that are in *front* of us. We may have learned from our mistakes in the past, and we may even avoid making some of them again in the future, but there are other mistakes that just seem to be waiting for us to make them.

That isn't negative thinking or the sign of a defeatist attitude; it's simply a fact. Unless we do something genuinely *different* this time, we could find ourselves once again, a year from now or five or ten, wishing that we had a second chance and that we could do it all over again.

In this book we are going to discover that we *do* have a second chance. But more important, we are going to uncover the truth about why, when we want so badly to succeed, we all too often fail. We'll discover what stops us, what holds us back, and what we can do about it.

And we're going to learn about something called "Inner Youth" and what the finding and nurturing of that Inner Youth can do for us for the rest of our lives. There is an energy, a "spirit of vitality" that lives within each of us—or tries to. Some people aren't aware that they have an Inner Youth, or that it exists at all. Other people sense a little of it but don't know what to do to bring it to life—to bring *themselves* back to life. And along with the discovery (or rediscovery)

16

of your own Inner Youth, don't be surprised if you also discover a renewed spirit of adventure for living the life that is ahead of you.

Searching for the Truths

During the past few years I have followed a quest to find answers—truths—about *us*. My quest, and the discoveries I found along the way, led to the writing of several books in which I wrote what I found. In those books I told about how the human brain and the subconscious mind get programmed, and how we act out those programs. I wrote about what we call "Self-Talk," and how individuals can use it to change or override old programs—how to consciously and simply create new programs that would help us live in a better way.

I had spent years finding and fine-tuning the human behavior breakthrough of Self-Talk. Eventually, I saw Self-Talk being taught and used in homes, businesses, churches, and even in hospitals and schools. As a behavioral researcher, I thought I would stop there.

But as I was to learn, my interest in the question *"Why do we do what we do—and how can we do it better?"* did *not* stop there.

In meeting with individuals from every walk of life, and in talking with countless interested people during years of lectures throughout the country, one final question came to me time and time again: Why is it, even when we know we are living out the lives that our programs set up for us, and even though we have now learned how to change those programs—why do we still find it so difficult to make life *really* work?

What brings us to the point that we find ourselves

17

saying, "If I had it to do over again, I'd sure do it differently this time"? Why do so many people feel so frustrated in their lives? Why do so many feel generally unfulfilled? Why do so many marriages fail? Why do we so often find our jobs—our work—so difficult?

Why do we sometimes fail so badly at the simplest tasks? Why are we so often frustrated or unhappy, when we *know* it ought to be better?

I suspected that if we could learn what stops us, we could then find ways to overcome that human inertia and find the means to replace the energy we spend *surviving* with the energy that would be so much better spent on *living*.

Another Secret to Discover

The notion kept tugging at my mind that there was yet another step—another secret—in our own discovery of ourselves. If we are born with so much potential in front of us, I wondered, then why do we *lose* so much of that potential as life goes on?

Instead of growing older, getting wiser, and learning to make everything work *better,* I saw around me countless people with lives that somehow fell short of that unlimited potential we see so clearly in the eyes of a newborn child.

I found myself living in the middle of the most successful human society we have ever known—a society filled with good, sincere, hardworking people who had no idea why marriages were failing, why masses of people including children and young people turned to drugs, why society at its best, with everything life had to offer, was ultimately *unfulfilling* for millions.

As I pointed out in my book, *What to Say When You Talk to Your Self,* we had already been given many solutions. We had gone through an era in which the rediscovery of individual potential became a popular pursuit. We lived through the "me" generation, and began to learn about the importance of "self-actualization." Each step of the way, the message became clearer: There is *more* to live in one lifetime than most of us are living.

The researchers and writers who had gone before me had given us a lot to chew on. There were many good books that gave us answers, told us how to live better, and encouraged us to do so. There were so many philosophies, so many leaders and thinkers who had told us their answers, that it seemed to me that by now we should have figured it out.

But it was clear to me that we were still missing something. So with a reasoning mind I continued to search. Having already found that it is the physiological programming process of the brain that had proved to be a good part of the answer, I began to study in earnest the questions, "What might be missing? We have learned so much, but could there be more—another secret that we have not yet discovered?"

I now know that there is an answer to those questions. And it is an answer that many of us must surely have known was there but never quite touched for ourselves. It is an answer that can create powerful and beneficial changes in our lives.

The answer I discovered you will find in the pages that follow. What I learned gave me more than inspiration; it offered a bright new perspective for our lives, and a renewed sense of hope for finding a way to make our lives work better.

You Can Find the Secret for Yourself

Had someone simply sat me down and told me, "Listen to me. This is the secret, and once I tell you, your life will be forever changed for the better," I would have made no discovery at all, and I doubt my life would have actually *changed* at all. *The secret that you find when you put on those magic glasses of very real "truth" can be found only by discovering the secret for yourself.* It is not hard to find—you have to know only where to look, and be willing to see the truth when you find it.

Instead of offering in this book the kind of "cure-all" solution that we find in so many so-called self-help books, in this book I suggest a different approach. It is an approach that summarizes what I have learned from more than a decade of work and discovery in the field of human potential.

To adequately share with you this discovery, I have to ask something of you. I have to ask, for the present—throughout the time you read this book—that you agree to "put on hold" any old "programs" of disbelief that you may have, believe with me that there *must* be a better way, and test for yourself the discoveries we will find together.

When we put on the glasses now, we do not find the confusion and bewilderment that so troubled young Clyde. Because we are prepared, we are able instead to see and to step into the real life that waits in front of us.

Imagine walking through the world with the glasses on, taking a journey through a few days or weeks of your life and seeing the world in a whole new way. If you do that, it could prove to be a remarkable journey!

And once we've worn the glasses of truth, though we can take them off and put them away again, I doubt we are ever quite the same. Some of what we learn will stay with us always. The things we learn can give a new sense of meaning and life to every day we have in front of us.

Let us begin by putting on the glasses of truth and seeing for ourselves what stands in the way.

3

•

THE MYTHS THAT SABOTAGE
OUR LIVES

•

*"We have learned to believe in the myths,
we have learned to live them,
and the myths have changed our lives."*

It is amazing what believing something is true when it *isn't* true can do to our lives. From the days of our earliest fears of the saber-toothed tiger being held at bay by mankind's campfires, we have lived with myths—beliefs that we thought so clearly to be true at the time when they were never true at all.

A Look at the Myths We Have Believed
in the Past

"Myth," as we are using it here, means something that we collectively *believe* to be "true," and because enough people believe it, we accept it as "truth."

People sometimes live their entire lifetimes without ever figuring out that a lot of what they thought was true really wasn't. Myths about our lives and about the world we live in have always been with us. And by now, of course, we've learned that some of those myths are just that—myths.

At one time most everyone thought that the world was flat. It was a worldwide mental program, a worldwide belief. It made no difference at all to the people who lived at that time that the world was round; they believed it was flat, and so they lived their lives as though it were flat.

Ancient mariners steered their ships away from the open sea, knowing for certain that if they ventured outward, they would sail off the edge of the earth. To those of us who are living today, that was a foolish notion, but to those who lived at that time, it was a "truth."

Those same well-meaning and often quite intelligent people from the past also thought at one time or another that the earth was the center of the universe, that they had to pray to the sun lest it would not rise again in the morning, and that illness was an evil spirit that invaded the body and could be driven out with chants and dances. It was a time when people believed in myths.

Later, as humankind became wiser and more aware, entire nations believed that comets foretold disaster, that kings were appointed by God, that "bleeding" patients and putting leeches on them was the high mark of medical science, and that there would never be a vehicle on the road that could move without being pushed by hand or pulled by horses. People then, too, believed in myths.

As unthinkable as it seems to us today, there were even times—not too long ago—that the greatest scientists of the land would go down in history as saying that the human voice would never be carried without wires, people would never fly, and that we could never fix a failing valve in a human heart.

The myths of humankind led our forbears to live lives of what we would consider almost unimaginable folly. There were times when patients who suffered from depression were locked away, and children who could not hear or speak but who could dance were given to circuses. Inventive individuals who suggested that steam could drive a train were derided and thought to be fools.

When the first human set foot on the moon, and the pictures of that glorious event were transmitted to our living rooms, there were still those who were convinced by the myth of their beliefs that it was all done on a Hollywood set and we had never gotten to the moon at all. As late as the second half of the twentieth century, there were those who said that communism would never end, and masses of people in Communist nations would never accept the truth of democracy; they said freedom could not work.

Motivational speakers, seeking to inspire the imagination of their audiences, have often told the story of how the United States patent office was almost closed at the turn of the twentieth century because, as it was said, "everything that could be invented already has been."

When we think we have it figured out, it's a good idea to look at the myths that so many others in the past believed in so strongly—when they, too, knew that they had "figured it out." They believed that:

- The world is flat.
- Dragons devoured ships at sea.
- Thunder is the sound of God's anger.

- Peasants are meant to be peasants; kings are meant to be kings.
- Famine is caused by disobedience.
- Children are born by miracle, not by conception.
- Women are weak; men are strong.
- An eclipse of the sun is a frightening message from the higher being.
- People with emotional disorders should be locked away.
- Spouses and marriage should be determined by parents.
- Man will never fly.
- Mankind will never reach the moon.
- Polio will never be cured.
- There are born losers and born winners.
- The automobile will never survive.
- We'll never be able to see inside the body without cutting it open.
- Children should be seen and not heard.
- Rock and roll will be here today and gone tomorrow.

Astounding, isn't it, what we have believed to be true. How much harm societies have created in the name of a myth that was thought to be true at the time. It's an almost unthinkable thought. They should have known better, but they didn't. They believed in myths.

It is important to recognize that the people who believed in myths had as much intelligence as we have. And yet they believed and fostered the myths. It was not their lack of intelligence that caused them to believe in the myths; it was the *programming* that formed their beliefs.

Because of the way that our "beliefs" are imprinted or recorded electrically and chemically in the brain, it is those programs that drive our lives. Our programs tell us who we are, what we *can* do and what we *can't* do, what we think about, how we perceive things, how we see the world around us, what we accept as truth or fact, what's important to us and what isn't, and literally thousands upon thousands of small but important beliefs about the world.

We live our lives based on what we believe about our lives. That is a profound thought. It is especially profound when you consider the fact that almost all of us live based on notions we were programmed to believe. These notions—those beliefs—not only *affect* us; they control most of what we do and most of what we think about anything.

Knowing that we are programmed to believe that what we believe is right, or true, or the best way, if we are thinking persons at all, we must suspect in some corner of our minds that at least part of what we believe to be true about ourselves and about life in general is probably not true; it is probably a myth.

If people have believed so many myths in the past, isn't it possible that we are still buying myths today and accepting them as truths? The truth is, not only do we *still* believe in myths today—we *live* by them!

What do you suppose the people who will live even fifty years from now will say about us and about what we believe today to be the absolute truth? They will look back in amazement at the myths that you and I are living with *right now*.

Some of the Myths We Believe In Today

If you were to put on the magic glasses of truth, even for a moment, for the singular purpose of discovering what some of our most cherished myths are, you might be astonished. Until we think about it, few of us ever recognize how many of life's truths—the truths that we *live by*—are not *true* at all.

When I began to search anew for an answer that would make all of our lives *better*, I also began to collect a list of the myths that *get in our way* and somehow, in the long run, tend to make our lives *worse*. These are just a few of the myths that make things more difficult for us instead of making things better.

Some of the myths on this list you have no doubt recognized as myths a long time ago. The more of them you recognize as myths, the more you've already been wearing your own pair of magic glasses.

At first glance some of them appear to be "truths." They are things we were told, things we were taught to believe. Within them there may be a truth or two, but most of them have very little truth in them at all. Here, then, from my collection of myths, are some of my favorites:

- There is a "they" out there who make things tough for us.
- People are *born* "leaders" or "followers."
- Having problems always creates character.
- There is always a right way or a wrong way to do anything.
- No pain, no gain.
- *Risk* is a negative word.
- You are measured by what you accomplish in life.
- Being first makes you better than being second.
- Nothing good ever lasts.
- You can't teach an old dog new tricks.
- If it comes too easily, it's not worth anything.
- What you think doesn't really count.

- It is best to always clean your plate.
- Younger people are more attractive than older people.
- The one who ends up with the most toys wins.
- There is no Santa Claus.
- There is never enough time in a day.
- Patience is always a virtue.
- Toys are only for children.
- Older parents still have the right to tell their grown children how to run their lives.
- Playgrounds and swing sets are only for children.
- People who daydream are wasting time.
- Money *can't* buy happiness.
- Money *can* buy happiness.
- Rich people are bad.
- Poor people are not as good as rich people.
- Ignorance is bliss.
- Opposites attract.
- Other people are better than you are.
- We're *supposed* to be the way someone wants us to be.
- It's not okay to be yourself.
- You're not good enough.
- Looking good means you have to look like someone else.
- People like you more when you do everything right.
- Some people are born creative; some people aren't.
- Things that cost more are better than things that cost less.
- You can never do enough.
- Other people have all the fun.
- Other people have fewer problems than we do.
- Democrats are good; Republicans are bad.

- Republicans are good; Democrats are bad.
- Some people have all the luck.
- They'll never cure the common cold.
- Some people have it and some people don't.
- Some people are lucky in life and unlucky at love.
- That's just the way it was "meant to be."

All the above are myths. Are some of them true some of the time? Yes, they are. But because they are true some of the time, we accept as "fact" that they must be true the rest of the time. Those are myths that we believe to be true while, in fact, they have value only now and then.

Why do we do it—why do we continue to believe the myths? We do it because that is the way we were raised; that is the way we were taught; that is the way we were programmed to believe.

The Future Disproves the Myths of Today

Time takes care of most of our myths for us. Time and experience eventually prove the myths false and get rid of them. I would not doubt for a moment that those who live after us will look back and see our lives quite differently from the way we see our lives now. There is no doubt that the generations to follow us will look back and see the myths we are living now just as clearly as we see the foolish myths of *our* ancestors.

You don't have to step too far into that enlightened world of the future to get a good picture of what our descendants will believe and think about us.

We still have telephone and electrical poles holding wires that hang over our streets. Will they be there in the future? No, they won't. Will television pictures come to us from a screen on the front of a clumsy box in our living room? No, they won't. The children of our future, without a doubt, will watch television in a true-to-life hologram of three-dimensional images with such sagas as the Civil War being fought in front of them as though they were participants in the battle.

Will doctors struggle with disease the same way they do today? To put a foot down and strongly declare, "They will never cure this," or "They will never cure that" would be foolish for any of us to say. Without a doubt, science and medicine will move on and we will somehow conquer most of the ills that plague us.

And in that world of the future it is also likely that those who live there will look back at us and see us as those beings who first began to uncover the myths of our own human behavior. But will we conquer the myths in our own lives now—or will we continue to live them out?

How to Recognize the Myths

In order to stop living out the myths that create difficulty in our lives, we must first learn to recognize the myths for what they are. How do you know what to question? How do you know where to start looking? If some of our beliefs are myths, and some of our beliefs are not, how do we find out which is which? The solution to those questions can be an adventure in itself. The answer is to start questioning. Start looking at everything around you. And don't just stop with what you see on the surface—look deeper than that. Remember, another word for myth is "untruth," and another word for untruth is "lie."

Whether you are talking to a friend, buying a car,

looking at yourself in the mirror, assessing your life, watching a commercial on television, listening to a speech, or thinking about your own beliefs about yourself, look for the myths and look for the truths.

Here is a list of questions that will help you determine what is a myth and what is a truth:

1. Does it really sound like the truth?
2. Is this something that I know I really ought to question?
3. Does my better judgment tell me I'm kidding myself?
4. Is buying into this perhaps nothing more than wishful thinking?
5. Do I have an uncomfortable feeling about this one?
6. Do I somehow "know better" deep down inside?
7. Do I suspect that I might be wrong?
8. Do I have to argue the point to be right about this, or is it really and clearly self-evident that what I believe is the truth?
9. Do the most sensible people I know agree with me or disagree with me on this point?
10. If I had a pair of magic glasses and put them on—and it were the last day of my life—what would I really think about this? *What would I tell someone else if it were the last thing I could say?*

Why Should We Look for the Myths in Our Lives?

If any of us ever makes a significant mistake in living, it is probably in the mistake we make of living with the myths. Because of the programming we received as we grew up, we accept many so-called "truths" when they are not truths at all! Somehow we come to believe that it is up to the others, who we think are more intelligent and capable than we are, to decide what is truth and what is myth.

The real reason to seek out the myths in our lives is that *by giving up the right to decide the truth for ourselves, we deliver control of our lives to someone else*.

It is an evident fact of social life that most of the leaders we have known controlled our societies almost entirely by their *might* and by their *myths*. We have labored in their fields, lost sons in their wars, toiled in their factories, voted them into office, believed in their truths, and "under-lived" our lives—and all because we were taught to believe in things that had no truth in them at all.

And so we have fought wars, won or lost them, accepted the rules of society because we "knew them to be true," and, as the poet first wrote it, "lived out our lives in quiet desperation."

The 10 Greatest Myths of All

There are many myths—false mental programs—that affect us, of course. A book that examined *all* of the myths which we live with today would be a book too lengthy for us to read! But some myths are more important than others.

In the many myths that I discovered, I was able in time to distill them down to a short list of the most powerful myths of all. These myths touch everyone—no one escapes them. Even if we see through them and outwit them ourselves, we are surrounded by others who continue to believe them as truths.

These are the myths that affect us the most, for they are the myths that guide and direct our most significant thoughts and actions throughout our lives. These most important myths are:

1. We are destined to be the way we are.
2. Unimportant things are incredibly important.
3. Being upset is natural.
4. Other people have it figured out.
5. Other people's opinions count the most.
6. It's not okay to be different.
7. It's too late to change.
8. You have no choice.
9. There will be time enough tomorrow.
10. There is no fountain of youth.

It Is Time to Get Rid of the Myths

The easiest way, of course, to get rid of every myth or untruth that we live with, at least for the moment, is to stop and put on the magic glasses— because magic glasses shatter myths. When you wear them, you see things as they really are. When you see things as they really are, you give yourself the opportunity to make choices that count—*choices that are based on truth rather than choices that are based on myth*. And when you do that, you give yourself the chance to change your behavior. <u>That is how we become more effective as individuals.</u>

Let's put on the magic glasses and take a look at those myths for what they *really* are. When we learn the truths behind them, we give ourselves the chance to discover an even *greater* truth about ourselves. But to get where we are going we must first get through the myths.

PART

II

THE
10 GREATEST
MYTHS OF
OUR LIVES

4

•

Great Myth #1:

•

YOU ARE DESTINED TO BE THE WAY YOU ARE

•

*"If there is a script that is written
for the story of your life,
the one who writes it is you."*

Let us begin with one of the greatest myths of all. It is the myth that says, "You are destined to be the way you are."

Entire societies have risen and fallen because they believed in this one myth. What an unfortunate belief it is to think for a moment that we are somehow set up to succeed or fail—as though some of us have what it takes and others of us, by <u>destiny</u>, do not.

We are all, by our nature, destined to succeed.

That is the way life really is. No one, no matter how much we may think it might be so, is given a golden spoon and a silver cup. No one is given rags and is expected to wear them. A human life is a human life. And in each life is an undeniably unlimited potential. If there is a destiny, we are taught to create it for ourselves.

For just a moment put on the glasses of truth and look at the people in the world around you. It is filled with people who win when they understand their potential and *choose* to win. You will also see people who never win at all. They were not destined to lose; it is only that they had never learned from others or from their experience that they could have been one of those who destined himself or herself to win.

This myth is important. If you want to find for yourself the treasure we are seeking, you will first have to recognize that some people believe that who they are and what they are and how they live out their lives is based entirely on the "fact" that they were *destined* to be the way they are.

The Very First Myth

Over the years, I have come to the conclusion that life is as difficult as it is to get through because we believe so many of the wrong things. Most people believe (and I agree with them) that life should be easier—better somehow. I know many people who see life as a struggle, a not-too-well-laid-out plan that is both difficult and ultimately temporary.

It is as though in heaven there are two lists. On one list are the names of those for whom life is destined to be easy, a "piece of cake." On the other list are the names of those for whom life will be an unending series of problems and difficulties, with only an occasional rest period or reward.

If there were two such lists, I suspect most of us would believe that the first list—the one headed "People Who Get to Have a Good, Rich, and Rewarding Life"—would be a very short list. The second list, headed "People for Whom Life Will Be Tough or Disappointing," would be a very long list.

I've thought about those lists. I have even wondered, if I were given a chance to look at those lists, where I would find my name. Where would you find yours? Or, more important, on which of the two lists would you look first?

That there are two lists—prewritten and somehow directing our lives from some "heavenly" place—is, of course, a myth. It is one of many myths that so many of us unknowingly live by. You and I may not think of our lives as the result of our names being on one or another list, but I suspect that we could find example after example of times when we live as though that is *exactly* what we believe.

During the past few years I have had the privilege of talking with groups of people throughout the country. I have watched many individuals come to grips with the notion that when it comes to personal destiny, personal success, and happiness, *"some have it, and some don't."* It is exciting to watch what some of those individuals do once they come to the realization that there was *never* a list in the first place, and that making the best of life was actually up to each of them.

The problem here is that when first confronted with the notion that our lives are somehow dependent upon some special genetic code that either works for us or works against us, many of us either deny that we believe such a thing or never think seriously about it at all. Yet confronting your own beliefs about whether you are "designed" to achieve daily fulfillment or not can make a profound difference in whether you let the rest of the world control who you are and what you do with your life.

What Do You *Really* Believe About Who Is in Control?

Here is a list of statements that will help you determine what you believe about who—or what—is really in control of your life. Read each of these items and determine whether it is true about you:

1. I am generally willing to go along with the crowd or let other people tell me what to do.
2. I seldom take responsibility for my own choices, large or small; I prefer not to make my choices for myself.
3. I believe that for the most part, I will live out the life that fate has in store for me.
4. Some people seem to get more "breaks" than I do.
5. Life is the way it is, and there is little I can do about it. The way my life is, is the way it was meant to be.
6. I believe that I can make a little bit of difference in directing my own life, but most of what happens to me depends on things that are beyond my control.
7. I just am the way I am and there's not much I can do about it.
8. Some people are just destined to have things better than others.
9. No matter what I do, I can't seem to get ahead.

10. Some people are born with more potential
    than others.

If even one of the items on this list sounds like
you, you may want to think about your own personal
beliefs about who is in control of your life.

Many people believe that their position in life is
not really up to them. They believe the myth. And
because they believe it, they live as though it were
true. People who believe the myth that control lies
elsewhere—somewhere outside of themselves—always have someplace else to lay the blame.

As long as you can say, "I'm doing the best that
I can; I guess I just wasn't born to be any better"—as
long as you can believe that, you never have to try to
win the race: "It just wasn't meant to be." After all,
if something else or someone else is truly controlling
our destinies for us, then it's not our fault if we don't
succeed. Failure or unfulfillment becomes acceptable,
unavoidable—almost natural.

And it is with that belief that many people live out
their entire lives. That's unfortunate. Had they not
believed the myth, they could have found so much
more to live for! But as unfortunate (or alarming) as
that is, there is an even greater reason why believing
the myth of outside responsibility plays such a harmful
role in our lives.

Believing the Myth Destroys Personal
Responsibility

The reason this is so important to understand is
that *if we accept the myth that some people are born
to win and others are not, then we lose our will to
exercise personal responsibility every moment of every*

day. It is when we do not believe we are completely responsible for ourselves that we assume that somebody else is in command.

The more we believe someone else is in command, the more we give in to the influences from the world around us. And it is those influences that slowly but surely attempt to convince each of us to get in step, stay in line, and go along with the crowd. That is what mediocrity relentlessly urges us to do. And it is when we give in to mediocrity that we *lose*.

We lose our enthusiasm; we lose our excitement for living; we lose most of the potential we were born with and could have lived out; we lose self-esteem; we lose our energy for getting up and living in a fresh and vigorous way every day—in short, we lose that magical, wonderful quality that could have kept us not just walking around, but truly *alive:* we lose our *"Inner Youth."* As we shall learn, there is a direct mind/body relationship between our attitudes and the energy we have for getting up and living in a fresh way every day.

How many times have you heard someone say, "Oh, but I could never do that!" when you knew that they could? In many instances, we learn later that they could, because with encouragement they end up doing the exact thing they said they could never do. The point here is that time after time we buy the myth that "we could never do that" as though it were foretold, as though it were some kind of destiny.

It isn't destiny at all. It's a myth. It is an untruth that is so subtle, so beguiling, and yet so powerful that when we accept it as truth, we lose an essential part of our *selves*.

There is a voice that cries out from within us. It is a voice that begs us to listen, to take our own stand, to breathe for ourselves. It is the voice of one who loves us, who pleads with us to throw off the shackles of self-doubt that have bound us. It is a voice that challenges us, encourages us, implores us to *live*. It is the voice of our Inner Youth.

5

•

Great Myth #2:

•

Unimportant Things Are Incredibly Important

•

*"If one day you will be gone,
and what was important to you while you were here
will no longer make a difference,
then why not make the best of it
while you are here?"*

When we stop and take stock of what's going on in the world around us, we have to wonder from time to time if the entire world isn't living out life engaged in the game of trivial pursuit.

I'm not referring here to the popular board game; I'm referring to a much greater game that we are playing out in our lives. Look at the trivia, the mundane concerns, the unnecessary drives that rule our lives. We place so much value on things that have so little worth! We believe in the importance of unimportant things because we were taught to believe they are important.

Since this is a book about putting on the magic glasses of truth, this is a very good time to put them on. Go ahead—spend the next while seeing the truth about how incredibly *un*important *important* things are.

This is one of the myths that cleverly and quietly seduces us into giving up our time and expending our valuable energies.

On our deathbeds years from now, all of those incredibly "important" things that we took so much time caring about will suddenly not be important at all.

What were you doing on September 15, 1972? What were you doing on October 12, 1975? What were you doing on the morning of May 15, 1983? What did you do, *that you can remember,* between the dates of February 12 and July 16, ten years ago? What did you accomplish? What major strides did you make in your life? What mistakes did you make? What, if anything, did you do during that time that embarrassed you the most? What did you learn? What arguments did you win or lose, and what difference did it make?

A Myth That Most of Us Live with Every Day

A friend of mine told me the story of how her mother had always cautioned her not to worry about the minor things in life. "Twenty years from now it won't matter," her mother told her. And, of course, she was more than right. Most of what happens to us in our lives does *not* matter twenty years from now. If you think about it, most of what happens to us won't matter in ten years from now, or five, or even in a year or a few months in the future.

But most of us are very good at fooling ourselves; we buy the myth by believing that little things really matter: who won the ball game; which dress to wear; what the boss said at work; who cut in front of you on the freeway during rush-hour traffic; whether the food or the service in the restaurant was up to par; whether or not you got the promotion; who finally won the spelling contest at school; whether you really looked astonishingly beautiful in the dress you wore to the company party; which team won the Little League pennant; whether or not Aunt Harriet married the man she was dating; what the kids got this semester on their report cards; whether or not you got to watch the Academy Awards; what you had for dinner on Sunday night; how much you weighed when you stepped on the scale this morning; whom to invite for Thanksgiving dinner and what to prepare—should it be turkey, or should you add the ham?

Go Ahead—*Live!* Take the Risk and Make It Count

At the time, how drastically important things *seem* to be! And in the long run, how unimportant most of them really *prove* to be. What an incredible myth this is—living out the belief in how important some things are when in fact they are not important at all.

I will never forget the time when an older friend of mine—his name was Henry—was discussing with his wife what they should have for dinner. Henry and his wife Caroline were devoted to each other, and they seldom argued or had cause to fight with each other. But they had their times when they disagreed.

Henry worked in a butcher shop cutting meat for his clientele, and Caroline worked at the church mimeographing lists of songs for the congregation to sing during services on Sunday mornings.

On that particular night, Henry—who was tired of dealing with particular cuts of meat—wanted to stay home and have an evening meal together. Caroline, who had worked hard all week, wanted to go out for a quiet dinner. The two of them cared about each other a great deal, but because they disagreed, they argued a little.

Henry won the argument, and they stayed home; Caroline cooked their dinner. They finished eating in the early evening, and decided to watch some television. During the time that they ate, each of them talked about the day, what had worked and what hadn't— and both of them got past the argument. Eventually, they went to bed. It was nothing unusual. It was another night at the end of another day.

At about two in the morning, Caroline died. The doctor who came later never quite figured out to Henry's satisfaction what it was that had caused her death. She had sat up in bed, struggled to breathe for a moment or two, nestled her head in Henry's arms, and breathed her last breath.

What Henry had wanted to do for dinner no longer made any difference. What Henry had wanted to do the next week, or the next month, or the next year or five years or ten, made no difference at all. The things that had mattered so much just a short time before no longer mattered.

There is so much that we miss by spending our time fretting over things that are unimaginably unimportant. At the time, they seem to be things of great consequence—look what important demands they place on our lives! *The myth is that little things are more important than they really are. The truth is that when seen through the magic glasses of truth, things show themselves for what they truly are—things that seem to be "important" that are not important at all.*

This myth comes to us like a thief, quietly and almost unnoticeably stealing the richest moments of our lives from us.

If you were able to step forward in time a hundred years and read for yourself the words written on the gravestone that marked your passing, what would you read? If you were able to read a short biography of the life you had lived, what would it say? Would it deal with the trivialities of your life, or would it tell the story of who you really were and what you did while you were here?

How is it that we get caught up in so many unimportant things? Why do we spend so much time complaining about the inequities, telling the stories of our days in unending details as though somehow those details represented the substance of who we really are and what we are really all about?

It is because of this myth that many of us often miss out entirely on the opportunity to *live*. It is not only possible, it is often typical for this one myth to almost singlehandedly make people believe that being "busy" with things somehow equates to being productive and being worthwhile. It is a powerful sedative. It lulls us into the belief that because we are busy thinking about *something*, whatever is foremost on our minds is important somehow.

All we have to do is look around us. Millions upon millions of individuals have learned to substitute taking personal action in their lives with a television screen filled with athletic events. In the lives of millions, personal achievement has given way to the details of the latest stories in the soap operas on TV. Instead of every day living out our lives to the fullest, demanding the best of ourselves, any of us who chooses can live out our lives watching someone else do it for us on a television screen.

Our conversations are laced with stories of who did what at the office, which neighbor bought what new car, who is having an affair with whom, and why some person or other got laid off from his job.

These all can seem important, of course—they are all part of our lives. But how important are they *really?* The problem is that we confuse the importance of performing the trivialities of everyday life with the importance of "living" itself.

That's what we learned to do. That is what created the myth. And because we have accepted the myth, we also accept that it is normal for "exceptional" lives to be unusual or rare—when in fact *exceptional quality of life should be the norm.*

We actually believe, in time, that "great" lives are for living by others. As the first myth suggested, it is as though we believe that there is a destiny that puts others in the *running* while we are in the *watching.*

This Myth, Too, Can Be Broken

I am not going to suggest that you stop living out the details of life. The details of your life are important to you. What you think about and do and talk about *is* important—that, too, is part of living.

But it is also true that much of what we do keeps us in the here and now while it quietly keeps us from measuring our lives and the real values that are held within them.

You can probably think of someone you have known who stayed so "busy" that he never got anything done. I have known salespeople who constantly relied on the fact that they worked hard and were busy all the time—and yet the busier they stayed, the less they got done. I have known other people who filled their weeks and months with activity after activity, as though the activity itself proved to them that they were getting something done. And I have known other people who continually got so wrapped up in the goings-on in the lives of others and everything around them that I doubt they ever stopped to realize they were doing nothing more than putting off doing something worthwhile for themselves.

I am not suggesting that each of us has to have some "master plan" by which we should live. I am not suggesting that every moment of every day should be filled with the achievement of a set of goals.

But when we observe those around us who are the happiest, those who are finding that their lives are all too short because there are so many worthwhile things to do, and so many moments of achievement to live for—when we observe those people, we always find that they have somehow learned to get past filling their lives with clearly unimportant things. They have chosen instead to fill their lives with things that matter—things that *count*.

Put on the magic glasses of truth for a moment and look at just a few of the people around you or people you have known. Read the biographies and study the histories of people who made their lives count the most. In most of them we find a truth that is a good lesson for all of us: The best of them learned to *focus* on the things that counted the most. They learned to put aside the less important "here today, gone tomorrow," often interesting but ultimately unimportant trivialities of the life around them, and they focused instead on the art of living.

I learned the importance of the myth of "the incredible importance of unimportant things" and the importance of overcoming this myth almost by accident. I will never forget the lesson I learned. I hope it takes you less time to figure it out than it took me.

The Story of Blakeley

Many years ago I visited a city that no longer existed. The city was named Blakeley, and it was situated on the east bank of the Tensaw River at the upper end of what becomes Mobile Bay near Mobile, Alabama.

When I first visited Blakeley, I almost didn't find it. Blakeley, after a hundred years or so, was by then nothing more than a few dozen acres of wild undergrowth made up of vines, weeds, bushes, and gnarled old trees. Blakeley was, when I first saw it, an almost impenetrable forest of tangled growth.

Seeing it then, one would never have guessed that on that site once stood a proud city of several thousand inhabitants. After the city had met its demise through the misfortune of a yellow fever epidemic and other natural calamities that our early settlements tried so hard to endure, the land that Blakeley stood on was left for nature to reclaim.

The only way you could tell that a city had once been there at all was by looking at two long rows of ancient oak trees above the undergrowth. Withstanding the ravages of time, those gnarled but stately old oak trees still marked the causeway that had once been the main street of the town.

Other than those oaks and the here-and-there

rubble of a few pieces of old oven-baked bricks that had been the foundations of long-forgotten buildings, Blakeley was no more. That is, except for the scattered remains of what was still the last resting place of many of the people of Blakeley—the cemetery.

Under a spread of oak trees and growth at the edge of the town's area, there still stood in broken rows the weathered markers of century-old graves.

The Blakeley cemetery was in no better condition than the rest of Blakeley, except for the fact that marble and granite outlive bricks and mortar. But if you looked long enough, and if you didn't mind the sweat-drenching heat and the ceaseless attacks of armies of mosquitoes, you could still search for and find the grave markers. Some were standing, and some were fallen and broken and lying in the earth nearly covered over by the relentless reclamation of time.

On the gravestones that could still be read were the stories of the lives and the deaths of the people of Blakeley.

It was more than twenty years later that I was to visit Blakeley again. On this recent occasion, a friend and I took with us a tablet of large sheets of paper and a box of charcoal crayons. On this second visit to Blakeley, I had expected to find the same tangle of wild undergrowth among the oaks.

But at some time in the years that had passed, others had rediscovered Blakeley, and the once-overgrown land on which it stood had been mowed and trimmed. In place of an unmarked, meandering dirt road, my friend and I now found neatly painted road signs, a new gravel road, and a well-kept sign announcing Blakeley as a historical monument.

Carefully worked excavations defined the perimeters of what used to be the Blakeley courthouse, a hotel, and other once-important structures. The cemetery that had lain overgrown and forgotten now resembled a peaceful park with solitary marble or granite markers scattered here and there.

During the years since I had first visited Blakeley, antiquity seekers had scavenged most of the gravestones, robbing Blakeley's resting place forever of most of its memories. But among the monuments still standing in the Blakeley cemetery were a few old granite monoliths six or seven feet in height marking the almost-forgotten plots of land where an inhabitant or two of Blakeley had once been laid to rest.

What hadn't changed was the heat, and the humidity, and the armies of mosquitoes. But we chose valor over comfort, and bravely went about the careful process of making "rubbings" from the stones—laying sheets of paper over the words that were carved on the front of the stones and softly rubbing the charcoal crayons over the paper until the words beneath the paper stood out in clear relief, capturing the words on the paper sheets that we would take home with us.

There was a reason I had returned to Blakeley. When I had first stood under those proud old trees that lined the main street of the city and fought my way through the generations of undergrowth that had overtaken the cemetery and then found myself reading the history of people's lives on those old tombstones, I had learned a simple but immeasurably profound lesson.

When I finally returned to Blakeley years later, to stand again in front of some of those same "timeless" stories in stone in the Blakeley cemetery, I wanted to take their words and their message back with me. It is a message I will never forget.

The stories in the stones themselves were the true stories of people who had lived and fought to survive, and had lived their lives—most of them short lives—

and then died. In those stones are the stories of husbands and wives and children. Infants were born and died within hours of birth. Mothers passed away giving birth. Husbands worked to clear the land and make a home for the families they loved so much and fought so hard to protect.

One of the still-standing stones told the stories of two brothers who founded the city of Blakeley. On two sides of the same stone are carved the words which are all that remain of the two brothers.

The words on the first side of the stone read:

Maj. GEORGE P. PETERS
of the
U.S. Army 2d Son of
Gen. ABSALOM PETERS
of New Hampshire,
departed this life at
Fort Gadsden E.F.
where he was in command
Nov. 28th 1819.
Aged 30 years.

The words on the second side of the stone read:

DIED
in this place Dec. 1st 1822
JAMES W. PETERS, Esq.
3d Son of Gen. Absalom Peters
Aged 51 Years.
Who with his partner
RUSSEL STEBBINS
emigrated from New York
to this Country in 1816.
These two with a few other
enterprising young

> gentlemen from the North
> commenced in the
> wilderness and founded the
> town of Blakeley in 1817.

For George Peters there are 37 words; for James Peters there are 59 words. For these two brothers that is *less than a hundred words for two lives,* carefully chiseled in stone—left to tell the story of their *lifetimes.*

The Things That Matter Most

At the time they were alive, the people who lived in Blakeley were just as hopeful and courageous and caring and troubled and full of life as we are today. They were very real people, with very real dreams and problems. Like us, they saw the sun rising in the morning and setting in the evening. In many ways their days and nights were just like ours. They worried and hoped and wondered and planned, just like we do.

And today, other than the stones that may still stand to remind us that they were there, or the paper tombstone rubbings that are now carefully framed and hung in a special place in my home, the people whose lives are recorded in the stones are nothing more than images in our minds.

Each day, each thought, each moment that they lived that was so important to them then is not important now at all. The frustrations, the troubles that they must have known, the joys and the dreams that were so important to them during the moments they lived them have all passed away.

Their lives, and all the things that were so important at the time, aren't important now at all. If it weren't for a few curious modern-day explorers who wanted to rediscover the past of a forgotten place, *we wouldn't know they had existed.*

Given a little time, it is just as likely that what seems to be so important to *us* today, in only a few generations of time will be nothing more than the etchings on a stone that, unless copied on a piece of art to be hung on someone's wall, will never be noticed at all.

If It Doesn't Matter, Then Why Not Make It Count?

The lesson I learned was not that our lives—and our hopes, our dreams, our work, our problems, and our achievements—are not important. They *are* important—that is what makes up our lives.

The lesson I learned is this: If life for each of us will one day pass away—and it will—and in time not even be remembered, then why not really make the most of it? Why not take the risk? Why not live it out to the fullest? Why not excel, and do our best?

If you do that, you have nothing to fear. Some people may tell you that you *can't do it.* Some people may think you are foolish to try, and some people may laugh. But rest assured—*time* is on your side. Time will pass, and in time no one will question you at all.

Whatever story you would like to write for the rest of your life, go ahead. Write it. *Live it out!*

If you would like to find your Inner Youth, recognize the truth that we often spend too much of our lives paying attention to some of the least important things and too little of our lives spending time where it matters most.

For now life will be a lot more fun, and in time it won't make any difference. No one laughs at a tombstone.

If you ever get the chance and are ever in the area, pay a visit to Blakeley. It is a nice place for a picnic lunch on a Sunday afternoon. Some of the stones may still be standing. It's a good place to visit. It's a good lesson to learn.

6

•

Great Myth #3:

•

BEING UPSET IS NATURAL

•

*"If you could be given back
every moment you have spent
on unhappiness or discontent,
and those moments were yours to spend again,
what would you do with them now?"*

This is the myth of "disconsonance." If has to do with being "out of sorts" with ourselves and the world around us. It is the disquieting feeling of disharmony, as though the clear, simple melody of life is interrupted by discordant notes—as though the orchestra is suddenly playing out of tune.

It is because many of us believe that someone else is writing the music, and that someone else is conducting the orchestra, that we allow the harmonies of our thoughts and feelings to play on unattended and unrefined by our own better judgment.

But the harmony—or the lack of it—that we feel inside us is not ultimately up to someone or something else; it is up to each of us. We alone determine whether we are in balance and at peace with ourselves or not. And it is when we accept the myth that tells us we *have* to feel the upsets and the aggravations, or that they *have* to play a prominent role in our lives, that we begin to live a life that is out of tune.

Like the other myths we are discussing, the concept of personal "balance"—the internal harmony that keeps us in concert with our higher selves—is not a matter of some philosophical notion. It is a practical, everyday reality. We live each day and every moment of the day being either in tune and in touch with ourselves and our lives, or uncomfortably at odds with ourselves or with something around us.

It is unfortunate that this myth adds to the mistaken belief that it is somehow natural to *react* to what goes on in our lives instead of recognizing that we have the capability to *respond* to anything that happens in a way that builds harmony instead of destroying it.

In my books on the subject of "Self-Talk," I described an unusually effective way of learning to respond *positively* to circumstances instead of reacting *negatively* to them.

Learning to talk to yourself in a different way, in order to keep yourself fully in control of yourself, is a lot like learning a *foreign language*. We all grow up learning to talk to ourselves in a certain way. Some of our Self-Talk is positive, and some of our Self-Talk is negative, depending on the programming we got from others. But the point here is that it is our Self-Talk that determines how we react or respond to what goes on around us.

The result is that your own Self-Talk can cause you to *create* negative reactions—that is, your own Self-Talk can *cause* you to become upset, when someone else in the exact same situation, using better Self-Talk, will not be upset by the situation. Which of the two of you would be more in control? You are always the *most* in control when you are in control of your own Self-Talk.

It Isn't Natural at All

Many of us have convinced ourselves that being angry, upset, aggravated, or ill-tempered is a natural way for us to be. Not only are these emotions usually unnecessary, they are just plain *unhealthy*. Yet it is surprising how many people never see through this myth at all. To the contrary, I know many people who argue for the right to live this myth.

I have had people tell me that it is their right to be upset or angry anytime they want to be. They are right, of course. That is their freedom, and it is their choice. But what an unnecessary load of negatives they heap upon themselves! I am not suggesting that we should not exercise righteous indignation—when something is wrong and can be corrected, it should be. Each of us does have the right to stand up for ourselves and expect reasonably human treatment from the world around us.

Nor am I suggesting that we should never be angry or feel bad. There are times when the right kind of anger is not only natural, it is essential. There are times when we become genuinely frustrated by the problems we face, and keeping a cool head is not always the easiest thing to do.

But it is when the problems and frustrations take control of us and rob us of our more joyous spirit that it is time to take stock of what upsets us and ask ourselves who or what is in control of *us*.

Imagine for a moment sitting down at a desk with two sheets of paper in front of you. At the top of the first sheet of paper you write the words, "Things That *Have to* Upset Me." At the top of the second sheet of paper you write the words, "Things I Let Upset Me When I Do *Not* Have To."

Now imagine the things you would list on those two sheets of paper. Almost any of us who were to do that simple exercise would find that almost nothing *has to* upset us. But we let those things upset us because we think "that is just the way I am" or that it is "natural" or "normal" to be upset.

Your Attitudes and Your Health

This myth is unhealthy—both physically unhealthy and mentally unhealthy. When we give way to unnecessary anger or allow ourselves to feel bad when we could, if we chose to, feel better, we create physiological havoc for ourselves.

A few years ago we began to see an increasing number of books on the subject of the relationship between personal attitude and physical health. Some of those books predicted that scientists would soon find biological proof that the body responds to what the brain thinks.

Since that time, neurologists and behavioral and medical researchers have proved that what and how we think directly affects our immune system, our ability to heal, our energy level, and how we feel and how well we do physically and emotionally every day.

And while we have learned that the right attitude creates healthiness, we have learned that the opposite is also true.

The brain receives the mental message that we are upset, and that message triggers a chain reaction of chemical switches in the brain that can dump literally toxic levels of chemicals into our systems that will take hours to run their course and dissipate to the point where we are once again back to "normal."

That is not a theory—that is simply medical fact. We, by our own attitudes, adjust our mental chemistry upward or downward—toward healthiness or unhealthiness. Medical science has clearly proved the link between attitude, stress, and wellness or unwellness. It should not be difficult for any of us to figure out that when we get upset about something that we do not have to be upset about, we are in fact *causing problems for ourselves*.

Why would anyone want to cause problems for himself? Why would anyone want to make himself feel down, miserable, angry, upset, and eventually less healthy because of it? Is that natural? No, it is not. It is not natural at all.

Being Upset Is a Habit That Harms

Unfortunately, that kind of behavior—even among supposedly mature adults—may be "normal." (If so many people do it, it *must* be normal.) But that doesn't mean it's good. That doesn't mean it's appropriate, and that doesn't mean it's a healthy way to live.

The fact is, we live this myth because it's a *habit*. We weren't born with the genetic code that told us we had to be angry or upset about the least important things. But many of us just got used to being that way. Being upset or not being upset is a learned style. It is a conditioned response; we become programmed while we are growing up to see ourselves as reacting negatively—or the opposite—keeping a cooler head when a potentially unsettling situation crops up.

I have met people who are convinced that they have absolutely no choice in the matter at all. One man I met told me, "When something goes wrong, I blow my top. It's just the way I am, and there's nothing I can do about it." He was only partly correct. That *is* the way he is *now*. But there *is* something he could do about it *if he wanted to*.

None of us is born to be automatically irritated by the world around us. It is a habit, and it is a habit that is one of the most unhealthy and destructive habits we could possibly have. And yet, because we have the habit, we accept the myth—and it does not have to be that way.

Being Upset Is a Waste of Your Precious Time

The real problem with this myth is not simply that it is unhealthy and creates problems for us. The real problem is that accepting this myth robs us of so much vitality and time. There are so many more important ways to spend each precious moment that we have.

Instead of letting negative emotions have free reign—even now and then—how much better off we would be if those emotions were replaced with better emotions and attitudes of the positive kind: joy, peace of mind, contentment, happiness, understanding, tolerance, perseverance, and optimism.

For every moment we spend being upset about something we would not have to be upset about in the first place, we are losing a part of us. We are throwing away another moment, minute, or hour in which we could have gained control of our own thoughts and feelings, a time in which we could just as easily have excelled at living instead of making ourselves feel as though—for those moments—we are losing at living.

Getting upset unnecessarily, being in a bad mood, being down, complaining just for the sake of complaining, finding things to gripe about, getting frustrated by things we can do nothing about—those are all habits, and they are habits that are hard to break. And the stronger the habit, the more we believe the myth—the more we fight for the right to be upset and to let the world know that sometimes things just aren't fair.

Some People Practice the Art of Being Unhappy

Some people seem to be masters at always being able to find *something* to get them upset or make them angry. These people have perfected the art of being down in the mouth or unhappy most of the time. And unfortunately, because they are so good at it, they are like the carriers of an illness that soon spreads to others.

People often react to negativity with negativity, and the result is that anger creates anger, frustration begets frustration, and what started as one person's habit of easily becoming upset soon spreads throughout the family or to those nearby in the office.

Some people have gotten so good at being upset with something so much of the time that instead of lines of laughter in their faces, we see the furrows of frowns as nearly permanent features of their countenance. Others, of course, live this myth to a lesser extreme. They are those who are not upset about something *all* of the time—just *part* of the time.

And then there is that group of individuals who have figured it out, and very seldom allow their emotions or their temper to take control of them. These are not people who are hiding their emotions or living life by avoidance; they are people who have gotten in touch with the better part of themselves, and have learned that happiness and peace of mind are up to the individual.

How Much Do You Accept the Myth?

There are some simple questions you can ask yourself that will help you determine how large a role this myth may have been playing in your life. Each of the following questions can be answered "almost never," "occasionally," or "frequently."

1. How many times in a day do you become upset?
2. How often do you *notice* yourself getting angry?
3. How often do you find it necessary to raise your voice or yell at someone for any reason?
4. How many times a day do you smile?
5. How many times a day do you laugh out loud?
6. How often do you say something to someone else that you later wish you had not said?
7. If people who knew you were asked to rate you on your level of maturity and coolheadedness, how often would they say that you were completely mature?
8. How often do you get upset about something you can do nothing about?
9. How often do you verbally complain about something just to get it off your chest?

10. How often do you find yourself defending your right to be in a bad mood?
11. How often do you start an argument?
12. How often do you feel depressed?

You, of course, will have to be the judge of how much of this myth you let live in your life. And you, of course, are the only one who can do something about it. For the moment, it may be sufficient to recognize that *having* to be upset is almost always a myth. That's good to know, because it means that it *doesn't* have to be that way. We don't have to buy into it.

You Can *Choose* to Not Be Upset

A woman once told me how upset she got with her husband on an almost daily basis because her husband had the peculiar habit of yelling at the television set. If he didn't like the news, he let the *TV set* know it—he yelled at it! If he didn't like the way the ball game was going, he let the TV and his whole household know it. If he could find anything wrong with any program that he watched, he would express his aggravation at the imperfections he found or at the disagreements he came up with by making sure *the television set* knew exactly where he stood on just about everything.

I suggested to the woman that it was also her choice to get upset about her husband's habits—and it was her choice to let it pass if she wanted to. But I know how difficult it can be to overlook something that is upsetting you when you are married to the "something" and it shouts a lot.

I'm not suggesting that the woman's husband

should put a stopper on his enthusiasm every time he sits down to watch a ball game on television. How he lives and how he reacts to things around him ought to be up to him. After all, that is his personal responsibility and no one else's. On the other hand, I do hope his wife gives him a photocopy of at least a few pages of this chapter.

I would love to see that man who spends so much of his time being aggravated about everything spend one weekend wearing the magic glasses of truth and seeing his life and what he's doing with it as clearly as other people see him.

Of course, you don't have to be thirty or forty years old to live this myth. Kids can learn it at an early age. It's too bad that so few schools actually teach classes on attitude. We would all be better off if we had all gone to a class on the benefits of *smiling* more!

I'm not implying that any of us should avoid real problems or have a "Pollyanna" attitude about anything. But when in doubt, why not give ourselves a break? Those wonderful words of wisdom that tell us to "lighten up—life is short!" offer us some of the best advice about our attitudes that we could ever find.

Which "Look" Do You Wear Most Often?

Take a moment and imagine a photograph of *yourself,* a picture of your face. Now, in your mind, draw an imaginary line that is curved up in the shape of a smile across your mouth. We'll call this the "Type A" look.

Next, draw a different imaginary line, a straight line, across your mouth in the picture. That is a "Type B" look.

Next, draw a different line, this time a line across your mouth that is curved downward like a frown. That is a "Type C" look.

Now imagine that you had a computer that could tell you how much of your life in minutes, days, hours, and years you had lived with a Type A look, a Type B look, or a Type C look. Let's say that this special computer could give you an accurate figure of the actual percent of your life you had spent with each look on your face. The message would be obvious.

It is not the circumstances of life alone that determine the face we wear or the attitude we carry within us. The attitude we carry with us is the direct result of our *programs*—of the *habits* we have learned.

How foolish we are to ever let this myth take any of our energy, our joy, our enthusiasm, or our youthful spirit from us! If we want to find the best in life, this is one myth that is clearly worth breaking.

The undoing of this myth does not ask any of us to be perfect—far from it. It asks us instead to take better care of our attitudes. We deserve the best, and by getting rid of this myth, each of us individually can give ourselves more of the best in our lives.

7

•

Great Myth #4:

•

OTHER PEOPLE HAVE IT FIGURED OUT

•

"If you choose to lead,
lead yourself first and always.

If you choose to follow,
follow the lead you have set for *yourself.*"

I would like to introduce this chapter by quoting directly from a page or two of the old book itself. Written in that small, beautiful book with the gilded title *The Fountain of Youth* are the words:

Until you wear the magic glasses for yourself,
you may think that other people have things well

figured out. The truth is, few of them do. Other people, especially those in positions of authority, only *seem* to have things figured out. In reality, they are just as confounded and as unsure as the rest of us. But they pretend well. They stand onstage and deliver their lines with an eloquent bearing that would have us believe they must surely know more than we.

Throughout history, kings and queens and presidents and prime ministers have taken the lead and we, thinking that they knew where they were going, have followed the paths they presented to us. History has also shown us that few of them had any idea of what was truly right.

There has always been an invisible conspiracy among leaders at every level from the highest to the lowest that demands that they appear to know what they are doing, whether they know what they are doing or not.

Parents in households, teachers in schools, employers at work, captains of infantry, lawmakers, and journalists all present the profound appearance of knowing exactly what they are doing. They offer to the common man the security of belief that someone is in charge.

I believe there is an essential truth in those words. It is as though we want so badly to be secure in the knowledge that *someone* has it figured out, we accept it as truth when they tell us it is so—when in fact it is not true at all.

I suppose that for those of us who would like to believe that there is a captain at the helm of the ship during the storm, it can be a frightening thought to question whether there is really a captain there at all. That is one of the reasons why every society that we know of has found a spiritual reason for being—a religion of one kind or another to follow.

The implication is not that we should question our religious pursuits. We need to "believe," and those of us who choose to will find a spiritual path to follow.

But we want to believe that somehow, some-where, *someone* has figured it out *for* us, someone who must know something we do not has been given the "secrets of the universe," and we are taught that if we follow the teachings that are handed down to us without asking too many questions, we can rely on the wisdom that someone *else* has been given.

It is no surprise, then, that as individuals we have such a struggle learning how to take personal respon-sibility for ourselves. In our enlightened time, we are clearly learning that *personal responsibility* is the basis for all true "success" in life. It is in the taking of personal responsibility that each of us is given the opportunity to reach the potential that we were born with.

But it is this one myth—believing that *other* peo-ple know more than *we* do, and have life somehow figured out better than *we* have it figured out—that calms us into believing we are somehow secure in the acceptance of *someone else's* truths.

Questioning the Myth

Over the years, as I have watched the presidential press conferences on television, I have imagined what those presidents must say to their wives at night when they are discussing the problems of the day. If we could listen in on them, I think we might be jolted out of our complacent belief that they *must* know what they are doing. They may know politics and protocol, but when it comes to being any kind of a wizard, even our presidents are no different from the rest of us.

It isn't that our leaders are not capable. It isn't that they are just as human as we are. They know no more about life than you or I. They, too, are just doing the best they can with what they have to work with.

Because we live in societies that are governed by leaders at the top, that same acceptance of leadership filters down to the acceptance of other people who *appear* to be "in the know" in every area of our lives. Depending on how civically or socially active we are, we can make sure that our individual voice is heard, especially in matters of laws, government, education, and the like. Yet we somehow accept the myth that other people have it figured out.

When we go to school, we are taught the basics of science, history, mathematics, literature, and philosophy. Other than the precise sciences—those things that can be proved as fact—what we receive as an "education" is really nothing more than a collection of other people's ideas.

The beliefs that other people hold, in their final analysis, are nothing more than *beliefs*. Those of us who are living at this incredible time today are more fortunate than those who lived before us. Because of mass communications, radio, television, and a constant barrage of questioning from media journalists, questioning the dictates and the viewpoints of others has become an acceptable way to think about what is going on around us.

Questioning the myth that other people have it figured out better than we do does not suggest that we should discredit our leaders, always question the boss, refuse to accept knowledgeable input, or develop a sense of personal anarchy. That would serve no purpose at all. But because we are born as humans in this life, we have with that birthright been given some rights of living that should never be taken away from us.

The question here is not whether those around us in positions of control are right or wrong, or know what they are doing at all. It is a question of whether *we* think for ourselves.

It Is When You *Think* for Yourself That You Begin to *Find* Yourself

One of the most dehumanizing concepts I have ever encountered in the field of personal growth has been the generally accepted concept that there are born "leaders" and born "followers." Because of an almost ingrained belief in a social hierarchy, many of us have come to believe that we were born to live at one rung of the ladder or another. In spite of the obvious fact that in a democracy anyone who wants to achieve something can attempt to do so, we still accept a form of social "casting."

There is an accepted but unspoken belief that we are born with a quality control tag strapped to our wrist that says something like "This is a Model 318 human being. She is designed to be a wife and a secretary," or "This is a Model 407. He is designed to be a mechanic in an automobile service center," or "This is a model 1035. She is designed to be a medical doctor," or "This is a Model 104. He is designed to do nothing more than get through high school and take whatever job he can find."

I would think those few examples were a little extreme if I had not met so many people over the years who have literally told me that *that* is who they were—that is how they saw themselves. And they felt powerless to do anything about it.

The truth is that there is no hierarchy of quality among individuals. Some people may not live out their potential and seem to waste their lives away, but they were never branded at birth as a Model 104 or 318 or 1035. If there is a social "cast" that we think we fit into, it is a mold that we created for ourselves. Not everyone can be president (there are very few slots open for that particular position), but any of us, given the right self-belief, could reach almost any potential we wanted to by the mere fact of deciding *that* is what we want to do—and then pursuing it.

The result of social casting is that many of us end up believing that who we are and what we are is "the way it is" or "the way it was meant to be." In Chapter Four of this book, we talked about the myth of accepting a prewritten script of our lives. We come to accept as fact that there are certain levels of living that we are expected to attain, or that we expect from ourselves, and we fail to recognize that the life that each of us lives is limited only by the ultimate picture we have of ourselves.

In doing that, we accept the myth that other people know more than we do—they have life better figured out than we do. In believing that, we do ourselves an incredible injustice!

No One Can Ever Live *Your* Life for *You*

The truth is that when you take responsibility for yourself and for the life you are living, *no one* will ever have your life figured out better than you can figure it out for yourself! No one has the right to tell you how you should live, or the right to expect that you will live the way *they* would like you to live it.

Destroying this myth is a huge responsibility. It

asks you to think for yourself, breathe for yourself, and live for yourself—without anyone else having the right to tell you what you *should* do, *ought* to do, or *have* to do.

The myth that makes us believe that other people have it figured out has little to do with presidents and congressmen and bosses at work and leadership in general. It has to do with personal responsibility. You were born with *your* life to live. No one else has ever had the right to dictate the direction of that life. That was, always should have been, and always will be, up to you.

When you think about this myth, it helps to put things into perspective. It helps to pause for a moment and look at the truth—as though you were wearing the magic glasses—and to see individuals, whatever their position, as they really are. The truth is that even the strongest people we know are often unsure and, even when they are "sure," they are often wrong. The truth is that because people want to be right, they often spend a lot of time and energy positioning themselves to *appear* to be right—even when they are wrong.

At one time, when I was young, I thought that there were so many people who knew so much that their enlightened knowledge would somehow take care of the rest of us and make everything okay. I thought that they had the world and life and everything in it all figured out. I thought that if I didn't know what to do, they would tell me. I thought that they had gained some universal insight that made them better or more knowledgeable than the average individual who was busy going to work and buying groceries.

In time I met many of those individuals whom I had at one time had such a great belief in. And in time I recognized the truth. They were just like us! They, too, were just going to work and buying groceries.

If they were politicians, they were trying to get their points across. If they were business managers, they were trying to make their businesses work. If they were educators, they were trying to do their best to teach what they were expected to teach.

In all that time the only individuals I have ever met who I personally believe actually had it "figured out" were wiser, older people who had lived long and done so much; yet *they* were the *first* to admit that they had nothing figured out at all.

If you think that you don't have the answers for yourself—take heart. When others admit the truth, they will readily admit that they know little more than you do.

Who Really Has It Figured Out? Ten Simple Questions

I began this chapter with a quote from the original old manuscript of *The Fountain of Youth* which Clyde found. In that book there was a list of ten wonderful questions. They ask each of us to look at some of the most profound questions of life to determine if we—or anyone else—has ever found the answers. These questions are not meant to confound us; they are meant to make us think.

Who is it that really has it figured out? Who is it that knows the truth of life and has the right to tell us how to live? It is probably the individual (whom I have not yet met) that could answer every one of these questions. They are some of the most important questions anyone could ever ask.

Here is the list of ten questions written in *The Fountain of Youth:*

1. Why are you here?
2. What is your purpose in life?
3. Who or what is in control of your destiny?
4. What would you like to do or be that you are not now doing or becoming?
5. Is the human race getting better, getting worse, or staying the same?
6. What is the real shape, form, meaning, and substance of God?
7. What is the one political or social system that would end war and create peace among humans?
8. What makes people do what they do?
9. What could you do that you are not doing now that would make your life work better for you?
10. What is stopping you from living your life in the most worthwhile way?

Learn to Call on the Wisdom You Hold Within You

It is true that we get so busy going to work and buying groceries, taking care of our households and taking care of our lives, we seldom stop to think that what happens next is almost always up to what *we* do next. If we accept the myth that other people have our lives figured out for us better than *we* do, we have missed an important part of living. We have failed to recognize that it is our own personal choice—our own personal sense of self-responsibility and *self*-management—that governs most of what goes on in our lives.

The conclusion of this myth is that there are few people you or I will ever meet who will ever be able to figure *our own lives* out *for* us better than we could have figured them out for ourselves. It is when we rely on the *imagined* wisdom of others that we fail to call upon the wisdom that *we* hold within ourselves.

You and you alone have been charged with the responsibility of taking control of your own life. If you live always waiting for the answers and the solutions of others, you will never get anything more than the dictates of someone else's beliefs.

Living at the suggestion or direction of someone else usually leads to nothing more than a feeling of unfulfillment and frustration. The adage is true: You have your life to live—they have theirs.

If others had found the answers for us, then the people of the world around us would not be struggling as they continue to struggle today. A quick glance at the headlines of any newspaper should signal the truth: No one has found the final answer.

Many young people think that the people who have it figured out are the people who are *old*. Meanwhile, many older people believe that anyone who is *young* and vital must be right. Neither of these beliefs is necessarily accurate, of course.

The true answer must certainly lie in knowing that any adult, whether young or old or in between, lives closest to the truth when he learns to take responsibility for the direction of him*self!*

There will always be wisdom and knowledge and good advice available to us from others. We may even find leadership that we want to follow. You may choose to listen to the ideas and the direction of others. But always remember this myth, and always remember to think for yourself. When it comes to making the decisions about how you would like to live, the one individual you should listen to most is *you*.

8

•

Great Myth #5:

•

OTHER PEOPLE'S OPINIONS
COUNT THE MOST

•

"If you want to listen to the opinions of others,
wait for the opinion of a wise man.

If you do that, you will wait a long time:
the wiser the man, the fewer opinions he will give."

During the time that I was preparing to write this
book, I asked people as often as I could what they
thought about the importance of other people's opinions. Even though I should have expected the response I got, I was still surprised. Most people—
people from every walk of life—were quick to answer,
and there was no question about their beliefs in the

matter. Almost all of them told me that the opinions of other people are *very important*.

I didn't argue with any of them. I just asked them, "Why?" I did not take the time to tell them that I suspected they were buying a myth which, when it was examined, had almost no grounds in truth at all.

This is one of those myths that many people would argue endlessly to support. As we were programmed to see life, as we were trained to look at ourselves, most of us have come to believe that what other people think about us and about what we do counts.

I suspect that even a quick rereading of the story of the gravestones of Blakeley would suggest to us that it is just possible that the opinions of others—those opinions that we take so much stock in during our everyday lives—have far less value than we might have thought they had.

There are certainly opinions that count, of course. The banker has to think you are worth the loan, and the boss has to believe you are up to the job. The husband or wife has to have the opinion that the mate is important, and the opinion of the professor in college can, without a doubt, play a role in the grades of the student. The buyer has to have the opinion that the salesperson knows what he or she is talking about, and the shift supervisor evaluates the productivity of each employee based at least in part on his or her opinion of that employee.

But none of those examples are the kinds of opinions we are talking about here. We are not talking about the appropriate, educated "evaluation" of something. We are talking instead about the myth that tells us that the thousands or tens of thousands of opinions each of us receives in a lifetime from generally self-serving or unsubstantiated sources should in any way affect our thinking as to who we are, how we are, or how we should live.

Without even thinking about it, we give undue prominence to the opinions of others even when those opinions ought to have *no bearing* on our thoughts or behavior at all. Throughout a lifetime we are told by so many people what we should wear, how we should look, what we ought to say to someone else, how we should behave, or even how we should raise our kids or what we should do for a living.

Seeing Opinions for What They Really Are

Imagine what the magic glasses would show us if, when we put them on, we could see every opinion we received for what it really was. If, through the glasses, we could see only truth, I wonder how much ultimate truth we would find in almost *any* opinion.

It isn't that people aren't well-intentioned. Many of the opinions we receive are well-meaning. Giving opinions, after all, is a habit. A lot of the people we know and live with are more than happy to give us their opinions on just about anything.

Unfortunately, few of those opinions are well-thought-out, structured analyses filled with pertinent, objective recommendations based solely on our individual situation or needs. For the most part, the opinions we hear are random thoughts that are nothing more than shared prejudices and beliefs based on the programming that the opinion-giver has received.

People give us their opinions because it seems like the normal thing to do. Yet, when you think about it, there are only a very few times when an opinion is really warranted at all.

The first instance when an opinion is warranted is

when we ask for one. We'd probably all be a lot better off if the only opinions we got were the opinions we asked for. But most opinions aren't asked for—they're just given. And it seems that they're usually given whether we want to hear them or not.

The second instance in which an opinion seems to have some value is during the course of an objective meeting of some kind wherein people are asked to share their ideas or recommendations, such as in a business meeting or a planning meeting. In situations like that, the opinions given are usually (or at least ought to be) more measured, well thought out, or considered.

But few of the opinions you and I will ever hear will be opinions that are offered either when asked for or during the course of a strategic planning meeting in which a valued opinion is needed and requested. Most of the opinions we hear will come from someone whose opinion we did not ask for in the first place, or from someone who feels obligated to impress their notions or beliefs upon us.

Who we really are or what we really want, and what is genuinely best for us—not from someone *else's* point of view, but from our *own* point of view— is almost never at the heart of the motivation of the person who gives us the opinion in the first place. Most of the advice and opinions we receive are given to us by people *whose own lives may be in no better shape than our own.*

Which Opinions Really Count, and Which Don't?

If you would like to know which opinions count and which opinions don't, and how to undo the myth of living by the opinions of others, there is a simple test to which you might like to put any opinion you hear. The next time your hear an opinion that is directed at you, ask yourself the following questions:

1. Is the opinion I just heard an *"opinion"* or a *"fact"*?
2. Does this person know more about this situation than I do?
3. Do I genuinely value what this person has to say?
4. Is this something I should decide for myself?
5. In the *long term,* will this person's opinion really count, or do I just think it's an important opinion at the moment?
6. Is what I am hearing "intelligent advice" or an opinion from someone else based on the beliefs of his or her own past programming?
7. If I did not get an opinion from anyone else, what would I think for myself?

If you'd like to know more about the effect the opinions of others have on your life, there are some additional questions that will help you figure out where you stand. As you read the following questions, instead of just reading through them and going on with the book, stop for a moment and think about each question—and give yourself an answer.

These are questions that will tell you how important the opinions of others are in your life right now. Answer each of the questions as objectively and as honestly as you can. Each of the questions in the following quiz can be answered with the words "never," "sometimes," or "often."

Let's find out how you rate yourself on accepting the opinions of others.

1. I place a high value on the opinions of others.
2. I listen to others more than I listen to myself.
3. I make it a point to consciously assess the real value of other people's opinions.
4. I let other people think that I agree with their opinions even when I don't.
5. I wish other people would keep their opinions to themselves.
6. I really believe that the people around me have more answers than I do.
7. I generally believe that other people are more intelligent than I am.
8. I let other people's opinions affect what I do.
9. I believe everyone has a right to his or her own opinion, and should state it at any time, even without being asked.
10. Trying to live up to other people's opinions or follow other people's advice makes my life easier.
11. Whether I do anything about it or not, I would like to tell other people to keep their opinions to themselves.
12. I really believe that other people's opinions should play an important role in my life. I think or act a certain way because of what I think someone else's opinion of me will be.

It is true that we live in the midst of others. Many people have ideas that count. *Many of them have opinions that don't.* Separating the two is a true test of individuality. At any time, in almost any situation, stop and ask yourself, *"Is this what I believe? Is this what I think? Is this what I want? Or is this what someone else wants me to believe?"*

There Is No Natural Relationship Between
Opinion and *Truth*

We would probably all be better off if we had been born with a switch with which we could turn our mental "receiver" on and off. Anytime anyone started to give us their opinion, we could just flip the switch to off. If we never listened to the opinions of others, we might miss an idea or two now and then, but I doubt that we would miss that much.

What we *would* miss, however, would be a lot of misinformation, inaccurate beliefs, and bias.

The problem with opinions is that they so often have little truth in them. People see the world through their own eyes, through their own prejudices, through their own programming. When they give us their opinions, it doesn't make any difference how helpful they are trying to be; they are, in fact, sharing their *prejudices* with us.

We have learned from the study of how the mind becomes programmed that it doesn't make any difference to the brain whether what is programmed into it is "true" or not. The mind believes what it is programmed to believe. Just because someone *believes* something to be true does not mean that what they believe is true at all.

In fact, I suspect that a study would reveal that *the more it is opinion, the less it is fact*. The reason for this is that our opinions have our attitudes built into them. When we state an opinion, our ego has a vested interest—we want to be right! And so we state opinions as though we *are* right, when we may not be right at all.

Have you ever known someone who stated his opinion strongly, as though he was telling you the truth, when it was obvious that this person's opinions were completely inaccurate?

I have known people whose opinions were almost legendary for being absurd, yet they were opinions—and *strong* opinions nonetheless. I have known others who fought for an opinion one day, and then reversed it the next—they changed their mind and then fought for the *new* opinion just as hard as they had fought for the *old* opinion.

Considering for a moment that most opinions are nothing more than that—opinions and not really truths—it is unfortunate that so much grief has been caused by the sharing of them. Marriages have failed because of the opinions of one or both of the partners. Parents have disowned sons or daughters; brothers and sisters have refused to speak to each other—even for years—because of opinions. Teachers have failed one student and passed another; friendships are foiled, and meaningful discussions turn into meaningless arguments—all because of opinions.

Elections are won or lost not because of facts, not because of truth, but *always* because of opinion. Was the politician really honest? Did he keep his campaign promises? Why did we believe what we believed about him before the election? For the most part, it was opinion.

When there are two evenly matched baseball teams, how is it that one of them is "incredible" and the other is worth cussing about? Is it fact? (No, we already know they are evenly matched.) It is all—one hundred percent—opinion.

On any night of any even passingly important ball game, somewhere a fight will break out. Two grown, supposedly mature individuals will toss the lessons of several thousand years of civilization aside and end up shouting or physically *fighting* because of some sporting event taking place between two ball teams on the TV screen in the corner of the room. Is "truth" the cause of the fighting? No; once again, it is nothing more than opinion.

Many Opinions Do More Harm Than Good

Not all opinions give way to open hostilities, of course. Some of the damage that opinions cause is much more subtle, but just as destructive. As an example, I know parents who would have done far better to stop "parenting" years ago, once their children were grown and were capable of making decisions on their own.

But even though the kids were now adults, the parents could not let go. And since they could no longer tell their sons and daughters what to do and when to do it, the parenting tactic changed from "These are my rules and you have to follow them" to a more subtle control measure called *"parental opinion."*

The belief somehow is: "I am your parent; therefore, I have the right to continue to tell you how you should run your life—and if I can't do it with force, I'll do it with opinions." No one gave the parents that right, of course. And unfortunately, some of those same parents never figure out that by trying to direct their adult children's lives, they are doing something that no one ever has the right to do to anyone—and that is to take their personal responsibility away from them.

It is no wonder, then, that the children of those parents, in one way or another, will rebel—either outwardly or inwardly—or they may just get sick, or let their lives fall apart. But because of the unnecessary and irresponsible opinions of their parents, their lives become "less," not more, and they fail to live out even a fraction of the potential that once was theirs.

I am sure you can think of other situations in which someone's opinions, even if they were offered with the best of intentions, did nothing to help and, in fact, only made the situation worse.

Learn to Discern the Difference

The important point here is that we learn to discern the difference between what is valueless opinion and what is important input. The problem is that so much opinion is dressed up to look like important advice—or, worse yet, it is disguised as fact. Learning to tell the difference can take some practice.

But if you are a person who believes in yourself or who wants to believe in yourself more, who wants to think at least somewhat independently, and who would like to know the difference between opinion and truth, then you can be sure that if you look for it, you will find it.

If you were to put on the magic glasses and see through them clearly, it would not surprise me to find that nearly *all* opinions would look different to you— because you would see only the truth in them, and none of the myths. Some of them—especially those we ask for, and that come to us in the way of supportive ideas rather than opinions—do have value. But those asked for and given in the right way are more "ideas" than opinions, and we can usually tell the difference.

Putting on the magic glasses suggests that if we listen to the opinions of others at all, we should, in every case, examine them carefully.

Are they accurate? How much truth are we really hearing, or how much are we hearing the biases or demands or even the wishful thinking that lies behind them? The next time anyone gives you an opinion (or the next time you hear yourself state an opinion), ask yourself a few questions like these:

1. Is what I am hearing an opinion or a fact?
2. If it is an opinion, do I *really* agree with it?
3. Does this opinion have any real value in my life?
4. Am I going to let this opinion affect me in any way?
5. If I disagree with this opinion, what should I do next?

Is It "Truth"—or Is It Opinion?

Here is a short list of statements that people have made at one time or another. See if you can tell, just by reading through them, which of the following are likely to be *truths* and which of them are *opinions:*

- "You look best in the color blue."
- "Timmy, math just isn't your subject."
- "The movie wasn't very good; if I were you, I wouldn't waste my time seeing it."
- "I'm sure everything will work out all right."
- "I just know this won't work."
- "I'm telling you, she's not your type; if you know what's good for you, you'll stay away from her."
- "Tradition is the most important thing we have."
- "Spending all that time knitting is a waste of time."

- "He couldn't possibly care about you."
- "There's nothing that will ever come close to skiing (or golf, or tennis, etc.)."
- "The best food in the world is French cuisine (or Mexican, or Italian, or Chinese, or German, or Greek, etc.)."
- "They were born to be poor, and that's the way they're always going to be."
- "That's women's work."
- "You'll never amount to much."
- "You'll just have to accept the fact that girls are better at math than boys."
- "That doctor doesn't know what he's talking about."
- "She has no taste at all."
- "Today just isn't my day."
- "You should be a doctor (or a lawyer, or an engineer, or a teacher, etc.)."
- "I know what I'm talking about."
- "Here's some good advice."
- "That's just wishful thinking."
- "You'll regret this for the rest of your life."
- "There's nothing like living in the city."
- "There's nothing like living in the country."
- "You'll always be a slow learner."
- "I wouldn't try it if I were you."
- "Take my word for it."
- "You're much too old for that."
- "She's a delight to be around."
- "You talk too much."
- "You should try to be more like your older sister."
- "No one could find him interesting."
- "It's too cold this time of the year."
- "He's just a troublemaker."

- "Blue eyes are the prettiest (or brown eyes, or green)."
- "You'd be well advised to listen to me."
- "I wouldn't be so sure about that."
- "You read too much."
- "No one with any sense would do that."
- "I'm too set in my ways."
- "There's nothing I can do about it."
- "That's the most you can ever hope for."
- "That's just the way I am."

What do all those statements have in common? All those statements are opinions. At the time they were said by the individuals who said them, some of them may have been at least partially true, but they were still opinions. And most of them were not true at all. And yet how often our lives are influenced or swayed, how often our actions are directed by opinions just like these!

I am not implying that we should not get good advice when we need it, and take counsel when it's appropriate to do so. There are educated opinions from people who have the experience, and it should always be our choice to listen to them. We're not trying to throw the good out with the bad, but it helps to recognize the difference. It helps to put the glasses on and see all opinions for what they really are.

It's Time to Stop Letting Opinions Stop *You*

The most successful people I know have learned the skill of thinking for themselves instead of living their lives based on the opinions of others. It's a good habit to get into. It can be a refreshing day when you wake up in the morning and say to yourself, *"I choose today to let no opinion get in my way."*

What others think about you, and what they would have you believe is best for you, is nothing more than what *they* believe is best—and that is always based on *their* beliefs, not *yours*. Over the years, I have known people who were totally crushed or who allowed an entire day to be ruined by the chance opinion of a total stranger.

I have known people who, though they badly wanted to, would not get up in front of a group and give a talk because they were afraid that people in the audience wouldn't like them. Without even thinking about it or figuring it out, they were allowing the opinions of others to stop them from doing what they wanted to do.

I have known children with great promise who grew to adulthood listening to the inaccurate beliefs and opinions of others and allowing those opinions to shape and affect years of their lives. I wonder how they might have lived differently had they seen the truth.

Finding the true identity of yourself means that you will have to listen to yourself more than you listen to the words of others. Since others cannot and should not ever live your life for you, that is the way it should be.

What would it be like if, throughout your entire lifetime, no one ever gave you an opinion unless you asked for it and valued it? What if you could live your entire life without ever once hearing an opinion that stopped you or held you back, held down your potential, or diminished your dreams? What if you could live an entire lifetime hearing the positive truths about yourself instead of ever hearing the random, subjective, misdirecting, off-target opinions of others?

Would you find more of your true self if you kept

your own counsel? The answer is, you probably would.

Always remember this: Most all opinions you will ever hear are "opinions," not *facts*. What others would have you believe is never anything more than what they believe themselves. What they believe may be right for them (though it often isn't), but what they believe may not be at all what is right for you.

Trust yourself. Listen to your own inner voice rather than the external voice of others. Listen to the voice within you that tells you who you are and what you want, and disregard the voices around you that tell you how *they* would like you to be.

Their Advice—Your Opinion

If you would ever like to break through this myth, there is one final suggestion which will help. If you ever want *advice*, ask for it. After you have heard it, decide for yourself whether you will take it. But if you ever listen to another *opinion*—make sure that it is your *own*.

The next time you hear an opinion from anyone else, without even telling them you are doing so put on the magic glasses that show you the truth. Think for yourself. Listen to the reason of your own mind. They won't know what you're doing, but that won't matter. *You'll* know what you're doing. You'll be taking another step in getting rid of the myth and taking control of your own life.

Other people's opinions do not count the most. *Yours do*.

9

◆

Great Myth #6:

◆

IT'S NOT OKAY TO BE DIFFERENT

◆

"When you find yourself
going along with the crowd,
ask yourself if the crowd is
going in the right direction."

The myth that says "It's not okay to be different" is
a major myth that affects the lives of almost all of us.
Of course, we have been told that it is fine to be
unique, that there is something important in being the
best.

But being different, in the context of most of our
lives, has almost nothing to do with being the best. In
our average, everyday lives, the idea of being "different" is not so popular. Being "different" has attached
to it the signature of being "odd"—as though being

different means that not fitting in is somehow akin to not being accepted, not being okay.

It is the same preprogrammed, insecure style of thinking that at one time caused people to believe that the world was flat that now tells us it is better to fit in and to be like everyone else than to be different. It is amazing that we could even consider accepting this myth, and yet we do.

How aware do we have to become before we finally recognize that Thomas Edison did not fit in— and that as great a poet and writer as Walt Whitman was thought to be odd, obscure, or "different"? How long will it take before our enlightened society will realize that "going along with the crowd" is one of the singularly most meaningless endeavors that any individual could ever undertake?

Before we criticize others for living out this myth, we should look at how solidly we have demanded obedience to this myth of ourselves and of others in our lives. Look at the programming we have received that has tried to keep us in line. If there were a list of programs, it would read something like this:

- Color inside the lines.
- Don't take risks—risks are bad.
- Look like others look.
- It was good enough for me—it's good enough for you.
- This is the way things are done.
- Being different is being odd.
- There is safety in numbers.
- Keep up with the Joneses.
- Don't make waves.
- Change causes problems.
- Don't call attention to yourself.
- Don't cause conflicts.

- Don't ask why.
- Don't question higher authority.
- Don't talk back (even when you're right).
- Do what you're told to do.
- Don't cause problems.
- Stay in line.

I have often wondered how many new inventions we might have had if our parents and teachers had not taught us that it isn't okay to be different. How many Thomas Edisons become less than they could have been—young men and young women who ended up *creating nothing at all* because they were taught how important it is to stay in line?

Schoolchildren, even today, are taught to stay in the lines when they color in their coloring books. What a foolish notion that is! Because we believe the myth that it's not okay to be different, we destroy creativity in most of us before it even has a chance to live. We have gotten so good at telling children what they "should" do and what they "ought" to do, that we all too often fail to tell them what they *could* do.

The truth is that it is okay to be different; it is probably the *best* advice you could ever give anyone.

We Have Learned to Be Less Than We Really Could Be

To get through this myth, we do not have to change everything about the way we think and suddenly believe that we *always* have to be different. But there are times, many of them, when we would be far better off if we put the magic glasses on, saw things as they really are for *us,* and followed our own direction.

We've already suggested that "going along with

the crowd" has its consequences. Failing to see things our *own* way, just because we were taught to see things *other* people's way, creates untold misdirections in our lives. The myth tells us that it's best to stay in line. It is one of those general rules of living that seems so safe—so "right."

But it isn't always right at all, and it certainly isn't always safe. Part of taking responsibility for yourself is seeing things for yourself, making decisions for yourself, and acting on them in your own way. If you were to adhere to the sensible rule that says, "I always take responsibility for myself," there would be many times that you would do things differently from the way other people do them or the way other people want you to do them.

From earliest childhood we are taught to act and think and be as much like others as we possibly can. There is, of course, some merit to that teaching. We do have to learn to fit in, to follow the rules in the classroom, to put our name and class number at the upper right-hand corner of the page just like everyone else, to not talk out of turn, sometimes even to dress just like everyone else dresses, and to behave the way we're expected to behave.

For years of our upbringing we are taught to conform. There are times as children that when we do something differently from the way the group does it, we are singled out, ridiculed, or made fun of. It takes a strong constitution in childhood to stand up to it. Many of those who, when they were young, stood up to it, soon learned it was not the thing to do.

And while it may not be better to always be "different," we begin to get the idea that it is better to stay in line.

A Natural Reason for the Final Rebellion of Youth

There is a reason that every generation struggles with the rebellion of its youths. In every generation, toward the end of their teenage years, the youths of that generation find some way to tell the rest of us that they'd like to be different.

There is a reason that, throughout history, we have witnessed so many minor revolutions on college campuses. Young people refusing to accept the status quo and wanting to change things for the better are not a recent occurrence—they have been with us throughout history. And they are trying to tell us something.

It is not just that youths rebel; it is that those youths know inherently that the "old" way is not necessarily the *best* way. What we see as youthful rebellion is nothing more than a final attempt by those youths to think for themselves.

In time, those youths join together under the banner of some common cause, and within the safety of their numbers try their best to get their message across. And their message has been the same generation after generation: *"The old way of thinking—the old ideas—are not necessarily right. The old way of doing things hasn't worked that well. Why not let us think for ourselves?"*

The "more mature" adults (who earlier went through the same thing themselves) learn to believe that it is nothing more than an unimportant, natural rebellion of youth which will pass with time. (It usually does.)

Few of us, as adults, ever figure out what that rebellion is really about. Because we don't look for it, or because we have been taught that it is something else, we fail to recognize the truth.

The truth is that the rebellion we see in our youths is the combined result of the unified voice of youth trying to be heard for the last time before it is stifled and subdued by the acceptance of the rules—and the *myths*—of adulthood.

Within those youths, one by one, the flame of *Inner* Youth begins to die out. The last pictures of youthful independence and identity begin to fade. Adulthood—and what we so carelessly call "maturity"—begins to step in and take over. The dreams and hopes and most of the potential that burned within those young hearts and minds begin to flicker out. Another generation of humankind is learning to "stay in line."

In time, the pressing demands of daily living, working at a job, raising a family, and dealing with the details of life will take over and cement their new lives in place. Soon, most of those young minds will learn to accept the "fact" that *this is the way life is*." Another entire generation has found its way into adulthood, leaving behind them much of what they could have been. They have learned their lessons well; they are staying in line.

We Are Not Taught to Live— We Are Taught to Stay in Line

In that process, the number of lives, the number of brilliant ideas, the number of individuals who could have been *individuals* throughout the rest of their lives, the number of good and reasonable and workable dreams that were lost by the wayside, is incalculable. We do not teach our youth to live. We teach our youth to stay in line.

So, because it is necessary to teach kids in classrooms, to deal with them in groups instead of seeing them as individuals, because it is necessary to maintain the status quo and keep society moving smoothly, we grow up being programmed to believe that being "different" is not quite okay. And the lesson is learned all too well.

With each new generation, the myth is taught and learned again. What a tremendous disservice this one myth does to humankind! Isn't it odd that while it is clear to any of us who thinks about it that almost all our greatest achievements, our inventions, our successes, our breakthroughs in life end up coming from those who were *different*, we still continue to teach our own children the myth that it's not okay to be different?

And the worst damage that this myth creates is not that it stops the budding Einsteins from discovering new theories of relativity, or the Madame Curies from discovering new medical breakthroughs. The worst damage that this myth creates is within each of us.

While this myth, like the other myths, causes problems, diminishes potential, and kills off a part of the Inner Youth, it also subdues us. It walls us into complacency and makes us think that going along with the crowd is okay, that the greatest value is in "sameness."

Of course we want to "fit in." Of course we want to be accepted and be a part of the people around us. But what happens when that need for acceptance gets in the way of our need for personal growth and fulfillment? The teachings we learned as children are in conflict with the needs we have as humans.

How subtly we learned that "sameness" was

good, while at the same time we *failed* to learn that taking control of our own lives is *essential*.

It is no wonder that psychologists tell us that one of the biggest problems we have in our society today is a feeling of *unimportance*, that quiet desperation that makes us question whether our lives have any meaning at all. Those psychologists tell us the most common problem they find is that people feel their lives are "empty" somehow. They have lost the "meaning" in life.

But how can you expect people who have always been taught to fit in and not truly think for themselves to find the real value in their lives when the *real value* in life begins only when they think as *individuals?*

That sounds philosophical, but it isn't philosophical at all. All we have to do is look around us. Common sense tells us that the people who are happiest, the people who are achieving, the people who are living a life of personal fulfillment, are always those who are thinking for themselves.

Can You Fit in and Still Be Your Own Person?

The answer is, yes, you can. But you have to *start* by being your own person. If you are your own person, then you are fitting in when you choose to, and standing apart from the crowd when that is the best choice for you. So we are not talking here about extremes of behavior that would label you on one hand "rebel" or on the other hand "conformist."

When you break through the myth that tells you it's not okay to be different, it would make no sense at all to force yourself to be completely different and never fit in. Having to be different for the sake of difference is just as much a myth as believing that it is not okay to be different.

But getting rid of the myth and thinking for yourself shows you that you can fit in and still be your own person. When we look around at the most well-adjusted, happy, and successful people that we know, isn't that exactly what we see? They fit in when it is appropriate to do so. But at the same time, they stand up for themselves.

If Necessity Is the Mother of Invention, Daring to Be Different Is the Father of Invention

Most of us think the way we think because somebody taught us to think that way. I first learned the message of the myth that it's not okay to be different when I was very young. It was the first time I learned that it might, after all, be better to think for myself. It is a lesson I learned and a story I will always remember.

Some people are lucky: Somebody hands them a pair of magic glasses *when they're still young*. They put the magic glasses on, learn to see the world in a different way, and are able to spend the rest of their lives figuring things out a little bit better than the rest of the world.

My father was like that. He must have tried some magic glasses on at some time when he was young. By the time I came along and got to know anything about him at all, it was clear that he looked at *everything* in a special kind of way. I'll never forget the summer when everyone in town learned firsthand from my father what you can do by looking at things a little differently.

The project my father had decided to undertake was to build a new foundation under a very big, two-truck storage garage. In order to replace the old, broken stone foundation under the garage with a new, higher, stronger concrete block foundation, the entire building had to be lifted up and suspended in that position while the old foundation was broken away from under it and a new one put in its place.

My father had decided to do the job mostly by himself, and the entire project took weeks. The first step was simple: With a sledgehammer and pry bars, he knocked four two-foot-square holes out of the old foundation—two holes on the east side of the building and two holes in the exact same place on the west side of the building.

Imagine two giant wooden beams, each two feet square by fifty feet in length. My father's next step was to slide these two heavy timber beams through the holes in the foundation. At that point, the entire structure sat soundly on the beams, and he could knock the rest of the old foundation out from under the building while it rested securely on the new wood beams.

The next part of the process was to raise the building into the air by lifting the beams several feet straight up. He did that with the aid of four small jack hoists and some extra pieces of timber. By now, about two weeks into the project, he had the building four feet off the ground, resting safely in place on the beams, and was ready to lay a completely new foundation of concrete blocks under the walls of the suspended garage.

All of this took place in a small town, and quite a few of the town's 2,500 inhabitants had stopped by now and then to take a look at the progress of this important event, and to pass the time of day with my father while he worked. Some of the townspeople came by quite regularly—usually around coffee time—and made sure they were completely up-to-date on

FINDING THE FOUNTAIN OF YOUTH INSIDE YOURSELF

what was, at that particular time, the city's only major
construction project.

So it wasn't surprising that a number of the townspeople who stopped by each day noticed what appeared to be a serious flaw in the engineering end of
the construction. Since the building was suspended in
the air on top of the two large wooden beams, those
beams would have to be lowered back down to the
ground in order for the building to be brought down to
sit back in place on top of the new concrete block
foundation. And a number of those same townspeople
were quick to point out to my father that when he built
the new block foundation, he had failed to leave holes
for the timbers to drop through so they could be
removed after the building was back in place.

The foundation was flawless and complete, and it
was clear that there was nowhere for the big timbers
to go to get pulled out of the way. If you can picture
this very neat-looking foundation, on top of which sat
two gigantic wooden timbers, which were holding up a
gigantic garage, you would see in a moment that my
father ought to have had a dilemma on his hands.

How could he lift the building up, pull the timbers
out, and then set the building back down on top of the
blocks where it had to end up? It seemed impossible—
but as I said, my father had learned to look at the
world and everything in it in a slightly different way.

Most of this building project had taken place
during the month of June, and by now it was the first
of July. I can still remember the way my father stood
back and looked at his beautiful foundation and told
the assembled observers: "The hard part of the job is
done; the rest of the job will be easy."

But the townspeople didn't think so. They looked
at the heavy building on its two giant timbers from
every side, and shook their heads. "You'll have to get

104

a 'sky hook' to lift the garage up so you can pull the timbers out," they told him.

"No, I won't be needing a sky hook," he said— as if there really were such a thing as a sky hook.

"Then you'll be needing an act of God!" was one man's reply.

There was clearly no way to remove the timbers without lifting the entire building up into the air and pulling them out. If you pulled them out as it sat, the building would simply topple and fall, and undoubt- edly crush the foundation my father had so carefully built.

"No, sir," the people told my father, "you should have left a place in the foundation blocks for the timbers to be let down through." And they went home, mumbling about how maybe my father's special kind of thinking wasn't so practical after all.

The next day some people from the local news- paper came out to take pictures. At the time, I thought they were just interested, but I imagine what they really wanted to do was to print those pictures in the newspaper for the people in town to have a good laugh at. Even the editor of the newspaper, who had come out himself to look things over, told my father that there was no way to get the timbers out, so he'd have to build two more feet of concrete block foundation and just leave the building stand there, four feet up in the air.

So my father finally said, "If you come by at twelve o'clock noon on the Fourth of July, you can watch me pull the timbers out and set the building down on its new foundation—and I'll even set it down so that it won't be a quarter of an inch out of line with where it's supposed to be when it's in place."

The editor of the newspaper knew that my father had never said anything about being a magician, so he was keenly interested in coming by on the Fourth of July at twelve o'clock noon to watch the proceedings. He also intended to bring a number of his friends with him.

On the following day, the third of July, there were more townspeople than ever stopping by to look things over and shake their heads. Word got around fast, and it looked as though half the people in town were going to show up at twelve o'clock noon on the Fourth of July.

A time like that can be pretty unforgettable for a nine-year-old kid who knows that his father's reputation for thinking things through is at stake. I hated to admit it, but try as I might to figure out a solution myself, I found myself taking the side of the townspeople—what my father said could be done couldn't be done.

The next day, July 4, I don't think there were too many families having their Independence Day picnic lunches in the city park. To me, it seemed like everyone in town was celebrating the Fourth of July by standing around and looking at our garage.

I suppose bets were being taken, but I wasn't a betting person and didn't know much about bets in the first place, so I just sat back and watched.

At about a quarter to twelve, my dad came out of the house next door to the giant garage that was suspended four feet up in the air on top of the two giant wood timbers that were stuck there, and somehow, in spite of the impossibility of the whole situation, he looked very confident and at ease. He walked over to the newspaper editor and bid him hello, mentioning to a few people that he wished we had enough coffee to go around, but we didn't own a big enough pot.

Finally, just before noon, one of the city fathers,

who was an important man in our small town, came up to my father and said, "Well, it's just about noon; how are you going to do it?"

Instead of answering him, my father turned toward the gravel driveway that led up to the big garage, noticing that a small truck was trying to make its way through the assembled multitudes who were waiting for the miracle.

The truck finally got through and stopped right in front of the garage. It was an old, beat-up truck with a flatbed on the back, and on the flatbed was a bed of straw, and on top of the bed of straw there was a load of two-and-a-half-foot-square blocks of ice.

It was the same truck that delivered ice to a lot of homes in our town, these being the days when not every home had a fancy new refrigerator, and iceboxes were still somewhat in vogue.

Without saying a word, my father put on a pair of heavy canvas gloves, grabbed one of the large ice tongs hanging on the railing on the side of the truck, and began to help the iceman unload the blocks of ice and lay them neatly in place on top of the concrete block foundation under the suspended garage.

My father had used the four jack hoists to lift the timbers and the garage on top of them high enough to allow the placement of the blocks of ice, and in less than thirty minutes, the ice blocks had been placed all the way around the top of the new foundation.

Now my father lowered the building so that it was resting on the ice blocks, which were a full six inches taller than the timbers. With a little help from a few of the people standing around, the two giant timbers were pulled out, and we all stood there gazing in amazement and wonder at a beautiful new foundation of concrete blocks and a second ice-block "foundation" on top of that. We all watched as the noon sun on the Fourth of July began to melt the building into place.

As an added touch, my dad now took the same four jack hoists that had been holding the timbers up earlier, and turned the tops of the jack hoists in toward each of the four corners of the building. As the sun melted the blocks of ice and the building began to lower into place, my father moved from hoist to hoist, pumping the handle of one jack here and another jack there, applying pressure to one corner of the building and then another to make sure the building would settle into place on the concrete blocks being no more than a quarter of an inch off from where it was supposed to be.

I don't think anyone recorded the exact time of the final moment when all the ice was melted and the building was finally in place on its new foundation. I do remember running outside early the next morning to see if it was really there—and it was. It was firmly in place and intact, just as it should be; and so was my father's reputation for looking at things just a little bit differently.

Being Different Sometimes Means Being You

It is true that "being different sometimes means being you." If you are not being *you*, then how can you possibly live out the total experience of the potential you were born with in the first place?

It is your choice to accept the myth or not. If you choose *not* to accept it, there are some things you might want to do about it. If you would really like to stop living the myth that it's not okay to be different, put on the magic glasses and see the truth that says "being different sometimes means being you," then here are some ideas you might like to try.

Read through the list and try some of the suggestions for yourself.

1. At every opportunity, ask yourself the question, "Am I thinking for myself?"

Who is really in control of what you think and what you do? How much responsibility are you taking for your own life right now? This doesn't mean that there aren't rules to be followed—there are. It asks you to question why you think what you think and why you do what you do.

2. "What am I doing right now that I would like to be doing differently?"

What would you like to change? This can be anything at all. Are you fitting in with some "supposed to" status quo? Or would you like to put your *self* into what you're doing and try it *your* way?

The next time, then, you find something you'd like to do differently—and it makes sense to you to do it differently—do it and see what happens. If you are ever going to be yourself, you'll have to get used to doing some things differently, *your* way, not just to be "different," but because that's the way *you* are.

For the present, don't worry about what other people think about what you do (or say, or think)—just do it. Let *them* worry about their own ideas and their own lives. They have to take responsibility for themselves. You have to take responsibility for you.

3. Choose something you would really like to do your way, and do it.

Go ahead! Show your stuff. Don't wait timidly in the shadows while the rest of the world is out in the sunlight. Be yourself. Your *real* self! Show them what you're made of. Show your *self* what you're made of.

4. Give yourself the right "Self-Talk"—tell yourself the words—that say to you over and over again, "I am creative. I am me. I am creative. I am me. I am creative. I am me."

Creativity is one of the most important forces in our lives. It is unfortunate that many of us were taught that creativity is reserved for a few. We learned that artists are creative, writers are creative, sculptors are creative, and so on.

For many of us, most of our creativity was trained *out* of us when we were very young. Some of us, while we were young, were encouraged to be creative because it appeared as though we could draw or paint or write, and that meant that we were creative.

Creativity *is* important to the painting of pictures or the writing of poetry, perhaps—but it is so much more important than that! It is not the artistry of pen and paper that counts the most. It is the artistry of *living* that will ultimately count the most for each of us. Creativity is the final stuff of which dreams are made and lives that are lived most fully.

Never let yourself buy the myth that some people are creative and other people are not. Creativity is a part of all of us. We were born with it, whether we know it or not. *You are creative—you were born that way.* And *being* creative is one of the best ways you will ever find to give life to your Inner Youth.

5. Make the decision right now to never again criticize someone else for "being different."

While you're busy breaking this myth, give other people a break. Appreciate the creativity that other people are trying to express. They probably went to the same kinds of schools you did. They were probably taught to stay in line. They probably learned this myth the same way you did. When you see others who

110

are doing something different, don't criticize them or complain about them or hold them back. They're just trying to be the best that they can be.

6. *At every opportunity that comes up, put on the glasses and tell yourself the truth: "There is always a better way to do anything."*

No one has yet found, nor will we ever have, a final answer to anything. When we go to school, we are taught "the answers." They are never the final answers. There are always alternatives. There are always better ways to do *anything*. Never accept the myth that we already have it figured out, or that we will never find a better way. We will—as long as we have people who don't buy the myth—always find a better way.

We always need new thinking. We always need new ideas. Some of those new ideas should come from you.

7. *Question everything.*

If you keep the glasses on, you won't override your common sense. You'll be safe. But keep putting them on; look for the myths, figure out what they are, and make the decision to *not* live the myths in your own life.

Do Something Different

Never let your Inner Youth live in the shadows of life. Let it come out. It has been shown that none of us can live out our lives to their fullest potential by staying entirely in line. It is not only "okay" to step out of line; it is probably *essential*.

If you had a second chance to live your life over

again, there is no doubt that you would do some things differently the second time around; and there is no doubt at all that you would do some things differently from the way other people expected you to do them.

Since you are living out your "second chance" right now, I can think of no better time than right now to practice the marvelous art of doing it differently.

Do something different. Surprise yourself! Surprise someone else if you like. But do it. Write, paint, go back to school, submit an idea at work, change your plans and take an entirely different vacation; whatever it is, decide to do it, and *do it*. Break the myth. Live it out. The more you practice breaking the myth and living the *truth* out for yourself, the more of your true inner self you will find.

10

◆

Great Myth #7:

◆

IT'S TOO LATE TO CHANGE

◆

"It is not the roads you have taken in the past,
or how long you took to travel them,
that should determine your direction.

It is the destination you set *today*
that should determine the next road you take.

As long as you are still on the journey,
it is never too late to choose a new road."

The ability to *change* has *nothing* to do with age. It
has to do with self-belief—with our attitudes about
ourselves. The biographies of some of the most successful or self-fulfilled individuals are full of stories of
new directions that people found—often late—in their
lives.

Of course, we want to feel secure and to keep our security intact, and the words *change* and *security* often look to be at odds with each other. How can you live out changes in your life and still stay safe? How can you replace the old with the new and know that things are going to be okay?

Because change often has with it the deep-seated discomfort of fear of the unknown, it is easy enough to say, "I don't think I can do this; it's too late to change." That's a very natural way for any of us to feel. What we're really saying is: "I'm *uncomfortable* with this. I'm not sure about the outcome."

The Fear of Losing the Things That You've Got

One reason people don't want to change is that they are afraid of losing what they already have. For some, holding on to what they've got seems to be a safer bet than setting out on a new adventure and maybe finding something new. It is as though they look at their possessions and what is around them in their lives, and they say to themselves: "This is me. This is what I am and this is who I am. These are the things that make up what is *me*. If I want to keep myself, I'd better hold on tight to what I have."

Other people see themselves differently, of course. They recognize that they are not made up of what they have gathered around them, but that who they are is who they *really* are *inside* themselves. Fortunately, there are very few of us who have to make such an ultimate decision that we would be asked to forsake all that we have to seek our futures.

We are not asked to board some ship for places unknown and, never looking back, leave our life and friends and possessions all behind us (although you would think that is what you are asking some people to do when you ask them to spend a weekend doing something different). Finding your Inner Youth does not mean losing what you have. Exactly the opposite is true!

Finding your Inner Youth is *enhancing* what you have, adding to it, getting the most from who you've been and what you have to show for it. Seeking Inner Youth is starting on an adventure that *adds* to your life instead of giving in passively to the most unimaginative and unrewarding pleadings of the status quo. And what we protect as safety and security is often nothing more than the quiet and unseen numbing of our senses that lulls us into a sleep from which we may never awaken.

Living the Status Quo

As we grow older, many of us lose the youthful enthusiasm that allowed us to see life as an "adventure." In time, we get stuck in our ways. We get used to the way things are, and maintaining the status quo becomes far more important than seeking new adventure. After all, we've worked hard for the status quo. We've fought for the right to know what to expect, and we feel better knowing that we can count on it.

In time, if our lives have worked reasonably well, we come to appreciate that normalcy, a feeling that we can rely on what lies ahead. And that is as it should be. But along with that hard-won reassurance that living out the status quo brings to us, we also at times find ourselves living out a "sameness," a predictability that one day will be like the next.

It is at this point that some people—probably deservingly so—sigh a sigh of relief, feeling that they have finally "arrived"—and they have. They have found a sense of belonging, a feeling of staying in one place, and they are happy to have found it.

Other people who reach the same position in their lives also appreciate the levelness of the road and the straightness of the highway, but they find themselves frustrated, quietly trapped on a journey that has only one direction. They live out a life of frustration, secretly longing for a detour, a new direction, or a new road to follow.

They, too, when asked, "Then why not reassess, readjust your sights, set new objectives, and find the next road?" will often say that they *would* . . . "but *it's too late to change.*"

Even younger people, men and women in their twenties and thirties, find themselves in situations that create the same response. For them, too, as they see it, it is too late to change.

I remember talking to a man who had studied to become an attorney. He told me that even though he badly wanted to move to a different area of interest in his life that had nothing to do with law, he could not do so because he had spent so many years going through law school.

"I can't change now," he told me. "Look at all the time I already have invested in getting where I am today. I would love to make a change, but it's too late for me. I hate to admit it, but maybe I should just hang in there and make the best of it."

The man I was talking to was twenty-seven years old.

What Is It That Stops Us?

All around us there are people who stop short of living out their lives the way they could have lived them out because they think: "This is the way it is." We all know people who have stayed in unhealthy relationships or unrewarding careers because they believed—*completely* inaccurately—that for some reason or other they could not change.

What is it that keeps us going on one narrow road when there are so *many* roads to choose from? What do we lose along the way that once gave us our courage and determination, or a sense of knowing deep within us that life has *many* highways?

The truth is, we never run out of highways—we just run out of gas. We lose the dream. We lose the self-belief, the curiosity, and the inborn sense of spirit that tells us there is an entire incredible world out there just waiting for us to discover it.

A lot of that spirit gets programmed out of us when we are very young. We are more often told what we *cannot* do than what we can do in life. In time, for most of us, the programming works. We begin to believe it. People who have already lost the spirit teach us to accept their kind of reality, *their* kind of life—and all too often we buy it. We learn to follow the rules and fit in. We learn, in time, to ignore the nudges from our inner selves that tell us there ought to be more to life than what others around us are telling us there is.

It has been pointed out that less than 3% of all the individuals we will ever meet live a life of "true fulfillment." That would imply that the other 97% are filling their lives with something other than fulfillment. So where do we get our programming, our beliefs, from? We get most of our programming from the *average* 97%—the people who *aren't* living up to their own potential.

It is no wonder, then, that so much of our early programming and the programming we receive throughout the rest of our lives is exactly the *wrong* kind of programming to give ourselves if we would like to achieve something better.

And so, because we accept the programming we got from others, we lose something. We lose a part of ourselves. We lose a powerfully important part of who we really are. We lose our sense of adventure, our sense of discovery. We lose the belief in ourselves that, were it given half a chance, would almost never say the words "It's too late to change."

Yet when someone is asked "Why don't you do it? Why don't you live it out? *Why don't you reach for the rest of your dreams and make them happen?"* they will almost never say that their dreams were impossible in the first place. Instead, they will tell you why it cannot work. And what they tell you next will sound like a litany of unfulfillment, filled with reasons to fail in some of the most important measures of their lives. They will say:

"It's just the way I am." "I've already invested too much to change now." "I'm too old." "It won't make any difference." "I should have done this a long time ago." "It would take too long." "I've already made my decision." "I wouldn't know how to do it any other way." "I've already gone too far to change now."

People will tell you these and any number of other excuses for stopping in place—halfway through the race—and giving in to the status quo.

The myth that says "It's too late to change" is a myth that affects all of us. We have heard others say it, and we hear ourselves saying it.

What Is It That Takes Us Out of the Running?

If it is true that "the race is won not in the winning, but rather in the running," then why would we want to step out of the race before it is over? Why would we ever want to give in to the self-imposed demands of daily living and think for a moment that those demands are somehow more important than *we* are? Are we so distracted by "survival" that we lose sight of *living?*

What *did* you want to do with your life? What did you want to become? When you were young, what were the dreams you had about the life in front of you?

When you were a newborn infant, only a few days old, lying in your cradle and looking at the world around you, you—like me, and like everyone else—were given the birthright to live out your fullest potential. Not half of your potential, not a quarter of your potential or a tenth—but your *full* potential!

At the age of eighteen or twenty, I suppose that any of us could have thought that being who we were, we would now live out a life that was for the most part scripted by the programs and the conditioning we had received from birth. At the time we might have said that it was already too late to change. Fortunately, though, most of us didn't say that. We knew that somehow change was inevitable.

Even at that early age, however, some people gave in; they followed some imaginary "system" for getting a job, getting married, and living in a manner that showed indifference to achieving the potential that each of them was born with. Some individuals at that point—so early in their young lives—got out of school, took a job, and proved to themselves that they would never change. And they were right. They didn't.

But not everyone stopped there. Others who had more support and better means went on to establish careers. They had the benefits of a good education and the added encouragement of goals and objectives. Yet many of those who were brought up to believe a little more strongly in their potential made it no further than through a first or second marriage and the first or second phase of their careers before they, too, readjusted their sights and stepped out of the running. They, too, were no longer contenders.

Life went on, of course, and they managed. But that's all they did. They gave in to the completely inaccurate myth that told them that for *them*, it was too late. Like those who had stepped out of the race of life earlier, there was nothing wrong with the lives they were living. They went to work, raised their families, paid their bills, and, in general, did okay.

But did they live out their potential? No, they didn't. They stopped when they believed that "life was the way it was"—it was too late for them to change.

At a slightly later stage, we find people who have already put it together. They have done it. They have raised families, gone through their careers, and have gained a great deal of experience in the art of living. They did what they set out to do. And many of them, in spite of the problems they may have met up with along the way, experienced most of what could be experienced in a single career or in raising a family along the way.

Many individuals who make it to this point in their lives have the satisfaction of knowing that they accomplished something, and along with that they made it to where they are today. The youthful terms of living—adventure, curiosity, potential, and achievement—give way to more practical considerations.

The word *retirement* takes on a new importance. And for many, finding enduring stability in personal and family relationships begins to become more important than it may have been in years. The "wiser years" of life impart a need for lasting stability.

Making New Plans for the Rest of Your Life

Over the years I have conducted seminars throughout the country dealing with the subject of personal programming and making "choices" for finding individual direction in life. I have always noticed the number of individuals who have attended those seminars who are already old enough to have lived out a good portion of the early and middle years of their lives.

I always especially enjoy talking to young people in their fifties and sixties and beyond who are there because they are planning the *next* important years of their lives.

But I have wondered about the people of that same age who are not there. It is not as though the others who do not attend should be going to some seminar somewhere to reassess their choices in life. But I do wonder what they're doing about setting their sights anew for the years to come.

Through the years I have received thousands of letters from people in all walks of life who wrote to share with me their thoughts and their questions about their own personal fulfillment. During that same time, and in my travels, I have met many people who wanted to be young at heart but somehow felt they were old in years. They believed—as did the graduate student or the middle-aged career person—that by now it was too late to change. They, too, were living with the myth.

It is astounding what the simple, natural act of getting older can do to dampen our self-belief! Because we are growing older, we somehow develop the notion that change is less available to us, more difficult, or just maybe not possible at all.

On the other hand, I have personally known other

people, also older, who had lived what they thought to be an entire lifetime avoiding change and doing their best to fit in and get by—only to finally throw the "status quo" away and make marvelous and profound changes in their lives, *regardless of their age*.

It Is Almost *Never* Too Late to Change

Throughout the years, I have learned that it is almost *never* too late to change!

Regardless of your age, while there is still breath left within you, you *can* reach out and find the potential you held when you were that beautiful infant that looked at the world in wonderment from your cradle all those years ago.

All too many of us stop living and accede to life long before our fire was meant to be spent. It's too bad that we buy the myth. It is deeply unfortunate that some of us think that it is too late to change—to grow—to live.

It is almost never too late to do something new. It is when we do that that we take the chance of living beyond our past—and just maybe living up to more of the potential we were born to live in the first place.

Making today work is important. But set your sights on some new goals and rekindle them. Give them the same kind of energy that you had in your youth. Go ahead—dream your dreams. Live your life. If you are still here—it's never too late.

11

◆

Great Myth #8:

◆

You Have No Choice

◆

> "It isn't that we have no choices,
> it is that we fail to see the choices
> that are in front of us.
>
> One of the reasons we fail to see them
> Is that we fail to believe they are there."

In my work in the field of human behavior, I became so convinced that our individual choices control our successes or failures that I wrote an entire book on the subject. The book *Choices* is about how to recognize what your real choices are, and how the choices we make create the mental programs that set up our daily lives and our futures for us.

But as I have continued to examine the myth that

tells us "we have no choice," I have wondered how many people will ever recognize it as a myth at all. It is as though this myth has so completely won us over that we really *do*, at least at times, believe *"that's just the way life is."*

People really do spend entire lifetimes living out the script that they believe someone else or the rest of the world writes for them. People really *do* live out tremendous frustrations and unhappiness because they somehow got convinced that they had no choice.

But what is even more unfortunate is how many people accept this myth that they have no choice and, while they never really fail, they never really *succeed* either. For so many people life becomes a process of putting one foot in front of the other, getting through it and doing okay. But it could have been—*it still could be*—so much *more!*

How often this myth puts blinders on our truth! How many times have we failed to follow the right path because we believed there was no right path to follow? In an earlier chapter we discussed the myth that we are destined to live a life in a certain way or to be as we were "meant to be." But this myth, the myth that says *you have no choice*, goes even further to blind us and confound us.

We have all known people who—because they felt they had no choice—stayed in jobs they didn't like, stayed in a relationship that could not work, said yes when they wanted to say no, or gave in to the "ought-to's" and "supposed-to's" of life, simply because they felt they had no choice.

It's too bad that it takes so much living—so much experience—and added years of age to finally begin to see through this myth. But that, of course, makes sense. People who are older and have gained more experience are able to look *back* at life. In hindsight, the alternatives become obvious. "Of *course*," they say, "I *did* have other choices—I just couldn't see them at the time."

The truth is, we *do* have choice—a lot more choice than we give ourselves credit for. I'm not suggesting that there are not demands and obligations that have to be met; there are some things we have to do. We have to do them either because we agreed to do them or because we feel the responsibility to do them.

The line between "I *have* to do this" and "I *choose* to do this" can be hard to find. But what if you could look at every one of your obligations and responsibilities through the crystal-clear perception of magic glasses?

How Can I Change If I Don't See the Choice?

Sometimes our choices are hidden from view. It is easier to say "I don't have any choice" than it is to find the choices that are hiding somewhere in front of us. But by making the statement "I don't have any choice," we feel like we are taking action, as though that should be the end of the matter. And, of course, by making the statement "I have no choice," that *is* often the end of the matter.

We can get so good at doing this that we don't recognize that by saying "I don't have a choice," we are making a choice—and likely as not, we're not making the *best* choice. The best choice, the one that we could have made if we had found it, was one of those we didn't take the time to look for.

Always looking for the better choice is a habit. Some of us were taught that habit at an early age, and we have seen its benefits throughout our lives. Other people have gotten so used to believing that they have no choices that it is almost unthinkable for them to accept the fact that they are just like other people, and they have choices just like other people have choices.

People who *always* look at their choices find that it really isn't difficult to do. (People who hold that they have no choices spend more time insisting on what *won't* work than trying to find a solution that *will*.) Fortunately, there are some very practical and surprisingly effective techniques that can almost immediately put you in the frame of mind for finding good choices for yourself.

I won't try to restate all of them here, but I will say that if you hear yourself saying, "I have no choice," and at the same time are not taking *action* steps to help you find the right choice, then there is a good chance that either the matter is not important enough to deserve a solution, or you have somehow lost faith in yourself to do something about it.

Sit down and write about it; state the problem or the question, and write out as many choices as you can come up with. Have a talk with an objective outsider, and ask for their input. (Remember to look for what may be "opinion" and what is not.) On a sheet of paper, write the words, "What I really want is . . ." at the top of the page. Then list clearly and simply the outcome or the possible solutions you would *like* to attain.

Take some time. Think about what you're asking for. Don't disqualify an idea just because it sounds like it's improbable at the time. Be inventive; use your imagination and be creative. Of course there are circumstances in life for which, ultimately, there may be no solution; we may have no choice. But those are the *least* of circumstances that we will ever live with. In most situations we have more choices than we could ever imagine. If you want to find them, you have to look.

What Saying "I Have No Choice" Really Means

How many times might you say the words "I have no choice" when that simply isn't the truth at all? When we tell ourselves we have no choice, what we're really saying is:

- I haven't figured out my alternatives yet.
- I have to do it this way if I want to be approved of.
- I'm letting someone else do my choosing for me.
- When it comes right down to it, I really don't believe in myself.
- The choices I *could* make are hidden from my view.
- I'm not really *looking*.

What incredible difficulties we create for ourselves by accepting the myth—*at any time*—that we truly don't have a choice in the matter! Whole lives have been ruined or left unfulfilled because of this one powerful myth.

Students have gone into the careers of their parents' choosing, and lived out lifetimes of frustration and unhappiness, because they gave in to their parents' wishes instead of choosing their own lives for themselves.

I know people who ended up getting married to someone they should not have married, simply because after once saying "yes," they felt they were obligated to pursue the mistake, even though it might take years to untangle themselves from the relationship. And they allowed all of this to happen to them by telling themselves, "I've already committed; I have to go through with this; *I have no choice!*"

Have you ever known someone who did not want to attend a family function or spend Sunday dinner with relatives but then gave in and did it anyway? What will they often say? "I don't have any choice. I'm expected to do this."

How is it that the "have-to's" have come to control so much of our lives? How many of the so-called obligations that we live with every day are really obligations at all? Or have we just accepted them, gone along with them, and told ourselves we have no choice?

Can these so-called "demands" of daily living *really* be that important? *Many* of those demands we will one day learn were never important at all. How can you tell? Wait a few years, until the day when there is little time left, to that moment when life is nearly over. And then ask yourself the question, "What mattered and what didn't? If I had known then what I know now, could I have really chosen more of my life for *myself?*"

Some choices, of course, have only a short-term importance to them, while others have a long-term effect. What we're talking about here is being able to look at life through the magic glasses of truth in order to help us make choices that have the best possible *long-term effects* in our lives.

Some of the people who reach that point are seeing the truth for the first time.

I met a man who had recently undergone heart surgery. The operation brought Paul back from almost not living to having a *new life* in front of him. It was as though his doctor had handed him a pair of magic glasses and said, "Here, put these on and take a good hard look at your life." Not only did Paul's near-death experience cause him to take a good hard look at his life, it caused him to make changes that he would never have considered making just a few months earlier.

Paul had believed the myths that had told him that his life was the way it was and that there was no way out but to get up each morning, go to work, get tired, come home, watch TV, and get further and further out of shape. Then Paul had his heart attack. He suddenly learned that what he thought was so real and so important wasn't the way it had to be. He *did* have choices. As he learned the truth about choices, life became worth living again. Paul stopped buying the myth.

Seeing Your "Have-to's" Through the Magic Glasses

There are some things that we are obligated to do, about which we don't have much choice. But the father who *"has* to" work late at the office and miss his son's homecoming game will learn one day, probably when he's much older, that enough of those evenings and weekends away from his family in reality did only a little for his job, even less for his life, and may have cost him a son in the process.

The woman who "has to" play superwoman and run herself ragged trying to keep up with her kids, her job, her social life, and an endless list of built-in demands and self-expectations may be partly correct when she tells herself that if she wants to be happy in life, this is what she has to do. But she does herself a great injustice when she also tells herself she has no choice. She is buying the myth.

She has many choices, dozens of opportunities, an unlimited number of ways to find meaning in her life and achieve a sense of fulfillment without destroying herself in the process. Soon she will lose sight of her youth, probably get unhappy with her marriage, and eventually start to wonder what it's all for.

It would be fascinating to see what she would do if she were to wear the magic glasses of truth for even a week or two. Do you think she would see things differently from the way she thought them to be? I think she would find that almost *nothing* looked the same. Would she see that there were other choices, and that wearing herself out was not the only way? There is no doubt that she would.

A Very Short List of "Have-to's"

There is the belief held by some, of course, that says: *Everything, ultimately, is your choice.* You could, if you choose, find a comfortable chair, sit down in it, and never get up again. (I've known some people who looked like that's exactly what they did!)

If you choose to do that, I doubt that life would be very pleasant. But you could make the point that every step you take or movement you make is up to whether you choose to do it or not.

But that's not a real, practical philosophy to live by. If you did put on a pair of magic glasses and looked around you to see how much choice you really do have in the matter of how you live your life and what you do in every detail of it, you would find that there are *some* choices that are usually made for all of us.

I think you'll agree with me that when you analyze the true "have-to's" of life, the following list includes most of them.

We "have to:"

- Go to at least some amount of school.
- Wear clothes.
- Eat and sleep.
- Be mindful of traffic.

Whatever you might choose to add to that list because you feel it is a "have-to" in life that "has to" be there, add it to the list. You might be tempted to add "work" or "go to work" or "work for a living" to that list. I suspect, however, that working doesn't belong on the list of absolute "have-to's" in life. I have run across too many people who have never really "worked," and I suspect they somehow never will.

But however long the list becomes, it will never begin to approach the length of the list of the choices we have believed we have to make, when we never really had to make them at all.

That you have no choice is a myth. That you *have* choices—many of them—is a blessing for you to enjoy.

12

•

Great Myth #9:

•

THERE WILL BE TIME ENOUGH TOMORROW

•

"The most precious gems of time in a lifetime
are not made up of seasons.
They are not the years of childhood,
neither are they the years of middle age,
nor the golden years of later life.

The most precious gems of time
are the *moments*.
They are sparkling, beautiful, and magical—
and then they are gone."

Why would we ever have believed this myth in the first place? It is one of the most unbelievable of all the myths we have been taught to believe.

Of course there is time tomorrow. Of course there is time to do new things. There will more than likely be opportunities that lie in store for us.

But it would take someone with exceptional magic skills to give us back the time we spent today. If you could look at your life right now, today, through the magic glasses of truth, would they tell you to put something off, or would they tell you to get with it— to get moving and to do something now? I don't think there is any doubt about it. The magic glasses would tell all of us to live today while it is here.

We have all been told many times before that we should make the most of the time we have at hand. But how many of us do it? Life goes on, and few of us have enough time to stop for very long and think deeply enough about what we're really getting done— about what we would really like to achieve.

This may be the hardest myth of all to accept for what it is. After all, we all "know" that there *will* be another tomorrow. There will always be another time. There will always be another chance. But is that true?

We have all heard the admonition that tells us we should "seize the day," take advantage of the time we have now—after all, time is fleeting, life goes by, and none of us, no matter how hard we might try, will ever be able to relive the day we lived today.

Sometimes it seems that life goes on quietly, almost endlessly. One day moves into the next. We think we will always somehow have the time to write those thank-you notes, write those letters, make those telephone calls, visit those friends we should have visited more often, or take care of those details of our lives that seem to fleetingly slip by.

Send Flowers to the Living

I know that at one time in my life I always thought there would be enough time. Anything I wanted to do

I would have the time to do. I was living a life that was positive and successful, and I was getting things done. I had at the time put a few things off that I knew I should take care of, but I knew there would be time enough tomorrow—or, at least, I thought so.

Then one day, when everything was going fine for me, I received a phone call from a friend. In less than ten minutes on the telephone, one small but important perception of my life changed when I heard her story.

I had met Laura years before, and I'd always known her to be one of the most collected and together individuals I'd ever met. She had two fine young sons, and was in the middle of a very successful career. Laura was a regional sales manager selling electronics products for one of the largest companies in the business.

Laura was a dashing, energetic, highly professional salesperson who had discovered the skill of making sales in the face of every possible obstacle. Within months Laura's region had become the number-one sales region of the country, in spite of the fact that the region would have done well to be in third or fourth place. Life, for Laura, was going very well.

The telephone call I received from Laura came one day in the middle of what should have been one of her greatest successes. But the voice I heard was from a different Laura. Because of what had just happened, everything in her life had changed—and I heard it in her voice.

Laura's fourteen-year-old son had been killed. It was a tragic accident. It had happened at home, through no fault of anyone—but it had happened, and the shock of it happening was overwhelming. When she talked to me, the most important thing of all to Laura was a message she wanted to give me.

I suppose it is a message that Laura would have

told the world if she could have. Her message was this: *"Send flowers to the living."* Laura will always wish she could have sent flowers to her son while he was still alive.

That simple message changed a part of my life. How many times do we believe that there will always be time enough tomorrow? How secure we are in believing that life will always go on!

It is amazing what we put off doing because we think we will have time to do it later. It's not a question of procrastination at all; it is a mythical notion of our "temporal permanence." Few of us, until we face it, come to grips with our own fleeting mortality.

I have known many individuals who made the firm decision to do something important with the rest of their lives, and then watched them put it off. Eventually enough time passed by, and they did nothing at all.

The human spirit is an amazing contradiction. On one hand, we believe there is nothing we can do. On the other hand, we believe that we will always have enough time to do anything we need to do. And so we begin to buy the myth. We actually believe there will be enough time tomorrow. There will always be another day; there will always be another time when we can make amends, or somehow make up for past failings or inadequacies.

"There will be time," we think—when time itself plays a game with us. It passes faster than we can imagine. It undoes our chances. It upsets the best of our goals. And time always, inevitably, moves on—as though it cares nothing at all about our foolish attempts to hang on to it.

One by one, the opportunities pass, and we grab them and hold on to them or we let them go. A small son's or daughter's birthday, a wedding anniversary, a moment that should be remembered, an opportunity for a new direction in life, speed past us—and we watch them pass by.

A Lesson from Uncle Eli

In my book, *Predictive Parenting: What to Say When You Talk to Your Kids*, I related a personal story that bears sharing here. It is a story that carries a message I will never forget.

I was finally six years old, and it was the day of my birthday party. Among the family and friends who attended the party was my wonderful, wise old uncle Eli, who had become one of my most trusted friends. When Eli had something to tell me, I always listened, and I always learned something—though at times I was not always sure exactly what it was I was learning.

It was during the party that Eli asked me to walk outside with him. He had something special to tell me. Outside, sitting together under the trees by my home, Eli asked me how old I was, and I was proud to say, "I'm six today!"

Then Eli asked me if I could snap my fingers. Any six-year-old who can snap his fingers would be happy to prove it—so I did. I snapped my fingers in a clear, sharp *snap!* Eli told me I had done well, and then he told me something that made no sense at the moment but that one day would make exceptional sense for the rest of my life.

Old Uncle Eli told me that in one year, on my seventh birthday, he wanted me to go off by myself for a few minutes and snap my fingers just once. And then he asked me to do the same on my eighth birthday, and on my ninth, and on my tenth, and then on my fifteenth, and twentieth, and twenty-fifth, and on each fifth birthday thereafter for as long as I could. On each of these birthdays I was to go off by myself and snap my fingers just once.

I didn't understand, but I did agree to Eli's request. After he had outlined the idea to me, Eli asked me to snap my fingers once more. After I snapped my fingers again in a sharp loud *snap!* Eli asked me if I had noticed that it seemed as though almost no time had passed since I had first snapped my fingers several minutes before. I nodded, and I sensed I was learning something important, but it would be a year later before I fully understood.

Old Eli couldn't make it to my seventh birthday party that next year because he had passed away in his sleep one night during the summer. But true to my word, on the day of my seventh birthday party that fall, I went outside and sat by myself on the bench under the trees and thought about Eli and what he had told me. Then I looked up at the stars above me and snapped my fingers just once. *And it was then that I understood*.

Between the time I had snapped my fingers a year before and the time I snapped them again a whole year later, it seemed as though hardly a moment of time had passed. There was one brief *snap!* and then another, and the time in between was gone as though it had never happened at all.

The following year on my eighth birthday, I did the same thing again, and then again the following year, and then the year after that. Five years later, and each five years after, I went off by myself, thought about old Eli and thought about time, and snapped my fingers just once.

Not long ago I received a call from my son Tony the day after his own young son Anthony's seventh birthday. "It works!" my son told me. "Last year on little Anthony's sixth birthday I took him outside and told him the story about Uncle Eli, and I asked him to snap his fingers just once. Well, last night was a year later and we did it again. He understands!" my son told me, about *his* son. "He *understands!*"

It hasn't been too long now since the last time I celebrated one of those special birthdays and *snapped my fingers just once* under a blanket of crystal-clear stars in the night sky. And once again I realized that I had grown from a child to a man in nothing more than a few brief "snaps" in time. That *is* how life goes by.

In another couple of years I will snap my fingers again, standing somewhere under the autumn sky on my birthday, alone with my thoughts. I know that I will think about myself, and about how it was when, what seems like only moments ago, I snapped my fingers that very first time. I know that I will think about Eli. And I think that this time I will also think about another young boy, my grandson, who only a moment ago stood under the night sky on his birthday—and snapped his fingers just once.

13

♦

Great Myth #10:

♦

THERE IS NO FOUNTAIN OF YOUTH

♦

"The truest test of living is not
in how much we can gain while we are here.

The real test is in how well we can recover
the Inner Youth we have lost along the way."

I can almost hear someone saying the words: "Of
course there's no fountain of youth. We all know
that!" But they are mistaken—they believe the myth.
There may be no fountain of *immortality*, but there
most certainly is a fountain of *youth*.

How do we know that? We know that because all
of us have met someone in our lives who has *found* it.
It is that man in his eighties who still has that "spark"
and that sparkle. It is the young woman in her twenties

who literally glows with life. It is the child so filled with eager enthusiasm who does not yet know what he cannot do. Each of them has been enlivened by the fountain of youth.

There may have been those in the past who believed in the legend of a river of immortality. Not knowing that the fountain of youth of legend was actually a metaphor for the spirit of Inner Youth, they believed it existed as a physical treasure or a shrine, and that bathing in its waters would give them endless life.

But that is not our quest. We are looking instead for an energy that, instead of just attempting to help us live longer, keeps us young for every moment we are here. The true fountain of youth—that energy, that *spirit*—lives, or at least *wants* to live, in each of us.

Since even the term *fountain of youth* sounds a bit magical or legendary, let's put this myth into practical, everyday terms and see it for what it is. To say there is no fountain of youth would be to say there is no inner spirit. The fountain or the "source" of youth is the spiritual essence of life.

What we are calling the fountain of youth is, in fact, the source of our mental and physical vitality, our individual enthusiasm, the bright and affirmative awareness of our own personal essence. It is that awake and aware part of us that communes with our soul and sends us messages of our most instinctive higher needs to live and to grow and to be free.

It is that part of us that taps the shoulder of our conscience, that small voice that yearns to be heard that speaks to us in the deepest recesses of our minds and says, "We are one, you and I. You are my life and I am yours."

It is as though that inner self, that Inner Youth, tries desperately to make a deal with us: "You keep me alive and well, and I'll keep you alive and happy. I'll make sure you are fulfilled in every way possible in your life.''

That Inner Youth may not be well. It may be weak and wounded, and may seldom speak to us at all because we have forgotten how to give it life, or we have let its voice go unheard for so long that we no longer recognize the words that it speaks to us. But as long as we have a breath left in us, that source of light and youth within us lives also.

Don't think for a moment that there is no fountain of youth within us. It is not something that some people have and other people don't. We were all born with it. Some people keep it, and other people lose it or forget it's there—or the years and the problems beat it out of them. And we can always see when it is going away or is dying out.

When We Lose Our Inner Youth

It is when that spirit of Inner Youth begins to weaken that our outlook on life loses sight of the good and begins to behave as though we see only the bad. When the spirit wanes, then dark, unnecessary, troublesome attitudes and behaviors begin to step in and take over.

In its most obvious form, the loss of Inner Youth is evidenced by:

- negative attitudes
- ill temper
- shortsightedness
- lack of caring
- inhumanity
- selfishness

- an attitude of feeling defeated
- gloominess
- a lack of vision
- little or no time for genuine playfulness
- infrequent joy
- shallow or heartless laughter
- a general lack of energy
- frequent complaining
- frequent depressions that have no clinical basis
- a sour disposition
- often feeling bored
- a feeling of uselessness
- frequently going to sleep in a bad mood
- often waking up unhappy
- being generally critical of yourself or others
- seldom or never accomplishing anything worth-while
- never doing anything new
- not making new friends
- being constantly upset with others
- being narrow-minded
- being frequently angry
- feeling powerless or incapable
- losing hope
- losing faith
- not looking forward to tomorrow
- crying too much
- never crying at all
- being impolite to others
- putting yourself down
- being afraid without reason

There is a source of youth within us that, if it had its way, would have us be better than all that. Many of the characteristics on that list can be caused by other things, of course. But if too many of them occur too often, you can be sure that somewhere at the heart of the problem lies the loss of Inner Youth.

People who are alive, youthful in spirit, who like themselves, and who have decided to really live spend very little time giving in to the seldom necessary attitudes and behaviors that we just recounted. Most of the items on that list are almost *never* necessary! But they are a natural symptom of losing sight of who we are and *what life is all about in the first place*. Life is, after all, all about being *alive!*

Those Who Argue Against Inner Youth Have Already Lost It

There is more to life than just being alive, of course—even being *really* alive. But the amount of "life" you live determines how well you do at everything else. And those who are the least alive are those who live the least.

It is those who have most forgotten their Inner Youth who never seem to understand this point. If I were to give a talk to an audience of one hundred people and if, within that audience, there was one person who had completely ignored his Inner Youth for years, he would likely be the one person in the audience who would stand up to tell me that all of this is nonsense, that there is no fountain of youth, that Inner Youth is just some silly notion, that none of this makes any sense at all, or that this is unimportant or a waste of time.

It always seems to be that one person who has the least amount of sparkle left in his eye who is the first to exclaim "Bah, humbug!" He does not like to learn that he himself has been responsible for failing to nourish the most vital part of his own life.

I would never be critical of that individual, of course. But it is true that once you are aware of some of the symptoms of an ailing Inner Youth, you begin to see some people a bit differently. When you meet someone who is gruff or negative or soured on life, *he* may not know what has happened to him, but *you* will have some insight into the matter. *You* will know what's really going on.

I have never known a single down-in-the-mouth, surly person whose Inner Youth was alive and well. I have never met anyone who seemed filled up with self-importance and pompous self-righteousness who had not lost his Inner Youth somewhere along the line. I have never met anyone who lived in hopelessness and despair whose Inner Youth was still standing up, let alone running in the race.

And so we live with the myth that there is no fountain of youth—that there is no river of vitality that will give us life. Nothing could be further from the truth. Anyone who argues too loudly to defend this myth probably already senses the truth, whether they will admit it or not.

We seldom like to admit that while we were at the helm we may have allowed our own ship to go astray. Recognizing that we bought into the myth that there is no fountain of youth, and then worked at making that myth a reality in our lives, can be an uncomfortable thought. But don't spend an unnecessary moment worrying about it. We have all been doing our best, and few of us were told about this myth and the damage it could do. We just didn't know.

So you can expect, too, that others who do not see this myth for what it is will very likely go on thinking and behaving in the same way they have in the past. People will be shortsighted and negative and self-centered and self-deluded and critical and complaining and many of the other things that we have just talked about. It is one of the reasons that so many people are so unhappy. And they don't even know what they are doing to themselves.

Some People Don't Want to Know

If you don't know what the problem is—or that it's even there—it's hard to fix. It is possible that most of the people you and I know will never consider the fact that a light that should be burning brightly in them is slowly flickering out.

I have even met people who I am sure do not *want* to know. They don't want to face the problem, because then they would feel they have to do something about it. Or the beliefs they carry around with them are so strong and so confining that to break out of their shell and start actually living again would be too much to take.

That, too, is their choice. But the problem is that few people think about life in these terms, and as a result, they never give themselves the chance to make a choice at all.

The concepts we are discussing in this chapter and throughout this book are concepts we may hear about from time to time, but they are not what we think about as being in the "mainstream" of life. We are told that these are the thoughts that should be left for the poets and philosophers and clerics, and that it is far more important to get the promotion at work, have a membership in the country club, and drive a new car.

There is nothing wrong with promotions, country club memberships, and new cars—but that kind of thinking often displaces an important understanding of our own human nature. There are people who are so sure that their view of life is correct, they resist anything that would question even the most one-sided point of view.

Short of undergoing open heart surgery, losing a loved one, or having a few moments of reflection while on their own deathbed, they may never give themselves the opportunity to figure it out.

So many of us have been taught for so long that we have to be practical, realistic, and hard-nosed about life, we forget almost entirely that within us lives a soul and a spirit and a driving force that, were they not vanquished, would have opened our eyes and led us to seek paths in life that would take us far beyond a simple career goal or the healthiness of a bank account.

This, too, is why so many older people who, when they have the time to reflect on the purpose and value of their lives, often wish they could live some of it over again. There were, after all, more important things to do.

There were some things that may have made no difference to anyone else—but had they done those things, had they lived them out for themselves, had they kept that inner spirit alive, they would have done something for themselves that nothing could ever have taken away. They would have lived more of the life that once was in front of them and now was all but past.

But instead they, like we, end up living at something less than their best, never quite understanding that they are getting only a fraction of the happiness and benefits that were available to them, had they only learned how to keep finding them.

And while we are going through life and working so hard to get wherever it is we are going, when we fail to listen to our voice of Inner Youth and fail to recognize there is a fountain of youth that is slowly dying away inside of us, we fail to notice the signs and heed the warning—and we often do nothing about it at all. In time we become convinced that it is right and natural to just get older not only in body, but in mind as well.

It Can Be Found Again

To get rid of this myth, you first have to be willing to accept that it is there. Once you take that first simple step, there are some fun and exciting things you can do to put this myth away forever.

14

•

THE DISCOVERY

•

*"It is only when you see the magnitude of the myths
that you can see the magnitude
of the hope that lies beyond them."*

It was after looking through the magic glasses myself that I began to see the myths for what they really are. It became more and more apparent to me that if we actually accepted myths like those for truth, we could not help but give ourselves countless problems and misdirections.

Believing the myths *had* to give us an inaccurate picture of the way things were. It would be like getting ready for the swim meet by practicing diving, only to find out you were going skydiving instead. Or it would be like believing and behaving as though the world were flat.

Of course, not everyone believes all the myths. But it is safe to say that if all of us wore magic glasses all of the time, none of the myths would look the same as they had appeared before we put the glasses on.

The fact is, we *do* live day in and day out based on countless beliefs that have nothing at all to do with fact.

It is as if each of us is the central character in our own play, and the role we are playing is part fact and part fiction. For some, it is more fiction than for others—some people believe more of the myths. For others, the roles they play are more true to life. Each of us lives a role that is somewhere between the myths and the truth.

When you recognize that fact, you might also ask the question, "Why is that so bad? What's wrong with it? After all, maybe a little of the fantasy is what helps us get through life, helps us cope, and helps us get by."

That is true. A little fantasy can be an enchanting thing. But the myths are more powerful than that. They do more than enchant us like a night at the movies or at the theater. The myths paint over the truths and cover them up with new pictures that hide the best of us from ourselves. The myths give us a false picture of life and a false picture of who we are. And so we end up playing out a role that is not really us at all.

Understanding that we live with myths all around us and believe in many of them, it is easy to see why life can get pretty frustrating sometimes. When you think the game you're playing is basketball, and you suddenly find yourself standing in the middle of a football field and the opposing line is bearing down on you, the results are inevitable. We think life is one way, while life sees itself differently.

So I reasoned that it was the myths that caused us to make the *mistakes,* that caused us to have the *problems,* that caused us to wish we could have a second chance and do it over again. But as I was to learn, I was only partly correct.

The Myths Cause Disharmony and Destruction

It was true that the myths in our lives were clearly creating havoc. It was as though we were living a minor form of insanity—fighting one another in wars, killing people, destroying beauty.

But it was in the less obvious results that the myths created the greatest destruction. Home life and families lived in feud and disharmony, parents shouted and children cried, worthy careers became difficult struggles, whole masses of society hungered for independence and opportunity and found only hunger instead.

Person after person found life, though at times comfortable and pleasant, more often a civilized form of survival, and knew no more than moments of true joyous fulfillment.

No, these myths were not trivialities that did little worse than inconvenience us or get in our way. They were wholly pervasive; they touched us in every part of our lives, and once they had found us and had entered our lives, they came in and sat down to stay.

Seeing the world and its myths and recognizing all that those myths were doing to the world, I thought, must be the end of the discovery. After all, that was enough. Get rid of the myths, and we should get rid of at least some of the destruction, some of the unhappiness, and some of the unnecessary problems that had troubled our lives. Even getting rid of a few of the myths would help.

The Myths Have Hidden the Magic

But seeing the myths for what they were was only the first step. The more I looked, the more I saw the myths were doing something *else*. And they were doing it, in one way or another, to *all* of us. The myths were not only creating havoc and destroying beauty and lives; the myths were hiding from us the most important facet of our selves and of our lives: the myths, like a shroud, were cloaking our *potential* in darkness, hiding it from the light and from our sight. And with each new myth that we accepted, more of that potential was hidden from us.

Myth by myth, misbelief by misbelief, our potential was stilled. The light of our potential became dimmer and dimmer, and was no longer filled with bright and unlimited energy. What once had been the brightest light of promise in our lives now only flickered.

I realized that I had found another part of the discovery. "That must be it," I thought. "That is why myths are so terribly wrong to have in our lives: *Myths stop us from seeing our potential and living it out!*

But once again I was to learn that I had found only a part of the discovery. There was one more part that would be found before the discovery was complete.

The Myths Destroy the Youth That Lives Within Us

I understood how the myths we live with create turmoil and troubles for us. I knew they had much to do with wars we fought and loves we lost and beauty that we failed to see, and I had also learned that it was the myths that hid our potential from ourselves and made us think it wasn't there at all. But I was soon to learn the most disquieting part of the discovery.

By distracting and confusing us, by keeping us busy flailing at the inconsequential and meaningless trivialities of life, by seducing us into believing that our potential was little or nothing at all, and so causing us to give in to an acceptance of a lesser self, the myths dealt us their greatest blow: They took away from us the most essential ingredient of an exceptional life. *They took away the Inner Youth that lived within us!*

That incredible spirit, that wondrous vitality, that undefeatable curiosity, that *life* that coursed through our veins, was admonished to humble itself, and learned to be silent—to give way to that final myth that we would call "maturity."

For most of us, the spirit of our Inner Youth went away. It was beaten down, ignored, or simply lost somewhere one day in our past.

I'm not talking here about the child that grew and became the adult; I'm talking about the real, original, *true identity* that empowered the adult in the *first* place. I'm talking about a force of energy that is so essential to keeping alive that without it, we *cannot* live a life that is complete.

Without the spirit of our own Inner Youth—that magical self deep down within us—still encouraging us onward, we do little more than try to do our best, walking through our paces on the stage and wondering why things don't feel quite right.

What Regaining Your Inner Youth Will Do for You

What will regaining your Inner Youth do for you? The results of that one decision to regain your Inner

Youth, if you follow through with it, will likely be beyond anything you have seen so far. No matter how much we live while we are here, few of us ever do more than scratch the surface. Life has so much to offer! And yet we ask so little.

Imagine beginning tomorrow morning, getting up and looking at the whole world in an unbelievably bright, wonderful, and alive new way! Imagine seeing the sun as though you were seeing it for the first time. Imagine smelling the flowers, or catching the scent of new-mown grass, or tasting some delicious food as though it were the first time you had ever tasted food in your life, or hearing the sound of your own voice as though an entire life had suddenly been given to you.

Can you imagine what it would be like to live the rest of your life *without* self-doubt? Imagine getting rid of mountains of needless fears, and replacing brambles and briars that reach out and clutch at you to hold you back, with hands that encourage you and lift you up? Think what it would be like to live a life in which you believe in yourself, state your ideas and thoughts, and share them with others, never lose a moment of precious energy on needless arguments or unnecessary opinions, and spend each day reaching into your own unlimited creativity and dazzling yourself with wonderful new insights and new awakenings.

Think for a moment what you could do with an unquenchable energy of spirit that gave so much zest and enthusiasm to each waking moment that you would never want to sleep at all. Imagine having the precious gifts of laughter, happiness, and joy showered upon you from your own Inner Youth in an abundance that you had never before imagined could be yours.

If these riches seem to be beyond the embracing of any one human being, then how is it that others have reached out and found these blessings for themselves? They have done so by enriching themselves first, with the rebirth of their own inner spirit. And with that Inner Youth alive within them, they changed their lives. They found a greater measure of life than they had ever thought to be possible. And if *they* can do it—so can you.

Discovering that Inner Youth within each of us, and bringing it to life once again, is one of the most important discoveries that you and I could ever make. It is the search not for what keeps us alive and helps us survive; *it is the search for what makes us live!*

15

•

GROWING YOUNGER EVERY DAY

•

"Learning to live again
does not come to us by accident.

It happens when we refuse
to live with the myths
that have hidden our spirit of Inner Youth."

If believing in the myths creates problems for us, hides our potential, and smothers our Inner Youth, they affect all of us, whether we are aware of it or not. If we ignore the myths or pretend they aren't there, they don't go away. They are just as pervasive as ever.

But the problem is that one of the *myths* is that *the myths don't exist!* We're often too busy trying to live to recognize that the myths are there. As we discussed earlier, there are people who will argue forcefully that, while life may be difficult at times, "that's just the way life is, and there's nothing you can do about it."

Some people refuse to put on the magic glasses.

Their programs from the past have convinced them that the way *they* see life is the way life really is.

But this book is written for people who care enough about themselves to look a little deeper. It is written for people of an open mind. It is written for those of us who feel there might be something to life that we have been missing. And the more I have studied levels of happiness, achievements, and inner fulfillment, the clearer it has become that what, for many, has been missing is the *recognition* and *nurturing* of their Inner Youth.

We begin growing older when our Inner Youth is no longer alive and well. This process of growing older doesn't begin in our fifties or sixties or seventies. For some of us, it starts when we are very young. We can begin to lose our Inner Youth at any time at all.

The Loss of Our Inner Youth Has Nothing to Do with Age

The loss of Inner Youth first begins when the myths of living overtake our natural curiosity and energy for living. Some people keep their spirit longer than others. For them, it takes years for their Inner Youth to finally become lost. Other people never seem to lose their Inner Youth at all. They literally stay young every day of their lives; you recognize it in their eyes, and in the way they carry themselves, and in the way they move.

Many authors in the past have written about "the child that lives inside us." But what we are talking about here is something far deeper than that. It is a sense of self, a recognition of being, an acceptance of potential, and it is somehow wiser than the child *or* the adult. It is that part of each of us that has to do with joy and discovery and an eagerness for living.

The Inner Youth is not a "child within" that gets wounded or hurt. Inner Youth is the *spirit of life* in human form. It lives at the very core of our being. As long as it stays alive, we continue to grow. If it is very much alive—if our Inner Youth is *active*—instead of ever growing "older," we grow younger every day.

In some of the people that we meet, it is clear when we talk to them or observe the way they live that their Inner Youth is very much alive and active within them. It is wonderful to see that spark, that sparkle in someone's eyes, that *vitality*, when it is clearly alive and giving *life* to them.

It is unfortunate, however, to notice how many of those around us have lost their Inner Youth entirely. We look into their eyes and we can see that the sparkle is gone. The fire has gone out. The spark of life that made life so worth the living is no longer there.

Believing the Myths and Living Them Out Stops Us from Truly Living

It isn't that we stop moving around and breathing and getting through the day. The survival system built into the computer of our brains sees to it that we keep on living as long as we possibly can—*biologically* living, that is. But moving *through* life is not living. It's just getting from one end to the other, from birth to death.

There is a lot more to life than just getting through it. But we seem to live at different *levels*. Some people live with a zest and a passion, with an almost unstoppable belief and attitude about themselves and about everything around them. Other people do "okay"; they have their moments, and they get by. For them life isn't all that exciting, but it isn't all that bad, either. It's okay.

And then there are others about whom one wonders why they ever made the effort to be here at all, since they have made very little effort to live once they got here.

From barely being alive—barely responding to life, to getting by, to living to its fullest, there is every degree of "being alive"—or not so alive. Some people believe that that's just the way we are—that it's "chemical" or it's just biological. It is true that our genetic structure influences many of our personal traits throughout life. But our Inner Youth, from the moment of birth on, is nurtured and protected—or left undefended—not by our biological makeup, but by the programs we receive from others and by the self-beliefs and self-esteem that those programs create within us.

If you meet someone (of any age) whose spark has gone out, it is likely not his fault at all. Programming does that to a person. It is our programming and the beliefs that go along with those programs that create the myths. And the myths of living destroy our Inner Youth.

In Order to Get Our Inner Youth Back, It Helps to Know What It Looks Like

Most of us, if we think about it, would like to have more of that quality we call Inner Youth. In fact, I can't imagine anyone seriously saying, "No, I don't want to feel alive; I don't want vitality; I don't want joy in my life."

I've met people who feel that they don't deserve it, or that they'll never get it, but I've never met anyone who doesn't want it.

Catching hold of Inner Youth can be a difficult

thing. Because we can't see it or take a picture of it, we're not always sure what it looks like. But we know what it does, and we know the effects that it has on our lives. To get the best picture of Inner Youth that we can, here is a description. Inner Youth is the quality within us that:

- Gives us curiosity
- Keeps us interested
- Gives us a spirit of adventure
- Gives us a sense of humor
- Lets us experience joy
- Is the heart of our creativity
- Fills us with promise and hope
- Gives us our dreams
- Picks us up when we fall
- Makes us feel alive
- Gets us to believe in the best
- Gets us to come out and play
- Stays alive as long as we nurture it

All of those are what our Inner Youth does for us. But our Inner Youth can only do those things while it is still active, while it is still *alive*. It stands to reason that if we allow the myths of living to take away our Inner Youth, then the qualities that are on that list will no longer be qualities that we possess. And that is exactly what happens. Those are the qualities of living that we lose.

When you meet people who have lost their Inner Youth—or who have lost part of it—you will meet people who have lost (or are losing) their curiosity, their interest, their spirit of adventure, their sense of humor, their joy, their creativity, their hopes, their dreams, their ability to get up when they fall, their liveliness, their belief, and their sense of play.

Summing Up

So we are born and become programmed by the world around us. We are programmed to believe things about life and things about ourselves that are not true. Among these myths that we are taught to believe as truths, there are powerful myths that cause strife and problems, hide our potential from us, and destroy or take away our Inner Youth.

When our Inner Youth is destroyed or taken away, we lose precisely those attributes that are the *essential ingredients* of a good life.

Understanding this, we can see why just being told by someone that we should "recognize our potential and live it out" has done little more than encourage us; it seldom changes our lives at all.

It is another reason why external motivation may try to get us moving but never keeps us moving very long. You can't go anywhere in a car whose engine has stopped. You can push the car, or you can pull it, but until you can give life to the engine and it runs on its own, it will never go far at all. And it is our Inner Youth that is the spark which ignites life within us— the engine that drives us. Without that spark we may be pulled or we may be pushed, and we may even move a little from time to time, but we will never come close to being in the race.

Recognizing how the process works—how we lose our Inner Youth, and how important it is for us to keep it alive—and knowing a little bit about what Inner Youth looks like should help us figure out how to find it and get it back.

Your Inner Youth Is Still Within You

How would you feel about slowly but surely beginning to lose your curiosity? How well do you think you might do if you slowly began to lose your capacity for hope? What would happen to you if, one by one, the dreams went away and there were no *new* dreams to replace them? How would you feel about—year after year—feeling less and less joy? And when enthusiasm went away, what would you find to put in its place?

We let the world tell us how things are; we accept the myths to be true when they are not, and one by one, almost all of us begin to lose exactly those qualities that made life worth living in the first place. *That* is a description of getting older.

When you meet someone who is bitter or cynical or doesn't smile much anymore, you have met someone who has lost or is losing his or her Inner Youth. The spark of life is gone, or is going away.

It is when the spark goes away that we stop growing younger every day.

Whether, at this moment in your life, you are in your teens, in the middle years of your life, or in the years beyond, your Inner Youth is just as important to you as it was in the first years of your life. It may be hidden; it may appear to come out only now and then, or it may even appear to be gone entirely. But it is not gone. *It is still there.* And since it is still there, since it is an essential part of you—a part of you that deserves to be alive and active—it is time to bring it back to life. It is time to say "hello" and get to know your own Inner Youth.

Some of us lost that Inner Youth when we were only children; some of us don't remember having it at all. Some of us lost only a little of it. Some of us lost so much of it that we think whatever we had was nothing more than the foolish passing fancy of our early years. But it was nothing foolish at all. And whether we ever knew we had it, we cannot live up to our best without it.

Fortunately, having learned how we *lost* the Inner Youth in the first place, we have also learned how we can gain it back. And this is the beginning of one of the most fascinating journeys that any of us could ever undertake. For as we will discover when we find again that Inner Youth, along with it we will find something else. We will find something wonderful.

How do we start? We start by shattering myths—and beginning to *live*.

16

◆

GET READY TO FIND THE TREASURE OF YOUR LIFETIME

◆

*"The journey you are about to begin
is a journey of promise and joy.*

The treasure of your Inner Youth awaits you."

What do you do if you want to keep that inner electricity of life alive and well within you? What can you do to breathe new breath into your own Inner Youth?

The answer lies in whether or not you are willing to break through the myths and see life for what it really is for you right now, today, and in the days that follow. It is the false "mental programs" of the myths that took away the dreams and the hopes and the joys and the curiosity and the creativity and the self-belief in the first place.

To get them back, you must first get rid of the myths themselves. Can that be done?

The Myths *Can* Be Broken

The answer is, yes, it can. Others have done it. Some have done it without knowing they were doing it. Others learned about it and did it by themselves. Others got it back with some help. But it can be done, and *you* can do it. It *is* possible to live without the myths leading you astray.

They will always try to lead us astray, of course; that is the nature of pervasive myths. They are all around us, and most everyone else we meet will believe them to be true even when we do not. And that means—at least at times—we will see things differently from the way other people see them. We will do things differently too. Instead of living for the sake of the myths, we will be living for the sake of our better selves.

This does not mean that when we begin to break through the myths and once again find the Inner Youth and bring it to life we will be doing anything that is "selfish" (in the negative sense). Quite the opposite. What we will be doing is finding and taking care of one of the single most important responsibilities that you or I will ever have.

If you just follow the right steps, the right directions on the "treasure map" we are about to follow, you may be able to break through some of the myths in only a matter of days. You may, almost overnight, begin to see the world differently, find your inner self, fan its flame back to life, have more energy and enthusiasm than ever before, and find every day a joy to live!

I have to admit, though, that I have seen few people do that. I have seen people make an almost miraculous overnight transformation and literally see every day that followed in an enlightened new way.

One of them was my friend Paul, the man I told you about earlier who almost died during open heart surgery. Another was a mother whose teenage daughter was brought back to life after almost losing it to drug abuse.

There are many stories of those who recover from an operation or a problem and, in their recovery, find a new sense of faith and direction in their lives. But whatever lessons *they* learn that cause the change, *we* often fail to learn the lesson for *ourselves*—even if we're the neighbor next door.

Seeing the world from a new perspective, getting rid of the myths, is not a lesson that is usually learned just by being aware of it or watching it happen in someone *else's* life.

How many Christmases do we have to watch the Dickens classic *A Christmas Carol* to figure out that the story is about *us?*

It was not that Ebenezer Scrooge was miserly with money. It was that he was miserly with his *life*. What bits of life he still had left he kept like soiled coins hidden in a rusted old money box in some dark, dreary corner of his miserable life. And it was not until Scrooge, in his dreams, confronted his mortality and saw his life stillborn and wasted that the transformation occurred. His life—at least what was left of it— was saved.

Why Do We Take So Long to Figure It Out?

It would be a shame indeed if each of us had to wait to have open heart surgery or almost lose a loved one or rely on ghostly spirits parading through our dreams at night, to give us the message that *life is passing and we're missing it.*

When I was twelve years old, I had a friend at school named Dale. Day after day, I watched him get his dreams beaten out of him. I watched his ideas scorned and his self-belief wither and die just as surely as if I had seen a bright young flame snuffed out before it had had the chance to burn bright.

I saw Dale change from an inquisitive, happy, adventurous boy of great potential to a quiet, withdrawn, frightened, and beaten youth whose spirit would never ignite again. Parents can be cruel sometimes, yet Dale's parents never knew they had harmed him at all. You couldn't see that they had hurt him, of course. But if you knew Dale then, and if you had known him before, you would know that something had taken the light from his mind.

Not long ago I received a call from Dale. The routes our lives had taken had parted when we left school, and we had not talked in more than thirty years. As we chatted by phone and remembered together some of those early days, I listened carefully to hear if Dale had found himself again—if he had regained that spirit that had once made him so much fun and intelligent and bright and strong.

But it hadn't come back. And when finally I asked Dale the question, "Well, tell me—what has happened in your life?" Dale's answer was slow and said without emotion or feeling. "Nothing," he said. "Nothing has happened in my life at all."

It is as though someone had taken a wand of light, and where once had been a boy who was golden bright, they had taken the color away and left only gray.

Could Dale ever get it back? I've seen others do it. He would have to want to, and he would have to be willing to try. I'd like to believe that he someday will.

I know that many of us have experienced difficulties in life that caused us hurt and pain. Some of those experiences took some of the light away, and some of it never came back. To each of those that happened to, and to all of us, it would be wonderful to find ourselves again. Not just what we have left, but everything we started out with in the first place, and have a right to hold today.

It is a wonderful experience to feel ourselves brimming with energy once again, full of excitement and the zest for living, filled with curiosity, unable to wait to find the discoveries in front of us—so eager are we to be alive.

If you'd like to do that—if you'd like to get rid of the myths, uncover the potential that got hidden away, and bring back to life that marvelous spirit of your own Inner Youth, I'd like to invite you to go with me on a treasure hunt to find it. And while we are on our journey, you will have the opportunity to confront and destroy the myths that have been standing in your way.

Confronting the Myths and Finding Yourself

By going through the process of breaking myths and regaining your Inner Youth, you will be asking yourself to look at many things in what may be some very different ways. As you do this, you give yourself new perspective—or at least you give yourself the *opportunity* to gain the new perspective. If you keep an open mind, and want to succeed, chances are you will find that what you see through the magic glasses of truth *is* different from the way you had seen things in the past.

Not everything will be different, of course; after all, most of us do have some sense of reality about us, and we try pretty hard to keep our feet on solid ground. But when you see something new, or see something differently, it will help if you have made the choice ahead of time (right now, as an example) to always look for the *benefits* in anything new you discover.

Seeing Is Believing

I recall reading the story of a man who, at the age of forty-seven years old, received his sight for the very first time. He had been blind since birth. Of course, he had learned to make his way through life in spite of the impairment, and he had done well. He was independent, got around when and where he wanted to, and had a good job and a good home life. He had learned to "see" the world without the benefit of what we call "sight."

But nothing could possibly have prepared him for what he saw when one day, following the operation, the bandages were removed from his eyes and, for the first time ever, he *saw*. In the days and weeks that followed, his new vision opened windows and vistas of unimaginable delights and surprises for him. No matter how independent and self-sufficient he had been before, his life was about to change immeasurably.

We *can* learn to do what that man did. Let's take this opportunity to see our life as though we were seeing it for the very first time. Let us see what windows and vistas we will find in front of us. In this case, seeing *is* believing!

Let's see what happens when we put the glasses on, rediscover the truths, and live out even a breath or two of the life that waits within us. *Let us begin our journey to find the treasure of our Inner Youth.* For those of us who choose to do that, it is possible that life is about to change immeasurably.

PART

III

A

TREASURE MAP

TO THE

FOUNTAIN

OF YOUTH

17

◆

THE QUEST BEGINS WITH A
SINGLE STEP

◆

"Ask yourself whether there could be
more joy in your life.

Then ask yourself what you are doing
to create it."

STEP
1
◆

Finding Your Inner Youth—
CREATE MORE JOY MORE OFTEN.

Included in the pages of the old book that Clyde
found in the attic along with the magic glasses was a
list of directions for finding the fountain of youth. This
list is a treasure map to finding our Inner Youth.

It may have taken years to lose the fountain of youth, but it won't take years to find it. If you were to start right now and follow the directions that lead the way, you could find it in almost no time at all. And none of the directions are hard to understand.

Anyone can follow them. The directions are:

1. Create more joy more often.
2. Practice being curious about everything.
3. Always keep an open mind.
4. Do something different.
5. Spend time with people who are truly alive.
6. Smile more.
7. Enrich your life with a sense of humor.
8. Bring to life your sense of play.
9. Learn to learn again.
10. Always have something to look forward to.
11. Wear the magic glasses of truth.
12. Check your progress every day.

Those few directions make incredible sense. If you care about living your life more fully, it would make no sense *not* to follow them. And the more we explore each of these simple directions, the more important and valuable they prove to be. Let's begin with the first step—a step that will help *anyone* get started:

Create More Joy More Often

How much real joy do you feel in your life? How often do you feel it? Not simple happiness or "okayness," but real, breathtaking *joy*, the kind that makes you want to throw your arms out and shout—the kind that makes you want to jump up and down and laugh or grab someone and twirl them around the room.

172

Remember the kind of joy you felt when you were a little child, and that most incredible thing of all time happened—a wonderful present under the Christmas tree, the first time you got to go to that wonderful place you had never been before, or that marvelous birthday surprise? It is still possible to feel that way.

And yet I know people who have not felt that kind of joy for forty or fifty years. That's too bad; they have missed so much! And unless they change something now and make the choice to have joy once again, they will miss even *more*.

What Does Joy Look Like When You Find It?

True joy is certainly made up of the experience of being completely alive and sensing a "oneness" with life. We find joy when we change from casually observing our blessings to actively embracing them. We find joy when we intensify our spirit of appreciation for what we have and who we are. Joy is an exultation that shouts the news that once again, *"life works!"*

We feel it inside us when something happens that is so good that we can't contain the feeling it gives us. We sense it when we do something that is abundantly fulfilling, and we know that we have taken part in living somehow beyond the day to day, to a level that for the moment confirms our value and worth. Joy is the act of having, for that moment, complete and total appreciation for being *alive*.

The secret to having joy is *"appreciation."* It is learning not only to appreciate the good that life gives us, or that we create within it; the secret to finding joy is in learning to actively appreciate, to appreciate with enthusiasm, to focus all your attention and energy on the moment or the blessing at hand.

Some people are very good at doing that. They have figured out that having joy is not so much in what happens *to* them, but rather in how they feel about what happens. They have learned to intensify their appreciation for living. There are people who greet each day with that kind of intensified appreciation—just for having the day to greet in the first place. Those are the people who see more color in color, find more richness and meaning in the sounds they hear, look for the beauty in the patterns of the artistry of the world that greets their eyes, and find meaning and value in the smallest of things.

The people who learn to find joy are those who refuse to wait for good fortune to hand it to them. They don't need the winning of a lottery or the raise at work or the good news of good grades on a child's report card, or the delight of a surprise birthday party, or anything that would seem extraordinary at all. Those who have learned to find joy have learned to find the important meanings in everyday life, and they have learned to embrace and appreciate what they find. So the secret to finding joy in your life is in how you choose to *experience* life.

What do you see when you hold a baby and look into those marvelous, curious, questioning eyes? How do you feel when the dawn of a new day tells you that you are alive, and that this day is for you to live to its fullest? What do you find around you when you go to work, or make your way through the day? Do you find reminders of your appreciation for life, or do you see nothing but the gray tones of everydayness and little or nothing to remind you of the wonderment and greatness that was born within you?

It is no wonder that some of us feel old! When there is no joy left, life diminishes. It becomes a hollow shell of its former self. When the incredible excitement of being alive—grabbing life and dancing with it across the floor—goes away, it is no wonder that we feel something profoundly important is missing.

Joy Is Not Just for Children

But if the joy is gone, how do you get it back? Can you get it back? The answer is, yes, you can. You will have to look for it; you will have to demand it of yourself; you will have to start upon the quest and never give it up. If you truly want to have that exciting feeling that makes you want to shout at the top of your voice, *"I have found life. I am alive!"* then your quest will be more than worth the effort.

If you say, "But I have no joy in my life," or "I don't have *that* kind of joy in my life," or if you say, "I'm too old for that," or "That kind of joy is just for *children,*" then stop and think about it. Is that kind of joy really just for children? Have you ever heard from any wise source that that kind of joy is to be *lost* when maturity is *found?*

Quite the contrary. *That kind of joy is one of the reasons for living.* That is the joy that tells us we are not just existing, but rather that we are truly living. And it is without that kind of joy that we feel our lives settling into the quiet despair that makes us wonder why things don't seem to be the way they ought to be. That kind of joy—that immeasurably wonderful, powerful, exhilarating kind of joy—is meant to be a part of each of us as often as we can possibly have it in our lives.

In the old book, along with the directions for finding the fountain of youth, there is a passage that reads:

175

To have joy in your life there are five things you must ask of yourself: The first is that you must want to have the joy. The second is that you must learn from yourself what brings joy to you. Third, you must do things for others, and you must do things for yourself. Fourth, you must share; joy is seldom a feast that is enjoyed alone. And finally, you must recognize the joy and know you have it when you have found it.

When is the last time you spent an entire afternoon figuring out what really brings joy into your life? I don't mean the wishes and the could-have-beens. What could you find or create that would bring the exhilaration of joy into your life now? If you already know the answer, what could you do to give yourself more of it?

It's Time to Put the Joy Back into Your Life

Someone once defined joy as "happiness that is so intense that we can take only a little of it now and then." That may be true, but "a little of it now and then" should never be only once or twice every year or so. If we got used to it, we could stand to have some joy in our lives almost anytime. You certainly deserve to have it in *your* life.

If you have too little joy in your life right now, it is time to open yourself up to it, and let it in. If you already have joy in your life, now is a good time to have *more* of it.

18

◆

A WONDERFULLY CURIOUS CLUE

◆

"Curiosity is a gift that can be given only
from you to yourself.

It is a gift that opens your eyes and your mind
to all those things in life
that you have not already seen."

STEP
2
◆

Finding Your Inner Youth—
PRACTICE BEING CURIOUS ABOUT
EVERYTHING.

It is easy to tell people who are growing old from
people who are growing young. People who are growing young are those who are curious about almost

everything. People who are growing old have stopped being curious about almost anything.

It is inquisitive, natural curiosity that adds interest, speculation, and learning to our lives. You can probably find examples of this among people whom you know personally. Think for a moment about someone you know who is curious and interested in many things. Now think of someone who is seldom interested in anything, and who has no curiosity. Get a good picture of each of them in your mind.

Now ask yourself, "Which of these two people is more alive? Which of them has more Inner Youth?" We would not have to guess at your answer. Then look at yourself, and size up your own curiosity. Be honest without being critical. The amount of curiosity each of us has is always a good indication of the condition of our Inner Youth.

There Is a Clear Relationship Between Curiosity and *Living*

Over the years, I had often noticed that people riding in cars could be categorized into one of three different groups: those who took an active interest in things that were passing by outside the car, those who paid no attention at all to things outside the vehicle, and those who had only a passing interest in things outside the car.

Almost everyone I had reason to be driving or riding with in a car clearly fit into one of those three categories. For a long time, as I observed this, I didn't think too much about it. But in time I began to notice that there was a clear relationship between the level of each individual's *curiosity*—and how "alive" they seemed to be in the *rest* of their lives.

The people in category one noticed just about everything. They commented on road signs, noticed new buildings under construction, pointed out differences in license plates, contemplated the sequence of the stoplights at intersections, and were generally mentally active and alert. They were curious about everything.

The people who I placed in category two were just the opposite. We could ride together in the same automobile for five miles, or fifty, and throughout the entire trip they would give not a single indication that they were seeing anything at all.

It was not as though they were people who were preoccupied with something else; it was more that they had simply stopped thinking about anything other than perhaps their own innermost thoughts—and sometimes I wondered if they were even thinking about those! It was as though they had no curiosity at all. There was no sign of mental alertness and inquisitiveness that said "I want to see; I want to know; I want to understand."

It was not that they could not hold a good conversation. In many instances, these people were quite intelligent. But in some cases you would not have known that if you had observed only their reaction to what their eyes saw around them.

I noticed that the people who fit into category three noticed some things and were interested from time to time, but missed other things and their interest would lapse. They might comment on something they saw as we drove along, and then seem to notice nothing new for the next twenty miles.

It was years later that I was to become convinced that my first casual observations of the curiosity levels of passengers in automobiles held a strong relationship to the level of activity in the Inner Youth in passengers traveling through life. In my earlier observations, I had also noted that the curiosity level had nothing to do with the age of the passenger. Before a dozen years of life had passed by, the young people, too, already seemed to have developed a basic level of curiosity.

I also observed that some of those same people over the years would have a higher level of curiosity or a lower level of curiosity at one time than they had at another time. When their self-esteem, level of self-worth, and self-confidence were highest, their level of curiosity was highest as well. When they were down, depressed, or feeling unsure of themselves, their level of curiosity appeared to be lower as well.

Curiosity Is a Choice

During the next few days or weeks, make it a point to casually observe the behavior of people around you. Take mental note of their level of interest in things around them. Then ask yourself, "Which of these individuals has kept his inner light alive and burning bright, and which has not?"

In doing this, we are not being critical of others; we are learning to observe something that is also true of ourselves.

Curiosity is one of those things that is yours for the asking. It does not have to be conferred on you by someone else, or taught to you by an expert. If you want curiosity, you can have it. It may take some practice if you're not used to having it—but with practice, you'll have as much of it as you want. No one in the past may have told you that curiosity is a choice, but it most certainly is—and it is a choice that is yours to make.

Start noticing things—anything at all. Get interested! Think about things that you see. Question how things work and why they are there. Curiosity is a game with infinite answers, and it is a game that's fun to play. But far more than a game, it is one of the most effective ways we have ever found for awakening our minds and creating more youthful spirit within us.

How to Be Curious—A Marvelous Art

It should not be surprising that some of us (most of us) have learned *not* to be curious. About the only thing we were taught about curiosity is that it killed the cat—and we are left with the clear impression that *we* are the cat!

Another problem is that many of us *think* we are curious when we are not really curious; what passes for curiosity is often nothing more than a mild interest stemming from the fact that something, for the moment, got our attention.

If you want to get on the best terms with your Inner Youth, you will have to learn to be actively, enthusiastically interested! And that means a well-developed sense of curiosity. If you would like to do that, here are some tools that will help:

1. When looking at something (an object, a building, a part of the landscape, a book, another person, anything at all), *really* look at it.

Take a moment and focus your mind and give the object or thing you're looking at some *real* attention. Examine it. Think about it. Then tell yourself to find something about the object or thing that you've never noticed before. No matter what it is you're looking at, you will find something new.

This is a fun technique to practice, but it is more

than just having fun looking at things in a new way. Even a day or two of this simple practice will do wonders to heighten your awareness of your own curiosity.

2. Ask more questions in your mind.

Start asking yourself questions like: Where did that come from? How was it made? Who first thought of that idea? What is inside this? What does that look like from the other side? What does he really mean? Why does that always work that way? What causes this? I wonder what would happen if . . . How could this be made to work better? Why do I like that? What else could I use this for? If I had been the one to design this, how would I have done it differently?

Practicing curiosity is one of the greatest mental stimulations you will ever find. Mind-brain researchers and medical scientists have learned that the structure of neurons in the brain grows stronger when they are stimulated, and "dry up" when they are not. These billions of neurons and their connecting dendrites and synapses and neurotransmitters, these so-called "muscles of the mind," must be exercised. It is no wonder, then, that those who have the greatest curiosity, ask the most questions, and have the greatest interest in everything that is going on around them are also the most alive. They are, in their brains—neurologically, chemically, electrically—the most alive.

Through their curiosity, they are exercising their mind and brain, keeping them fit. And without a doubt they are also having the most fun.

3. If you want to find the "truth," you'll *have* to be curious.

The truth in everything around us, the truth that helps us rid ourselves of the myths and get on with our lives, usually doesn't have a sign on it announcing what it is. But curiosity helps us find the truth. Curiosity exposes the myths and reveals the truths that the myths cover up. Curiosity is what caused Clyde to put the magic glasses on in the first place. And because of curiosity, truth is what he found.

19

◆

OPEN MINDS OPEN DOORS

◆

"The one who holds the key to your mind
is the one who opens or closes
the door to your storehouse of knowledge.

Know well the one who holds the key to your mind:
The one who holds the key is *you.*"

STEP
3
◆

Finding Your Inner Youth—
ALWAYS KEEP AN OPEN MIND.

It is a delightfully accurate picture of life that says, "I have an open mind about everything that I haven't made my mind up about yet!" That is probably true of all of us—for some more than others.

I don't think I have ever met anyone who had a

completely *closed* mind—*and* a brightly burning Inner Youth at the same time. Nor have I ever met anyone with a completely *open* mind whose fire of Inner Youth had gone out. The link between a clear, open mind and a strong Inner Youth is evident.

Being Closed-minded Is Being Closed-*lived*

We have all seen, as an example, the stereotyped "terrible father" in the movies or on television who will not listen to anything his son or daughter has to say. The mean father, set in his ways, is the quintessential portrait of the closed-minded man. Usually, in the stories, it is his closed-mindedness that leads to disaster.

We don't have to look to movies or television to give us examples of closed-minded men and women. We all meet plenty of them. I doubt that most of them have ever given a moment's thought to the fact that closed-mindedness destroys a vital part of their inner selves. They are so sure they are right! They are so convinced that theirs is the only answer. They are so sure that theirs is the only way, that they often spend years of their lives defending it and attempting to prove it.

And it is such a waste of energy! It wastes time, and it makes life miserable for others. The behavioral style of failing to keep an open mind, refusing to recognize the possibility of alternatives, has walled people off from reality, stifled their lives, sabotaged potential, and smothered new ideas before they were ever born.

Can simply being closed-minded do all that? Yes, it can.

Without an Open Mind, Truth Is Useless

If you want to find the treasure of the youth within you, you will have to have an open mind. This one direction that leads to the treasure within us is vital. Without following it, we cannot stay on course—because if we don't keep an open mind, we refuse to accept the truth even when it is in front of us. Why put the magic glasses of truth on at all if we are not prepared to accept what we see? Why try to find the answers if we have closed our minds to seeing them?

So if we want to be completely alive every day for the rest of our lives, we have to open our eyes and our ears and our hearts and our minds at those times when in the past we would have closed them. This does not mean that we should immediately begin to accept everything at face value; that is never the case. Having an open mind does not mean giving up choice. It means giving ourselves *more* alternatives to choose *from*. It is when you close off your options that you close off your potential.

Yet how many people have we met who never seem to have an open mind about anything? And it doesn't make any difference how bright or intelligent they are. I know people who are brilliant and are still so closed-minded that their brilliance will never do them or anyone else any good. There is no relationship between closed-mindedness and how much intelligence one has or doesn't have.

Closed-mindedness is the direct result of programming. As we have learned, we were programmed to believe what we believe and to think the way we think. Those programs still operate within us. They set our course and direction, and even control the way we think and act today. But we have also learned that we can override those old programs by conscious choice. And if we have failed to be as open-minded as would have been best for us in the past, it will take a clear and conscious choice now to do something about it.

A Self-test for Open-mindedness

The next time the opportunity comes up for you to accept something *new*—a new idea, a new belief, a new solution—ask yourself these four questions:

1. What would I ordinarily think about this?
2. If I were *completely* open-minded, how would I look at it?
3. If I were closed-minded, how would I look at it?
4. Since I have made the choice to be open-minded in all that I do, how do I choose to look at this *now?*

Even if becoming more open-minded had nothing at all to do with Inner Youth (although it has a *great deal* to do with it), it would be worthwhile to practice the habit of open-mindedness for the many *other* benefits that it will automatically bring to your life. Perfect the art of being open-minded, and you will enhance the life that you are living.

This step in the pathway to finding the treasure of your own fountain of Inner Youth will help you live younger—and it will help you live *better*.

20

◆

TAKE AN UNEXPECTED TURN

◆

*"The fullness of your life
will be measured
not by the number of years you live,
but by the number of memories you make each day."*

STEP
4

◆

Finding Your Inner Youth—
DO SOMETHING DIFFERENT.

It stands to reason that if you are going to look for ways to create more joy in your life, have more curiosity, and keep an open mind, you are going to naturally find opportunities to do something different. Doing something different is one of the best ways you can find to get your own attention, and *convince you* to do some things differently from the way you might have done them in the past.

One of the reasons that people of any age grow older and their Inner Youth starts to die out is that there is too much "sameness" in their lives. They have confused "sameness" with "security," but the two are not the same. Sameness often leads to *dullness;* dullness leads to *boredom,* and boredom leads to *unfulfillment.*

It's not that we find it difficult to find something to do that is "different"; it is that we simply may not be used to doing it. If something is different, then by its very description it is something we are not in the habit of doing. And if we are not in the habit of doing it, it is out of the ordinary. So doing something different attacks our security, and our old programming tells us to be afraid or cautious and gives us reasons to put off doing the thing that is different.

We're not talking here about doing something different just to be odd or unusual. We're talking about adding *dimension* to our lives, adding more color and shape and substance to who we are and what makes us up. And we're talking about more than just styling our hair a different way or getting some new clothes.

Unfortunately, there is no list of "different things to do" that would automatically work for everyone. Every individual requires a different list. To some people, "doing something different" means doing something daring or dangerous. To those individuals, going skydiving or shooting the rapids alone in a kayak might seem to be exactly what it takes to bring the Inner Youth back to life. (To my way of thinking, it could also very quickly shorten it.)

Other people think of doing something different as making a change in a relationship, finding a new way to meet people, or changing the habits of years and taking a whole new kind of vacation. Others see doing something different as changing jobs or making a complete change in their career paths. Other people think about going back to school, starting a new hobby, or getting a new group of friends.

All of these may be fine; I am neither for nor against any of them as things to do that are different. That is always up to the individual. But I would suggest that the kind of "difference" that we are talking about here goes far beyond a single dramatic step such as a change in summer vacations, or the search for a new relationship.

Doing Something Different Means Making an "Attitude Adjustment"

In this step that leads us on a pathway toward our Inner Youth, we are talking about being *ready* to do something different anytime the opportunity calls for it. It is readjusting an *attitude* that might have once said, "I'm sorry, *this* is the way I do things, and *this* is the only way I am." Like the challenge we received in the previous step about keeping an open mind, this step asks us to look at opportunity much as a child might look at the rides at a carnival. There is so much to explore, so much to do, so much life that has not been lived yet!

It does not mean making poor choices or doing something that you do not choose to do. It means seeing the unlimited opportunities that are in front of you, and taking the risk to live at least some of them out. This direction suggests that we see risk not as a negative, but that we change the word *risk* to mean "the opportunity to live."

If you want to keep your Inner Youth alive, tomorrow do something different. Today do something different. Start with something easy. Eat something different at your favorite restaurant, or try a different restaurant. Get up at a different time in the morning. Watch something new on television, or don't watch television at all. Read a different kind of book. Call someone on the phone whom you don't usually call. Listen differently to other people when you're having a conversation.

Doing something different could be anything at all. Make your own list, and start by trying the first item at the top of the page.

This is not an exercise in trying to do something strange. This is getting us to grab ourselves by the shoulders, shake ourselves hard, and get our own attention. When we become complacent, we stop living a little. We subdue our Inner Youth or slowly lull it to sleep. It is time to wake it up.

21

◆

THE PEOPLE WHO SHARE
YOUR ADVENTURE

◆

"If your life is a reflection
of those you share your time with,
then share your time with those
whose lives you would most like to reflect."

STEP
5
◆

Finding Your Inner Youth—
SPEND TIME WITH
PEOPLE WHO ARE TRULY ALIVE.

People who are truly alive make *other* people feel more alive. People who have that spark and sparkle of Inner Youth, that zest for living, that enthusiasm—

those are the people who have the energy that seems to rub off on the rest of us.

None of us needs to be told that many of the people we are with the most are the people who influence us the most. And the more we've learned about the neurological programming processes of the human mind, the more we've learned that every "input" we receive from someone else *does* become imprinted chemically and electrically in our brain—and those influences *do* affect us.

Since we are in part the sum total of all of the programs in our brain, and since all our beliefs and attitudes are the result of those programs, then it makes sense that the people who program us—the people we associate with—play an important role in how we feel about ourselves.

What Spending Time with the Wrong People Can Do

Have you ever experienced a time when you felt great—your spirits were high, you were in an incredible mood, and everything was going just right for you—and then someone took that all away because he or she had a sour attitude or was depressed or upset about something? Sometimes spending ten minutes with the wrong person can ruin an entire day!

And not everyone around us understands that it is their own attitude that is making life miserable or difficult for them. They haven't learned yet that in order to keep your inner spirit alive, you have to get into the habit of being "up" instead of being "down." So we know a lot of people who sort of grouse their way through life, not ever too happy about anything, thinking that's the way it has to be and making our lives the worse for it.

Being around that kind of person can be draining, especially if you're trying to keep your own spirits high and find some joy and enthusiasm in life. Instead of complaining about inconsequential problems, a lot of those people who don't know how to live on the brighter side of life are just "there." Those people are all around us, and there's not much we can do about them.

We may live with them at home, or work with them in our job, or in one way or another we simply have to associate with them. We do our best not to let their negative attitudes rub off on us, and yet when we're around those people, we can feel their attitudes hanging heavily in the air like the oppression of humid summer heat. We can feel the weight of an unpleasant attitude as it dampens our optimism and saps our energy.

I know individuals who have lost so much of their Inner Youth, and who live the myths so strongly in their lives, that they carry an atmospheric depression with them wherever they go. They can walk into a room and change the atmosphere. We all sense it. They can walk into the brightest day and make it rain.

Fortunately, not everyone is like that. People and their attitudes create emotional climates that run the range from the sorriest to the brightest and everything in between. Some people have the habit of being gloomy only now and then, and bright and sunny now and then. Other people are almost never bright, optimistic, cheerful, enthusiastic, or joyous. And others see the world in a brighter, better way in spite of the problems that they, too, must deal with.

You can always spot these people in any crowd. They radiate a glow, the sparkling and colorful effervescence of an Inner Youth that is alive and well. They are the people who carry their own personal rainbows around with them. They are the people who give off a special kind of light. Those are the people who are really alive.

Who Would You Rather Be With?

Even as we ask ourselves the question, the answer is obvious. Who would you rather spend your time with, people who have lost their Inner Youth and have no sparkle left, people who aren't even aware that there is an Inner Youth at all and are just getting by— or people who are happy, excited about living, and very much alive?

It may be a simple question to answer, but the choices you make about the people you spend time with are among your most important choices. And it is not just because of the way those people influence you, what they say to you, what their ideas are, or what beliefs you might gain from them that these people become so important to you. It is also in how you *react* to them.

When you meet someone who has an interest in being alive, and who has an active personal energy, the two of your attitudes combine to create a synergistic force that both of you can feel.

When a person has no internal spirit, no self-drive, no internal power plant of self-generated energy, then that person must draw his vitality from the people around him. Why is it we feel so drained after spending only an hour or two with someone who is down or negative or has no inner spirit? It is because that person has no real energy source of his own to tap into, and he has to tap into the energy he finds in the people around him.

Some people who want to help others feel they

are doing good works or are being of service to their fellow man when they allow other people to draw energy from them. That is not a good work or service. That is simply allowing someone else to not take responsibility for his own internal spirit. We can *encourage* others, of course; we can believe in them and let them know it, and we can help others in many ways.

But we can never give our energy to others and expect that we can create *their* inner spirit *for* them. That is something that each person must do for himself. So when we spend time with others who do not have a healthy Inner Youth, they usually do little more than pull us down, as though our inner spirit would be buoyant and strong enough to hold both of us up.

We can do that for a time, of course—but any of us who has tried to keep someone else afloat, keep someone else happy, or add zest to his or her life finds that we can do it only for a very short time and then *our* energies, too, begin to ebb away. And it is important for us to be aware of that. But it is the opposite of ebbing energies that is the truly important message in this step toward finding and keeping our own Inner Youth alive.

The real message here is not so much to avoid entirely those who have lost their Inner Youth. Our goal now is to *seek out* others who *have* it, associate with them, spend time with them, do things with them, talk with them, share with them, and together build on the spirit of *living*—enhance the joy we feel within us, reach out and grab whole handfuls and armfuls of experience and sharing and growing and living.

Ask yourself the question we posed earlier in a different way: Would you rather spend a weekend with a group of friends who looked at life as being rather gray, average, or not too interesting, or a group of friends who were *alive, enthusiastic, curious, joyous, open-minded, full of belief, and full of life?*

Now ask yourself another question: Which of any of these friends would you rather spend even one hour with—or ten minutes, or five?

Spending Time with the Right People Will Add *Life* to Your Life

If you want your Inner Youth to be vitally alive, one of the greatest kindnesses you can ever give yourself will be to spend time—a *lot* of time—with people who are really alive. When we spend time with people who are clearly and actively alive, we surround ourselves with examples of success—models to follow—enduring proof that others can do it. And therefore, so can we.

When we spend time with people who are truly alive, we enrich ourselves with encouragement and support. We know that we are going to be shown a reflection of the best of ourselves. We know that the words we hear from those we choose to have around us will always be the words that build us up and never pull us down. They will be the words that add to our self-confidence and self-esteem.

In any relationship, there are two factors that make the difference. They are the principal ingredients that will make a relationship work for you or not work for you. The first factor is your own attitude and actions. The second factor is the person you choose to have the relationship with.

If you'd like associations, relationships, and friendships in your life to always be those that help you get the most from yourself, then put people on your list who are very much alive. People who are alive give you the confidence to do new things. Their age is completely unimportant. Where they've been or how much "status" they may have means nothing at all. *It is who they are and the status they carry with them in their own minds that counts.*

When you next meet someone and you consider whether that person may be someone whom you would like to get to know or to share some of your time with, look for the spark. Look for the glow. Look for the clues that tell you whether this person is *alive*.

Those may not be the criteria you choose to use in selecting every friend you make. But it is a simple fact that the more people you associate with in your life who have vitality and energy of their own and who see the world in a believing and self-fulfilling and prosperous way, the more you will find yourself in the midst of the group that is going somewhere that works.

I'm not suggesting that you get rid of old friendships or disavow present relationships and rush out to seek new friends. But you may want to take a look at the people you spend your time with, and ask yourself whether those relationships are really full of a healthy spirit or not.

Who you choose to spend your time with (other than the people you "have to" be with) should always be up to you. And since it *is* up to you, that means you are the person who can do the most about deciding who gets to share your time and who doesn't.

An Immediate and Wonderful Reward

If you were to make a list of all the people right now in your life whom you spend more than an hour a week with, and if you were to put a check mark beside the names of those in whom, when you looked at them and looked in their eyes, you saw that marvelous sparkle of Inner Youth alive and well, how many check marks would you make?

If you made a similar list, but this list was made up of those people you associated with completely by *your own choice*, how many of the people on that list would have a check mark in front of their names?

It is a facet of human nature that we tend to select friends that are most like we perceive ourselves to be. That would say that out of a list of ten people, if you have checked eight of them as having "the light," it would mean that you feel unconsciously that your own light—your own Inner Youth—is strong within you.

If on your list of ten friends *that you have chosen* there are only a few of them who have the sparkle, that might suggest that you do not feel as enthusiastic about your internal liveliness as you would like to—and you may want to practice all the harder bringing more of your own spirit back to the brightness that it deserves to have.

Most of us, when we look around us at the friends we keep, after only a moment or two of reflection, have a pretty good idea if we have chosen well. And spending time with people who are alive and filled with their own Inner Youth *always* makes life better for us every day we do it.

One of the most exciting things about following this step is that it offers a reward almost from the moment you decide to do anything about it.

This is not one of those suggestions for living that self-help authors often give us that if followed will eventually do some good. *Good comes from being with people whose Inner Youth is alive and well the moment we begin spending time with them.*

22

◆

THE LIGHT FROM WITHIN

◆

"The amount of life you allow yourself to *live*
while you are here on this earth
can be measured by
the number of times you smile each day."

STEP

6

◆

Finding Your Inner Youth—
SMILE MORE.

What a wonderful, magical thing a smile is!
And how remarkable it is that some people do it so
seldom.

Of all the gifts of human spirit, of all the simple
treasures that do so much to enhance our lives—to

make us feel better, to quicken our step, to give us an immediate lift in attitude or bolster our confidence or light up the day—there is nothing so attainable as a smile. What incredible, positive, uplifting power that one simple expression has in it!

It would be hard to imagine someone who had a great deal of Inner Youth who did *not* smile. Being alive, being in tune and in touch with life, feeling good about yourself, having strong self-esteem, having a great deal of curiosity and a lot of joy for living—those are the signs of Inner Youth. But the simplest, most powerful sign of all is the smile.

It Is More Important Than We Might Ever Have Imagined

Let's take a look at what something as simple as a genuine, heartfelt smile does for us when we see someone *else* smile:

- It creates an unconscious positive feeling.
- It shows us the person's attitude.
- If the smile is directed at us, it shows us we are liked or thought well of.
- It is a sign of friendliness or friendship.
- It is a sign of some level of happiness.

Even though we may take smiles for granted, we recognize them when we see them, and we are happy they're there. But a closer look at what happens to us—*within us*—when *we* smile may give us a better idea of how that simple smile we take so much for granted may be far more important than we had ever considered it to be. When we smile, we:

- Feel better
- Think more optimistically
- Are more open to opportunities and alternatives
- Immediately begin to affect our own attitude
- View problems more positively
- Give ourselves strength and encouragement
- Create positive chemical and electrical changes in the activity of the brain
- Improve our physical and mental well-being
- Improve our chances for having a better day

When you look at the *benefits* that the simple act of smiling creates in us, it makes one wonder why we don't automatically smile more.

Why People Don't Smile More Often

It isn't that some people smile because things are going well for them and other people don't smile because things aren't going well. It is almost a measure of balance in one's life to be able to smile when things *aren't* going all that well. In fact, it is often true that it is our good or bad disposition that makes things happen for us, good or bad, instead of the other way around.

If the habit of smiling can do so much for us, then why is it that some people have to be almost encouraged to do it? (And some people almost *refuse* to smile, no matter how much encouragement they get.)

Just as there are reasons that people don't take care of their health as they should, just as there are reasons that people don't treat others in a relationship as they should, there are also reasons that people don't treat *themselves* and their own psychological or mental nutrition as they should. Some of the reasons people *don't* smile include:

- They feel unhappy.
- They are too busy.
- They think they *are* smiling when they're not.
- They don't understand the importance of smiling.
- They never really learned *how* to smile.
- They have low self-esteem.
- They feel that life is unfair.
- They feel that they have been treated poorly.
- They can't think of anything to feel good about.
- They have a habit of looking serious.
- They think that smiling is reserved for certain social circumstances, such as smiling when it is "polite" to do so.
- They never really *think* about smiling.
- They will wait until sometime when they "feel" happy.
- They just *forget*.

What Smiling Does for Your Inner Youth

The art of smiling is more than the art of making yourself feel good or making other people like you. When you smile, you create strength of self, get in touch with your inner joy, and spread it like rays of sunlight for the world to see.

There are three manifestations caused by smiling—and each of them add life to our Inner Youth:

1. When you smile, you *empower* yourself.
2. When you smile, you *discover* yourself.
3. When you smile, you *release* your inner self.

Let's take a closer look at each of these manifestations and what they mean to us.

1. When you smile, you empower yourself.

The attitude or the state of mind that is automatically and naturally tied to a smile is one of increased self-assurance, feeling closer to your best, more capable, and more confident. A smile is so much more than just the repositioning of the right set of facial muscles around the mouth that create the smile in the first place.

The smile itself is the literal physical manifestation of a neurological and physiological phenomenon within the brain. Thoughts within the brain trigger powerful electrical and chemical responses that show themselves in our actions and in our attitudes. A positive, constructive thought creates a completely different set of human actions and moods from a negative or self-defeating thought.

You can almost see a living picture of someone's attitude by the way they carry themselves, the way they walk, the way they move, the way they talk, look, and act. That is also true of the way they smile, and how often or how seldom they smile.

But it is also true that the way a person chooses to look, act, walk, move, etc. *will, in turn, affect the person's attitudes and thereby the chemical and electrical reaction and response in the brain*. It can be said that if you want to smile more, create happiness. It is also true that if you want to create happiness, smile more.

It is physiological: People who are the happiest smile more. *And people who smile more create more happiness and well-being in their minds*—and thus are happier in reality.

Does that mean that the act of smiling itself actually creates more well-being in someone's life? Yes, it does. Happiness may create an expression of happiness on one's face, and the reverse is also true: *Creating the smile creates the result!*

Go ahead—try this for yourself. Right now, smile! Not just a little smile—*really smile*. A great, big, happy, "I like myself," "I feel good about myself" smile. If you can take a minute, and you have a mirror handy, look in the mirror. First look at yourself *without* smiling—and then smile. Not just for a second, or a flash of a smile, but really smile! Practice it for a few moments or until you get used to smiling at yourself in the mirror without feeling silly or uncomfortable. And then for a little bit longer, keep smiling.

If you can't get to a mirror at the moment, I trust you are practicing the smile while you are reading this. I assure you it cannot hurt you. And while you were smiling—especially if you smiled a great, big, happy smile—you stopped thinking about whatever it was you were thinking about just before you smiled. And if you were worrying about anything at all, for the moment *you stopped worrying*.

Go ahead—try it again. Don't try to worry, of course—just smile one of those bright, sunshiny, "I'm in love with the world and everything in it today" kinds of smiles, and see what it does. You can actually *feel* the chemical change taking place inside of you.

Neurologically, physiologically, you are affecting the mood mechanism of your brain (chemically and electrically) in a most natural and positive way. The human brain is conditioned to sense a smile as a sign of well-being. When things are going well with you, it triggers the mechanism that creates the smile you show.

In the same way, when you consciously choose to wear a smile, you send a powerful message to your brain that tells it to naturally and automatically *create the mood that is most often associated with the smile you are wearing*. That's *you* controlling the chemicals of your own mind! That is why smiling empowers you with extra strength, more courage, more optimism, and a feeling of well-being. It is a tremendous tool that you have at your disposal *anytime* you choose to use it!

2. When you smile, you discover more of yourself.

Smiling puts you in touch with who you really are. The reason this happens is that when you smile, some of your guards go down—some of the walls are broken through; some of the self-protections that we create to hide ourselves behind are broken through by the sunny rays of a smile.

A true, genuine smile has an innocence about it. It lets us see a part of ourselves that is not so walled off, not so afraid and unsure.

We're not talking here about the feigned smile or the "social smile," the turn-it-on, turn-it-off, expected smile that carries with it no real depth or sincerity. We're talking about the very real smile that all of us like to feel, all of us like to see—the smile that always makes things a little better.

It is that kind of smile that helps us discover more of the best of ourselves. It may not be true that people who like themselves the most or who have the highest self-esteem always smile the most. (The unfortunate truth is that many of them, too, simply never learned *how* to smile or have never learned the *value* of smiling.) But it is certainly true that those people who have the least self-esteem or who like themselves the least often smile the least.

They are not only unhappy about *things*, they are also unhappy with themselves. It can be hard to smile a real smile when you are unhappy with who you are. But one of the steps on the road to recovery is learning to smile again—practicing what it feels like to like yourself and to be happy with who you are.

Within each of us lives a very fine person. Learning to smile helps us discover that person.

3. When you smile, you release your inner self.

We have just seen that smiling helps us discover a part of our inner selves. It is also true that smiling helps us release that self, express it, and let it out into the daylight.

So much of the best of ourselves is bound up by fear and is hidden away within us! There is so much of our potential that never gets out! If we could just learn to discover and release the potential that is *already within us,* no one would ever have to tell us a thing about "how to" achieve in life. As simple as it may sound, the practice of smiling, honestly and openly, helps us release that potential and live more of it out.

This is one of those steps on the treasure hunt to finding your Inner Youth that sounds so simple that some will wonder how it could ever make any difference at all. Some people think it is an absurd notion to suggest that smiling more could ever make any real difference. The concept is so simple and so "within the ordinary" that it doesn't appear to be extraordinary at all.

People *learn to* smile, and they learn *not to* smile. The ability to create warmth and to show it through our smile is a habit. Some of us, when we were very young, had the habit. It had come to us naturally, and we exercised it well. For some of us that habit gave way to a different look at life and a different expression on our faces.

Eventually, when little or no time is spent practicing smiling, the smile becomes an occasional thing. It is there when required, or when something strikes us

207

in a certain way—but strike us it must, or we seldom smile at all.

Little did we know what a role this simple featuring of our faces has to do with keeping in touch with who we are inside. And once grown, with the innocent smiles and bright sparkling eyes of youth long gone, to learn to smile again—twice as often, ten times more often, or at every opportunity throughout the day— some would almost need to take a special class in smiling, and learn how to smile all over again.

With all the philosophically complex ideas that are presented to us, with all the deep books and intense seminars, I suspect that a simple one-day workshop on the art of smiling might teach us more. You would almost not want to admit to anyone that you were attending, of course. I can just hear what some people would say: "Smiling?! You're going to take a class on smiling? Why in the world would you ever want to do that? Everybody knows how to smile. Everybody already does it. What could you possibly learn in a class on smiling?"

But I also suppose whoever said that would not be wearing the magic glasses of truth—or they would know. They would know that we carry with us a tool that is so valuable that all we have to do is put it on and wear it and it changes things. They would not know that while our eyes may be the windows to our souls, *it is our smiles that are the reflection of the light we carry within us*.

Hints to Help You Remember How to Smile

It may be, of course, that you smile a lot already. As with any of the other steps and directions in this treasure hunt for the Inner Youth, you may have been on course long ago all by yourself. That is my hope.

But if the simple message of this chapter has made sense to you, and you would like to try the wonderful art of smiling *more* for yourself, here are some helpful hints:

1. Don't wait for an opportunity to smile. Smile anytime you want to. Now would be a good time to try it.

2. There may be times when smiling might not feel appropriate. You'll always know when it's good and when it isn't. Most of the time, it's okay.

3. The next time you feel bad about *anything* that you would rather not be feeling bad about, smile. I am reminded of the story of the man who learned about the physiological value of smiling, and the very next time he was stopped by a patrolman and given a traffic ticket, he cheerfully handed his driver's license and auto registration to the officer and smiled from ear to ear throughout the entire ordeal. He told me later that it helped, and that the patrolman never did figure out whether he was crazy or just enjoyed getting traffic tickets.

4. I would suggest that you not make it a point to tell someone else about your new experiment in smiling. Unless they understand, they may think it's a strange idea, and they'll question every new look that crosses your face, thinking, "Oh, my—here comes another smile!"

5. Learning to smile more is a habit. That means you'll have to stay with it. The more you practice smiling at yourself in front of the mirror (especially each morning), the easier it will get and the more natural you will feel about smiling more often for more reasons (or for no reason at all) throughout the day.

6. And finally, when you smile—for whatever the reason—for just a moment say these words to yourself: "I like who I am, and I'm glad to be alive," and then quietly or silently say "hello" to your Inner Youth. *You are about to see more of it.*

23

◆

A SERIOUS SUGGESTION

◆

*"Learning to laugh is not only
the result of a life well lived;
learning to laugh is
the beginning of a life well lived."*

STEP
7
◆

Finding Your Inner Youth—
ENRICH YOUR LIFE WITH A SENSE
OF HUMOR.

We have heard that laughter is one of the remedies
that "cures what ails us." Most of us from our own
experience know that is true. There is also no doubt
that the Inner Youth within us understands laughter

very well. It enjoys laughter. It waits for it. And it relishes laughter when it comes.

Laughter is such a hearty medicine! Good, heartfelt laughter has a marvelous effect on our bodies and our minds.

When we laugh, we feel different. When we *really* laugh, for whatever good reason, we feel a part of the joy of life that overwhelms us and lets us touch for a moment a feeling that almost nothing else in life gives us.

Laughter is good. But laughter is more than good. It is *essential*. Without laughter in our lives, there is little real feeling or expression of joy. Without laughter in our lives, the tensions of day-to-day living reign supreme, and there is little place for them to go. Laughter dissipates the stresses of daily life in a way that nothing else comes close to.

It is a therapy that each of us gives to ourselves that settles our nerves, subjugates and pushes aside the problems, and lets us know that, ultimately, all is well. Laughter in its truest form gives us a sense of inner relief. It lets us know that no matter how bad we think we have it, things could be worse. It tells us that no matter how bad things are that are going on around us, we are still here and alive, and instead of letting the problems of life get us down to some unbearable level, we can still see the light and take things less seriously.

And therein lies the key to this step in the finding of our own Inner Youth.

Some of the most successful people I have ever met are able to laugh the most. They have learned to laugh at themselves; they have learned to recognize the incredible inequities in the world they live in, and to see them for what they really are.

Are We "Designed" to Laugh Only a Certain Amount?

Some people believe that although laughter is a natural part of life, some of us are destined or "genetically" inclined to laugh more often than others. They believe that recognizing and expressing the humor of life is a genetic "given." They assume that some people get to laugh more than other people because that is the way they were born to be. And they end up with less laughter in their lives because of that mistaken belief.

But that isn't the way it is at all. Those same individuals who believe that laughter is natural to some, and allowed in only a limited form for others, fail to recognize that learning to laugh has little to do with some pre-set genetic personality. We are not born to laugh or not to laugh. We are not born to express our joy or hold it back. We are not born with a sense of humor or without one. All that is part of how we learn to live.

Just as we learn to speak up when we have something to say or learn to hold it back and seldom speak our piece, so do we also learn to laugh or learn to reject and subdue the feelings that we feel inside of us.

It is the same with crying. Some people learn to cry, and learn to know that it is okay to cry. When they feel bad, they express their feelings of disappointment or despair by crying, or they learn—usually from early childhood—to wall it off and hold it in.

We Learn to "Edit" Our Feelings

Year after year, day after day, we are taught what is "okay" to feel and what is not "okay." In time, we develop a pattern that is taught to us by others, and we learn to follow that pattern. Instead of learning to express joy and happiness when we feel it and how we feel it, we learn very early to edit our feelings and to display them carefully.

Countless children have been told that they should not cry when they are feeling bad. Those same children have been told to be quiet when laughter was ringing through the household. And so they learn a "truth" that was never really true at all. Instead of being taught to cry and to laugh, they learned to put their feelings away somewhere as though those wonderful feelings of sadness or hurt or joy or excitement were not quite okay to express.

For the sake of "controlling one's emotions," for the sake of keeping things quiet and level in the household or in the classroom at school, the relief of feeling sad or crying or the exuberance of laughing almost for no reason at all was mitigated by adults who, while they were trying to do their best, taught some of us to believe that self-expression must be controlled.

In part they were correct. To make life work, we do have to control our emotions. But for some, the control went too far. Learning to hide our innermost feelings was not good learning for any of us.

And then, as we grew older, along came life. As we grew up and began to deal with the "serious" side of life, most of us learned to quiet the extremes of our feelings. We learned to act in a way that was acceptable to others. Some of us learned not to cry too often or too much, and we came to believe that mirth and joy and laughter were only now-and-then things.

A movie or a joke or a comedian on television could make us laugh, but our own laughter for our own reasons—for our own sense of self-expression—gave way to the supposed seriousness of everyday living.

214

And in time not all of us, but most of us, learned to laugh less—not spontaneously as we did as children, but appropriately, when something was suitably funny or humorous and it was okay to laugh out loud.

So it is that we have come to believe that some people have a "sense of humor" and some people do not. That we are conditioned out of having a sense of humor does an injustice to the human spirit. There is an incredible amount of humor in life. But so much of the recognition of the humor that is there gets taught out of us.

Responsibility for Our Laughter Is Left to the Entertainers

Eventually, many of us leave it up to the comedians to show us the absurdities of life. When we see them in a movie or watch them on television we laugh at the foibles of living that they point out to us. A good comedian makes us laugh because he has fun with our flaws and our failings, and shows them to us as they really are.

When we are "thorped" in our heads with a verbal two-by-four of absurdity, we get the message— and their message hits home.

Jokes, comedians, and movie comedies get us to laugh. The service they perform is necessary because all too many of us have lost sight of or have never learned the fact that a sense of humor is an *essential* and basic part of every successful life.

I will never forget talking to an old man many years ago who told me, "Shad, there are three things that you have to have in order to live a good life. They are love, health, and *a sense of humor*. If you don't have a sense of humor," he told me, "you'll take yourself and your life too seriously, and you'll lose sight of what it's all about.''

The old man was right. He may not have read a book about Inner Youth, but he certainly knew what he was talking about. One of the strongest earmarks of a strong Inner Youth is a strong sense of humor.

Have you ever known anyone who was really successful as an individual who could not laugh at himself? Any life that is well lived is *full* of foibles and mistakes. It is through those foibles and mistakes that we learn almost everything that is not learned in a classroom. The school of life is full of misjudgments, blunders, and mistakes. When we take them too seriously, we lose. When we lighten up and see the humor in our own growth, we have a chance of getting through it all.

Learning to Laugh at Yourself

A quote from the old book *The Fountain of Youth* reads:

> *Those who learn to laugh at life and learn to laugh at themselves always live more of the lives they are given. Those who have learned to take life too seriously always live life a little less.*

There is a lesson in those words. It is when we take ourselves and our lives too seriously that we miss out on living the life that is in front of us. It should not take a comedian or a funny movie to *make* us laugh. It should be *us*. All of us have the ability to recognize that every day of our lives is full of laughable situations. *But we take ourselves and our lives so seriously!*

We learn to believe that every problem we have is

one of the greatest problems that anyone has ever had. We learn to believe that the travails and problems of life are so important that we must deal with each of them in dead earnest, as though what we think and what we do is unbelievably and seriously important.

It does seem that life, at times, plays games with us. Life—because we don't always know how to deal with it—makes us feel foolish or unprepared or insecure. When life does what it does to us, you and I have the option of feeling foolish or stupid or insecure or unprepared—or we can get the better of it. We can figure it out. We can laugh along with it.

The next time you fail to get the promotion, or burn the toast, or overcook the turkey, or the next time company arrives and the house is a mess, or you have to get someplace and the car won't start, or something doesn't work the way you wanted it to work, or you are disappointed, or you have a problem in your life that you cannot change, remember this: Lighten up—life *is* short.

What incredible stress we add to our lives by taking things so seriously! What amazing drama we create in the smallest details of our existence! All too often it is only later, when we look back on a situation, that we look at it differently—in retrospect—and laugh about it.

I will never forget a time in my life when something happened to me that at the time was so embarrassing that I thought I would never live past it. Later, it proved to be one of the most enjoyable experiences I had ever had.

A number of years ago I drove a car that I dearly loved. The car was a brown Cadillac Coupe de Ville, and it was big and spacious and comfortable. Driving it was like driving my living room sofa down the street.

It was always easy to count my blessings when I was driving that car. It made me feel good about things.

But one day my Cadillac got sick and I had to put it in the shop for repairs. I asked my wife if I could borrow her car for a few days while my car was being fixed, and she was more than happy to lend me hers. She drove a white Oldsmobile Cutlass with two distinctive red pinstripes down the sides. It was a car that was unmistakable when you saw it on the street.

You've probably had the experience, as I had, of driving a new car or a different car for the first time— you notice any other car on the road that looks just like yours. It is as though they are both the same car.

On this occasion, only a few days after I had put my car in the shop, I was stopped at a light on the way to my office in the morning, waiting for the light to turn green, when I happened to look over at the car in the lane next to me at the same stoplight. It was the *identical* car: a white Oldsmobile Cutlass with two red pinstripes on the sides.

Recognizing the coincidence of the similarity, and wanting the driver of the other car to notice it too, I tapped politely on the horn. The driver in the other car looked over at me, then looked up at the stoplight, and I could see in a moment that he had not understood. He didn't get the message.

I had thought, I suppose, that a special kind of "highway bonding" should take place; the two of us being in identical cars meant we had something uniquely in common with each other. But when he looked over at me and then looked away, I realized that he hadn't noticed. No bonding had taken place.

But I wanted him to get the picture, so this time I honked on the horn longer, and when he once again looked in my direction, I pointed at myself and my car, knowing that now he would surely understand. But he didn't.

Now I thought, "This is getting embarrassing. I've just honked my horn and pointed at myself—and he doesn't understand!" The other driver looked up at the stoplight a little nervously, as though he were hoping the light would change soon and he could speed away from this strange driver next to him who was honking his horn and making strange gestures.

With only moments to go before the light changed, I decided I'd better try again. So this time I honked the horn loudly and motioned for the driver of the other car to roll down his window. He looked even more nervous by now, but he must have been curious, because he rolled down his window while I pushed the button on the door panel to lower mine.

Just as the light changed and only moments before both of us accelerated and moved forward across the intersection, I yelled through the two open car windows, *"We're both driving the same car!"*

And it was at that precise moment that I realized I was back in my brown Cadillac Coupe de Ville and he was driving a white Oldsmobile Cutlass with two red pinstripes down the side.

As he sped away into traffic and I slowed my Cadillac down to an embarrassed crawl, I realized that there was no possible way he could have understood. I wouldn't be surprised if the driver of that other car took a different way to work every morning for the next two weeks.

Can you imagine what he said when he got to the office that morning? He had to say something like, "You wouldn't believe what happened to me on the way to work today!" I'll bet he even thought that the driver of the Cadillac *looked* like a businessman! (Maybe he thought, "I'll bet it's an author.")

To this day, the memory of that moment evokes a combination of shaking my head, laughing at myself—usually out loud—and the unforgettable experience of extreme embarrassment.

When I was in the studio taping one of my national cable television shows, I told the producer of the show that I wanted to tell that story on the air. The producer of the TV show said, "It's a great story, but why do you want to tell it on the show? It doesn't have anything to do with what we're talking about." So I told him, "I want to find the guy and *explain!*" He didn't let me put it on the show.

I have told that story in some of my lectures, and along with the delight from the audience at my unretractable blunder, I've always wished that I could find that driver and tell him what happened. I think I hope that by sharing the story with my audience, I might just be lucky enough that he'll one day be in attendance. So far he hasn't been.

You'll understand, then, when I tell you that I hope he reads this book. If he does, I hope he'll drop me a card and tell me I'm off the hook.

There are two morals to this story. The first one is obvious: We all make mistakes; we all get embarrassed. Learn to love it, learn to laugh at it—it means you're alive. The second moral is: If you're ever in your car on the way to work and some guy at a stoplight honks his horn, gets you to roll down your window, and yells "We're both driving the same car!" give him a break. Be nice to him. It could be me.

Making the Choice to Have a Sense of Humor

Learning to laugh at yourself and your life does not mean *not* taking important things as seriously as you should. It means learning to laugh at *life* as it really is. If you lose that whimsical, fun-loving perspective and forget that life is, after all, incredibly short, then you lose the ability to take life breath by breath.

So, knowing how important it is, why don't we lighten up? It is because we honestly believe that who we are and what we are doing at any given moment is so important that if we don't do this thing in this way, say the right thing, do the right thing, or act in the right way, someone will think less of us. In short, at whatever level, fear steps in. We may not recognize it as fear, but in the final analysis it is that same old internal fear and insecurity that stop us.

Imagine what would happen if you made the choice right now to live the next twelve months without having a single fear or a single disapproval from anyone else. Let's also say that during those same twelve months you set a goal for yourself to look at life as it really is, and you decided to make your number-one goal, for just one year, to have a sense of humor.

During that time you choose *not* to rely only on someone else to make you laugh; instead, you choose to give everything you've got to developing your *own* sense of humor, and to enjoy the next twelve months of your life more than you have ever enjoyed a year.

How many minutes of each day now do you laugh? How much of the real humor of life do you allow to touch you? If you have been taught and conditioned to laugh, this one will be easy for you. But if you have not remembered how important it is to laugh—really laugh, the kind that shakes you up and reminds you of the laughter you had in your life when you were younger—then this one will take some practice.

If laughter is not an everyday part of your life right now, then there is something you can do that will not only help you find your Inner Youth, but will help you come alive again every day that you have in front of you. *You can practice laughing!*

You Can Practice Having a Sense of Humor

What brings out the humor in you is up to you, of course. What is funny, and what makes you laugh, is an extremely individual thing. All of us have experienced a time when we laughed uncontrollably at something that the next person saw no humor in at all, and vice versa. So what you laugh at is going to be up to you. The question here is whether or not you're taking the time to *find* the things in your life that bring the laughter, and whether you're finding *enough* of them.

We are talking here about what one might call a "positive" sense of humor, of course. It implies looking for the humorous while still seeing the good in things. There are plenty of good things to laugh at; all you have to do is look for them.

Go ahead—laugh at anything you want. That's the whole point. And since laughter is healthy (it is physiologically and biologically one of the healthiest things you can do for yourself), do as much of it as you can.

Ask yourself the question, "What makes me laugh?" You may want to have a discussion about this with a good friend, or with your family. Make a list if you like. Figure out what makes you laugh, and *make the decision to do more of it*.

That sounds simple. It is. The problem is that we often confuse laughter or humor with a lack of responsibility; we are raised thinking that a strong, apparent sense of humor, and the laughter that goes along with it, might indicate a lack of seriousness or a lack of respect for "important" things in life.

The truth is that a sense of humor *is* one of the most important things in life. The people who limit their humor to below that of a reasonable level seriously limit their capacity to see the truth of life's foibles. The result is that they end up taking life too seriously. And when that happens, they take themselves too seriously. And when that happens, they begin to lose sight of the enjoyment of life and parts of living that matter most.

Our Inner Youth has within it the spirit of happiness and joy and laughter. There is a part of all of us that sees life as it really is. When we, in our outer world, take ourselves too seriously, our Inner Youth—if it is still alive—sees life as it really is and begs us to lighten up, loosen up, do our best, and have fun with the greatest experience we will ever have in this lifetime. That experience is the experience of "living."

If you can't enjoy life while you are here, then you will lose one of the most important reasons for being here in the first place. You will lose the joy of living.

True Laughter Is an Expression of the Joy and the Spirit That Lives Within Us

If you love life and are living it, you feel good about it. If you, right now, are glad to be here, glad to be alive, and thankful for the opportunity to be living right now, then you must also feel the almost childlike delight and exuberance in expressing that joy. If open, outward, joyous laughter does not come easily to you, then I encourage you to begin to find it.

Practice laughing. Practice feeling good. Practice

having fun with life every day instead of ever dreading another tomorrow. Doing that and living that way will always be up to you. Don't wait for the latest laugh-a-minute situation comedy on television to bring out the joy and the humor that you already have within you.

Make the choice right now to find the humor—for *yourself*. Find the joy for yourself. Learn to laugh at the good times and the bad times. Learn to see for yourself in your own life what is serious and what is not.

Life doesn't always have to be funny, but with the problems that it delivers to us, we ought to at least have the opportunity to make life fun. Go ahead—find the fun in it! Learn to laugh at the absurdities of life as the child you once were who was ready and willing to laugh at anything at all.

For the rest of your life you will either have fun with the days that you live, or you will not. You will decide to laugh and enjoy yourself, not take yourself too seriously, and find for yourself some of the better reasons for living—or you will not. If you do not make the choice to laugh at yourself and to put into perspective the life around you, you can never ever truly live out the best of yourself.

If you choose to see life for what it really is, to take things in stride and to experience the *fun* of living it, you will have learned an immeasurably important lesson in the living of life. As it says in *The Fountain of Youth*, "Learning to laugh is not only the result of a life well lived; learning to laugh is the *beginning* of a life well lived."

24

◆

THE GREAT RESCUE

◆

"Never put off loving life.
Every day that you put off
embracing it, enjoying it,
and having fun with it
is a day that is gone."

STEP
8
◆

Finding Your Inner Youth—
BRING TO LIFE YOUR
SENSE OF PLAY.

As children, most of us grew up with a certain sense of adventure. We learned to believe in the magical, in the exciting, in the wonderful—and the world in front of us was full of marvelous unknowns and great opportunities and the unlimited possibility of treasures to seek. We sensed that if we were lucky enough, we would one day find that pot of gold at the end of the rainbow for ourselves. If we were of a creative mind, we may have even imagined that we might one day receive an inheritance from an unknown relative who, in his passing, left us untold riches. Those were the dreams of children, of course. We dreamed them as we played and pretended and lived fabulous lives of fantasy in our minds.

But then we started to grow up, and the games we played as children became fewer and fewer and soon began to go away. And the treasure we already possessed—the marvelous imagination, the wonderful pictures of ourselves that we lived in our minds—began to go away with them. As we grew up, a new kind of reality stepped in and took over, and new games replaced the old.

Instead of living imaginary lives as princes and princesses, or astronauts, or pioneers, or doctors, or nurses, or quarterbacks, or deep sea divers, or presidents, or ballerinas, or movie stars, we were told to keep our feet on solid ground—to keep our heads out of the clouds and to get down to the practical business of earning a living, having two point three kids, two cars in the driveway, two weeks of vacation every year, and someday, at the end of the road, a few years of retirement.

We were told that the new games of adulthood were the real games—that they were much more important than the games we played as children. And so we learned how serious and how important those new games that grown-ups played were. But we never quite realized what happened when we began to be adults: The imagination went away and stopped the play. The *play* went away and stopped the *imagination!*

Cops and robbers and rolling in the grass and riding on sleds and doing somersaults and playing with model planes and teddy bears and electric trains soon gave way to driving cars and going to work and having families and attending meetings and paying bills and being busy and waiting for the weekend and doing okay and getting through another day.

There's nothing wrong with any of that, of course. Most of us have a lot to do. Grown-up games can be pretty demanding. And as we have pointed out in Part II of this book, when we discussed the great myths we live by, a lot of us come to believe that the grown-up games we are expected to play are so important that they are more important than *anything else*—even more important than *us*.

There is a difference, of course, between "personal responsibility" and taking it all too seriously. Learning to find more of the real value in life, and learning to enjoy life while we're here, does not mean that we are not taking personal responsibility for ourselves. Just the opposite is true. It is when you *are* taking responsibility for *you* that you create *balance* in your life.

There is nothing at all balanced about a life that is made up of too much drudgery, too much attention to the unsatisfying work ethic that says we must work hard every moment, lest the moment be gone. I know people who believe that the value is in how hard they work, not in what they do. That is a myth in itself, and it has driven many to early graves or to unfulfilled potential.

If you see work and play as opposites, then balance them out and give yourself enough of both. But if you go beyond the old and questionable clichés of "serious work" and "unnecessary play," then you will open a door that could affect the rest of your life.

The most sensible point of view tells us that it is when you find *joy in your work* and *rejuvenation in your play* that life ultimately works best. If you truly want to take responsibility for yourself, you *cannot* avoid the responsibility of nurturing yourself with the vital replenishment that only a full measure of play can give.

We have a need to play, and to play often, and to enjoy our play as we did as children. If we fail to recognize that need, we end up playing another game; it is the game that grown-ups play.

Playing the Grown-up Game

As adults, we literally follow the "rules" of games that seem so all-important that we forget they are only games. We forget that there may be something else that we are losing that could be far more important, far more precious—something wonderful that is slowly slipping away.

We live out the myth of the incredible importance of unimportant things. We live out the myth of believing that other people know more than we do, have it figured out, and have the right to set the rules that tell us how to play the game. We lose our sense of courage and confidence, and give way to the random and unqualified opinions of others as though their voices count more than our own. And so we give ourselves "second best" in matters that ultimately determine how successfully we live out the potential of our own birthright, and how well we follow the path to our own greatness and joy.

We are told what to do and how to live by so many people that we stop living *our* lives and end up living *their* lives instead! We lose touch with a reality and a hopefulness that we understood far better before we grew up and learned the rules of the futile new game. In the process, we lost touch with ourselves and with our innermost needs as humans. By getting in step and following the crowd and buying into the game that grown-ups play, we forgot the message of our soul.

We got too busy, ended up with too many things to do, got too wrapped up in going to school and finding jobs and raising families and trying to live out the picture that life around us expected us to be—and we forgot how to listen to ourselves, our real selves, deep down inside.

Of course we know better! Almost anyone will tell you that they recognize the importance of coming to grips with who they *really* are and why they are here on this planet. If you have a heart-to-heart discussion with someone about this, you will find that person *"knows"* deep down inside, *senses* that there is more to life than most of us ever admit. Yet we still follow the "rules" and move from game to game.

Shakespeare was right; we are actors, and we go from stage to stage—from play to play—until the curtain goes down and the final play is over. And how serious we learn to believe our lines in the script are! We come to believe that our lines—our role—the latest game—is the most important role or game of all. And we play it out in earnest.

Some people take themselves so seriously that one would think the game they have chosen to play somehow matters more than anything else in the world around them. And they take themselves and their accomplishments and their trophies and medals and diplomas and titles and positions and jobs and everything about themselves and their lives seriously—*incredibly* seriously, *dangerously* seriously.

Some people do this more than others. Some people only partly forget that one day they will be gone and, in not too long a time, almost no one will remember them—and then in a little more time their names and their jobs and their rules and their demands and their limited views of life will be forgotten.

Other people buy into the game so completely that they never once, in their entire lifetime, recognize that it was finally just a game, and the only people who won were those who figured it out and saw it for what it really was. Those who live—who really *live* while they are here—are those who recognize the game, learn to play it on their own terms, and learn to put this most dangerous game aside when it begins to take away from them the value and the meaning of their lives.

Defending the Myth

What would the person say who never wears the magic glasses? He would say, "Wait a minute! You're trying to tell me that life isn't serious." And then he would defend the game he is playing by telling us again what he believes: "Life *is* serious. We've got a lot of responsibilities. We've got work to do. We've got more to do than we have time to get it done. Life is no laughing matter. Oh, maybe a joke now and then is okay; we all need some time off, a vacation now and then. But if you want to get anywhere in life, you've got to buckle down to business. You don't want to end up at retirement with nothing to show for it!"

What happens is that the half truths stated by the person in that example can *sound* so convincing. But they are only half true. Of course it's important to take responsibility for yourself, to work for what you believe in, to raise a family or have a career or spend your time in the way that you choose. We do live in the middle of a society, and we are part of that society.

But the game goes too far. Half truths become "rules" that we are, for some reason, *supposed to* follow. The half truths that tell us how we should act, how much time we should work, how responsible we should be, how we should spend our time, and an unending number of other social rules that surround us create a reality that appears to those who live within it to be more real than any other reality. The ultimate and total "seriousness" of life becomes such a cold, hard fact of life that we actually become convinced that it is a "truth" when it is not a truth at all.

Is This Grown-up Game Really How It's Supposed to Be?

A close examination of most of the people you or I meet would reveal that their own spirit of Inner Youth may not have flickered out completely, but it is often injured or dim. Much of the Inner Youth they had years ago is gone, and they look at life differently now. They have learned different games. They have learned different rules. They have grown up and accepted life as they see it to be as an adult, and they have learned to leave the not-so-serious excitement and fun and joy of youth behind them.

Many of them would also tell us that this is how it should be. "That is, after all, how grown-ups are supposed to act," they will tell us. Some of them will go so far as to tell us that when you grow up, "serious is the way you are supposed to be." If you wanted to go out right now and find someone who thought that way, I suspect you would not have to go too far.

People who *lose* their Inner Youth believe that having one is no longer important! They believe that growing up, settling down, stopping playing, and being generally serious about just about everything is the right way to live.

It is when people have lost their Inner Youth and can now play only the game of grown-ups that they will fight the hardest to defend their belief in the game. They will give you every reason they can think of that being "young" is one thing and being "adult" or "older" is another. They would like you to believe that their way—no matter how much of a grind it is, no matter how illogical it may be to live the way they live—that their way is the right way; they would have you believe that their reality is the true reality.

If you were to say to them, "You ought to stop for a while and take a good hard look at where you are going in your life, and you should consider playing more. You should think about being young again," many of those who are playing the game of grown-ups would tell you that playing is for children—that games are for kids. But I would question them.

Is the Grown-up Game Really Working?

If the game of grown-ups is working so well, then we could assume that getting rid of our Inner Youth and learning to take life more seriously and buckling down to becoming an adult and learning to live by the rules of the grown-up games *would make life "work" for us*. It makes sense that if we have found a *balance* between youthful enthusiasm and grown-up seriousness, life should be *working*.

But those same adults who have forgotten how to play, and who have learned to take life with frightening seriousness, have little to show for the value of their grown-up game. It is unfortunate that they have never figured out that it may not be the right way to *"live"* at all!

We see entire households torn apart by yelling parents, unhappy mates, insecure children who are having every ounce of their self-esteem destroyed for them, battered wives and embattled husbands, runaway kids and high school dropouts fostered by untrained parents who are trying to follow the rules of being an adult. That is a very common—all too common—kind of adulthood that surrounds us today. *Is that making life work?*

We drive down the highway and watch supposedly mature adults play high-speed games behind the wheels of cars, venting their emotions by lying on the horn, refusing to give way in a gesture of simple, polite decency to allow another car to change lanes or enter the right-of-way. We watch other adults who have learned to play the grown-up game become so angry at being caught in a traffic jam that they pound their fists on the steering wheel in infantlike frustration, and shout obscenities through a closed window.

We drive through city streets with our ears so accustomed to the drone of ceaselessly honking car horns that we become inured to the fact that this mindless cacophony goes on endlessly day after day— a discordant aria of rushing, unhappy humans who believe that this grown-up game they are playing is a game they are supposed to play. *Is that living life to its fullest and making it work?*

We turn to the front pages of our newspapers and read headlines that should shock and jar us, yet we calmly read past them as though they are not news to us at all. By now, as adults, we have learned there is nothing new about the news: Another terrorist attack ewhere killed someone who was innocent; another state or city is in crisis because its jails and prisons have become filled to overflowing, and there is no longer any place for the endless legion of angry, socially misguided errants to go to be jailed; alcohol and chemical abuse are ripping homes and families and whole countries apart at their seams.

If the adults around us have everything so well figured out, it looks as though something must be going wrong. *Is this living a life that's working?*

Even in something as necessary and as ordinary as day-to-day jobs, we look around us and see business managers, owners, supervisors, and employees at every level following the rules of being grown-up, and becoming so entrapped in the game that they go home night after night and complain to their husbands or wives about how unfair the boss is, how things never go right at work, or that someone is trying to get past them or do them out of something they deserve.

Squabbles, bickering, complaints and infighting among adults are so commonplace that they go by almost unnoticed; *they are a way of life!* Instead of keeping alive an inner spirit of positive, open-minded, curious enthusiasm for living, countless adults play out their frustrations in the battlegrounds of day-to-day living.

Few adults are able to confidently shout out their excitement with their lives. Fewer than three out of any hundred adults even *claim* to be living a completely fulfilling, self-actualized life. Of the other ninety-seven or so percent of those who are *not* finding fulfillment in their lives, millions of them have gotten so good at getting rid of their Inner Youth that they have forgotten how to play at anything that really nurtures their lives.

Does that tell us that the grown-up game is work-

ing? Does that tell us that the rules of the grown-up game were written by anyone who had any understanding of life at all?

We Play the Game We Are Taught to Play

Those around us who take their games so seriously cannot be faulted for doing so. They are just doing their best to live by the rules *they were taught.* And unfortunately, they were taught rules that were only half truths. They were taught rules of living by people around them who knew no better than they what would work for them and what wouldn't.

Some of the people around us who try to teach others how to live a better life *do* understand. They know the secrets, and they do their best to share them with others. But all too often their far more sane and sensible words of true wisdom have been drowned out by louder, less-informed voices who believed that their own messages were more important and more right.

In time, most of us began to lean in one direction or the other. We either gave up most of our creativity, or we kept it. We either expanded our curiosity, or we began to push it aside. We either looked forward to life as an adventure filled with new discoveries, or we began to hope that we could make it through somehow without too many injuries or bruises along the way. We either sought out new things and looked for new things to do, or we found our sense of security in sameness.

We either sought out new friends whose lives and youth and insight would stimulate and enhance our own, or we settled for the more accidental acquaintances who ended up being our friends simply because circumstances put us together.

We either fanned our inner spark of life—that ...ne of *youth* within us—and kept it burning bright, or we let it go unattended—quietly struggling to stay alive but finally, slowly flickering its way toward nothingness, toward a time when it would become nothing more than a few almost-forgotten childhood memories in our now grown-up lives.

We have lost so much along the way, and it is time for us to get it back. We may not be able to give Inner Youth and life and spirit back to others, but it is certainly time to give it back to ourselves.

Rescuing Your Inner Youth

When it comes to trying to hold on to our Inner Youth, most of us at some time or other get lost in the playing of the grown-up games along the way. And the problem with playing the game of grown-ups is that we take it all so seriously, *as though it were going to go on forever.*

It is as though we set out on a journey to find a treasure of untold beauty and riches, and instead of looking for the treasure where it really is—in the bright, sparkling sunlight of ourselves—we stumble into a cave and find ourselves searching aimlessly through tunnels and caverns that lead us deeper and deeper into dimmer and dimmer light, farther and farther away from the brightness that was our youth, our imagination, and our play.

After a while we no longer remember what we were looking for. After we have spent years wandering the passageways just doing our best to stay alive and keep moving onward, the goal is no longer the treasure we were seeking. The treasure that we started out to find is replaced by a new set of rules, by a new game that is the ultimate game grown-ups play. It is the game they call "survival"—and *survival* becomes the new goal.

Life is like that. The demands of daily living can send us on the most incredible wild-goose chases; we think we are headed in the right direction and are on target, when in reality all we are doing is getting more and more lost. It's even possible to get so lost and to spend so much time wandering through the caves and caverns that after a while we get used to it.

When we were young, we still felt our potential burning strong and bright within us. But now, when we have lost our way in life, and have lost sight of where we were headed, we have forgotten all about the brightness and the hope we began our treasure hunt with in the first place.

What we need is to suddenly hear a shout in the darkness, to hear the sound of our name being called out and leading us up out of the depths and back into the light. What we need is to be rescued!

The Rescue

To rescue yourself (because no one can do this for you), you have to make some decisions about what you want next. You have to decide for yourself whether the grown-up games are the best for you. Are they healthy? Is the life you are living right now exactly the way you want it to be? Is it life-giving, or is it life-*draining*? Is it mentally and physically wholesome and nutritious in every way? Are you giving yourself what you deserve?

Is there a part of you that would like to—even now and then—break away, feel better, and feel happier with yourself?

Maybe it's time to make some changes. Maybe it's time to get some of that Inner Youth back again, and this time hold on to it for good. Or maybe it's time to launch a full-scale rescue operation, and get *all* of your Inner Youth back and start getting to know yourself again.

If it's really important to you (or you even think that it *might* be), then there are some things you can do that will help. There is a rescue team of activities waiting for you to get your program under way, and you can start right now.

When we were kids, we believed that someone or something would always come to the rescue. When we got older, we started to believe that there was no cavalry at all, and hoping that anyone would come to our rescue was probably just wishful thinking. In a lot of life, that's true. We *do* have to be practical, and there *is* a reality out there.

The problem is that we have allowed those practical, hard-nosed, unforgiving rules of the grown-up games to undermine our sense of hope and faith and belief and new discovery.

Help *is* on the way—beginning the moment you send for it. If you want to rescue your Inner Youth, you can do it. If you're tired of living by nothing more than the questionable reality of the grown-up game, and you would like to regain some balance in your life, you can have it. Not only is there nothing *wrong* about balancing responsibilities of your everyday adult world with the lively enthusiasm of Inner Youth, it is probably the most important thing you or I could do today to make tomorrow better!

We are about to discover that creating Inner Youth is one of the most enjoyable experiences we adults could ever have. And we are about to do exactly buckled Camden, who, once free, raced into the house.

Libby Bradshaw poked her head through Evan's open window. "Don't worry about a thing, son. Cam's fine here as long as necessary. You take care of Grace and concentrate on finding the person trying to hurt her and her sister."

"Yes, ma'am." Having grown up in a military family, he always used "ma'am" and "sir" when talking to his parents. "And thanks, Mom."

She kissed his cheek and hurried indoors.

He may never have a wife and Camden may never have a mother in his life again, but they had his parents and Lisa's parents. Evan had spent too long feeling sorry for himself and focusing on past mistakes, maybe it was time he started counting his blessings instead of his failures.

Backing out of the drive, Evan flipped on the siren and sped toward Porter Animal Clinic and Grace.

He pulled into a parking spot beside the other patrol car and raced up the outside stairs that led to the apartment, ignoring the neighbors and community members gathering in clusters on porches and outside other businesses. It was natural for people to be curious and concerned when a police cruiser, or two, showed up out-

SIX

A ringing phone shattered the early morning quiet. Evan woke with a start and pushed himself up into a seated position. Snatching his cell off the nightstand, he checked the screen. Blackberry Falls PD.

He was on instant alert. "Bradshaw here."

"Chief. There was an intruder at Porter Animal Clinic." Reba Franklin, the night shift dispatcher, had his full attention.

"Is Grace okay?" Jumping out of bed, he put the phone on speaker, tossed it onto the bedside table and hurriedly pulled on a pair of jeans and a T-shirt.

"We think so, sir."

"What do you mean you think so?" Why was his dispatcher talking in circles? "Tell me what you know."

"Dr. Porter called the station approximately ten minutes ago. Someone was outside the kennel. They made entry. At that time, we lost communication with Dr. Porter."

Fear gripped him. Why had he left her there alone?

The dispatcher continued. "When Officer Wilkes arrived at the clinic, the side door was ajar. He entered the building. There were signs of a break-in and a struggle, but the intruder had fled the scene. Dr. Porter had barricaded herself in the apartment. She's shaken up and insists on giving her statement to you."

"Is Wilkes with her now?"

"Yes, sir."

"Tell him to stay with her. I'm on my way." Disconnecting, he tried Grace's cell, but the call went straight to voice mail. He shoved his feet into a pair of running shoes and bent to tie them. Then he grabbed his wallet and keys off the dresser before crossing to the nightstand and retrieving his service revolver from the locked box. Time to roll.

He walked into the hallway and froze. Camden. He'd call his mom from the car and let her know he needed to drop him off at her house.

Evan entered the small room decorated in a superhero theme. His path illuminated by a Spider-Man night-light, he stepped around the toy cars and plastic dinosaurs littering the floor.

Bending, he grabbed a pair of tennis shoes

off the floor then scooped his still-sleeping, pajama-clad son up into his arms and headed for the garage.

"Where are we going?" Camden mumbled, his eyes still closed as Evan put him in the SUV.

"Grammy's house," Evan answered as he secured the seat belt across the booster seat.

His son's green eyes opened and peered at him accusingly. "You promised we'd go fishing today."

Evan groaned inwardly. He *had* promised, after missing the end of the school year picnic. Thankfully, school would be out for summer break soon, giving him one less thing to juggle.

"The day has just started." He ruffled Camden's hair, then climbed into the driver's seat and backed out of the garage. "First, you get to hang out with Grammy and Poppy, have breakfast and watch cartoons. Then, when I get back, we'll go fishing."

You, me, Grace and Barkley. If she's okay. Please, let her be okay.

He desperately wanted to turn on the lights and sirens as he raced to her, but he didn't want to frighten Cam.

By the time they arrived at his parents' house, his son was wide-awake. His mother met them in the driveway, wearing her nightgown and housecoat. She opened the back door and un-side a residence or business, but Grace would hate all the attention.

Tom Wilkes, a twenty-four-year veteran of the force, stood on the small deck outside the apartment. Evan raised an eyebrow, and the older man shrugged. "She wouldn't open the door. Insisted you were the only one she'd talk to."

Evan clapped his officer on the shoulder and jerked his head in the direction of the small crowd. "See if any of the residents who live nearby saw or heard anything. And while you're at it, try to persuade them to disperse."

"I'm on it." Wilkes ambled down the stairs and across the street.

Knocking, he identified himself, saying, "It's Evan."

He held his breath and waited. Finally, the click of the lock sounded, but the door remained closed. He puffed out the breath, twisted the knob and stepped into the apartment.

The tension he hadn't even known he'd been holding since the phone call that woke him lifted from his shoulders at the sight of Grace. She was sitting on the same green-plaid sofa they had sat on together the night before, only now it blocked the door leading to the clinic. Barkley rested at her feet with his head in her lap, soaking up the attention as she rubbed her hands over his head.

She glanced up, and her eyes shone when she saw him. A wisp of blond hair fell in her face, which was makeup-free, giving full exposure to the smattering of freckles across her nose and cheeks. She looked both hopeful and frightened at the same time, much like the twelve-year-old girl she had been the first day he'd walked into sixth-grade science class at Blackberry Falls Middle School. She'd been happy that day to have the new kid assigned as her partner because the experiment had made her queasy. He remembered teasing her later that same day at lunch when she'd shared with him she wanted to be a veterinarian when she grew up. If only this incident could be laughed away as easily.

Evan crossed the small room and sat beside her. "Want to tell me what happened?"

"Barkley needed to go out. It was still two hours until any of the staff would arrive, and I couldn't make him wait." She focused on brushing her fingers through the animal's fur. "I know you told me to stay inside, but I thought the kennel would be safe."

Evan put two fingers under her chin and lifted her head until her eyes met his. He bent toward her, stopping himself mere inches from kissing her, his heartbeat echoing in his ears. Could she hear it? To cover his near faux pas, he pretended he was only close to emphasize his point. "I'm not mad at you. You didn't do anything wrong."

She nodded, but sadness emanated from her silver-blue eyes.

He sat back against the cushion. "Now, tell me everything."

Evan listened as she recounted the story, how the intruder jumped the six-foot chain-link fence and busted through the door. As she spoke, her voice trembled with fear, pulling him into the scene. He had no difficulty picturing her executing the roundhouse kick that had saved her life.

He smiled. "I guess those karate lessons finally paid off."

She looked at him blankly.

"Remember? In eighth grade, you went through a phase of wanting to be a PI and begged me to take karate with you. Six months later, you got bored and quit."

"I didn't even think of that. I just kicked and hoped I could get away."

He was thankful she had kept her wits about her and had done what was needed to escape harm.

"Did you get a good look at the guy? Could you identify him?"

A frown marred her face, and she shook her head. "He wore a mask."

"Don't tell me it had an animal face screen-printed on it."

"No. Not this time. This one was a solid dark color. I couldn't tell if it was black or navy."

He'd look at the clinic's security footage later, but for now, he wanted to give Grace time to process everything. He knew how her mind worked. If he left her alone, she'd sit there replaying everything over and over in her mind, getting angrier with herself for putting herself in the situation by leaving the apartment. However, if he encouraged her to talk about it, she'd process what had happened with a clear mind and let it go.

"What about height? Weight? Build? Anything at all."

"See, that's the thing bothering me the most. The guy seemed different this time. Maybe it's because I didn't get a clear view of him." She shooed Barkley away, and turned to face Evan, tucking one leg under her as she sat sideways on the sofa. "I'm not sure if it's because I froze during the attack on Chloe, watching everything play out in slow motion, and this time, I was running for my life. Whatever the reason, the guy seemed taller. Broader." She bit the corner of her lip, as if contemplating whether to continue.

"And?" he prompted.

"I didn't see his face, but he seemed more agile…younger."

Whatever he'd expected her to say, that wasn't it. Could this attack have been unrelated to the other two? Was it possibly a foiled burglary? Completely unrelated to the attack on Chloe?

His gut said no. That meant only one thing. More than one person wanted Grace dead.

"There's been no change. Your sister is stable, and we're keeping her comfortable." The nurse's words were disappointing, but Grace hadn't really expected Chloe's condition to improve overnight. Suppressing her frustration, she disconnected the call. Although she yearned to be in Denver with her sister, Grace knew Blackberry Falls was where she needed to be. For now.

Crossing to the small vanity table, Grace gathered her hair into a messy bun at the nape of her neck and secured it with an elastic hair tie. Then she finished her look with minimal makeup—tinted moisturizer, a light coat of brown mascara and a pale, natural lipstick. Touching her lips, her heart raced. She'd thought Evan was going to kiss her earlier. And if she were honest, she'd wanted him to.

With a sigh, she slipped her feet into comfortable sneakers and walked into the living room.

Someone had moved the sofa back to its original spot, and Evan and an older officer were sitting at the small dining table in deep discussion.

She signaled for Barkley to follow her and headed to the door that led down into the clinic.

"Where are you going?" Evan's question halted her steps.

Grace turned to find him towering over her. Forcing a smile, she replied, "It's time to open the clinic."

"Oh, no, you don't." He took her arm and led her to a corner of the small sitting area. "The clinic can remain closed for the day."

Twisting out of his grasp, she squared her shoulders and pulled herself to her full five-foot-nine height, ready for a fight. She would not disappoint her father, even if he wasn't around any longer to see it. "No, it can't. The clinic was closed yesterday with most of the appointments being rescheduled for today."

"I don't care. Your safety is of the utmost importance."

"I agree, and I'd very much like to stay alive. But these patients' lives are important, too."

"You can send the urgent cases to one of the three vet clinics in Lincoln Park, it's only a thirty-minute drive."

"Only one of the vet clinics in Lincoln Park

is open on Saturdays, and they have their own patients to worry about."

"Too bad. You're not opening. I can't guarantee your safety if you do."

"Well, that is too bad, because I am opening the clinic today. If I were an MD, would you ask me to put my patients' lives in danger by postponing critical care?" He started to reply, but she rushed on before he could protest. "No, you wouldn't. Look, in addition to vaccines, there are two surgeries scheduled for today, an ACL repair on a nine-year-old greyhound and the removal of a mass on the liver of a twelve-year-old Burmese cat. These animals' lives are as important as mine. They're someone's family members. They're loved as much as any human, and I will not postpone their care."

Evan shoved a hand through his hair, frustration etched on his face. She hated to cause him to worry, but she'd taken an oath to provide the best care for any patient in her charge. And, whether she liked it or not, James's patients had become hers yesterday when he'd walked out of the clinic. Good thing she had already lined up several people, some newly graduated and some with experience, to interview as his replacement.

Actually, Grace planned to hire two veterinarians to replace James, not that he had done the work of two doctors, but the practice had been lacking. She'd hired someone to take up the slack after her father passed, but they'd only lasted three weeks before James had run them off, telling Grace and Chloe if they hired an extra veterinary assistant, he could handle the workload without another veterinarian.

If only she hadn't stayed away after her father's death… She might have been able to… to what? Stop James from being so controlling about the clinic? Save her sister's marriage?

"What time does the clinic close?"

"Um…what?" Lost in thought, Evan's words hadn't penetrated her consciousness.

"I asked what time the clinic closes."

"Oh. Ah, noon." Hope swelled inside her. "Then we're closed until eight o'clock Monday morning."

"Which gives you forty-eight hours to make other arrangements for the care of the animals of Blackberry Falls." He winked.

Unable to resist, she offered a saucy smile and replied, "Or it gives you forty-eight hours to find the person behind the attacks and put him in jail."

He sobered. "Believe me, that would be my preference. I'll do my best."

"Does this mean you won't fight me about working today?"

"It means I understand the importance of your work."

The older officer pushed away from the table and ambled over to them. "I can stick around and guard the doctor."

"Wilkes, you've just completed a night shift, you need to go home and get some rest."

"No, sir. I never go to sleep before one. Besides, Martha has gone to Albuquerque to visit our daughter and the grandkids, so I'll be going home to an empty house."

"Doesn't matter. I can't pay overtime. I'll pull a patrol officer to hang out here for the four hours needed."

"Well, sir, you do that, if you feel it's best." Wilkes turned to her and smiled. "Dr. Porter, since it's lonely at my house, would you mind if I come back here and spend a few hours hanging out with you and the animals after I've gone home and changed into civilian clothes?"

Evan watched the exchange, an amused expression on his face, and Grace knew he was awaiting her reply. Probably more than anyone, Evan knew she wasn't comfortable with people going out of their way doing things for her. How could she say no when he looked so proud that his officer had volunteered his free time?

She searched the older man's face. Something about the officer bothered her. She couldn't put her finger on it. Maybe it was the forced smile that didn't reach his eyes. She mentally shook herself.

What was wrong with her? Had she really started to suspect everyone? *Stop imagining things.* Evan trusted him. The man had worked the night shift. He's not being unfriendly, he's tired. Which might be a good thing. He could find a corner and sleep while she worked, and she could forget he was there. It wasn't like she needed a guard at the clinic anyway. The guy who was after her wouldn't make a move with her entire staff and clients present, would he?

SEVEN

Evan craned his neck for a better view of the exam room. The door was still closed. In the past hour, Grace had given vaccines to three dogs and one cat, and now she was stitching up a ferret brought in with a nasty-looking cut. The waiting area was empty for the moment but wasn't likely to stay that way for long.

Settling back into the vinyl chair, he glanced at the clock. It had been forty-five minutes since he'd sent Wilkes home to change out of his uniform and eat breakfast. The veteran officer should be back soon, then Evan could go to the station and follow up on leads.

In the meantime, he had gone over the security footage from the outside cameras, trying, to no avail, to identify the intruder. The man, or woman, had strategically avoided most of the cameras, and in the kennel where they couldn't be avoided, they had kept their back to them. Unfortunately, there were no cameras inside the clinic.

The bell over the door dinged, and Ben Hamilton came in with his Australian shepherd. He waved at the receptionist, Tina Layton, and headed into the waiting area. The animal tugged on his leash, trying to get to Evan for attention.

"No, Max. Stay," Hamilton commanded.

Evan laughed and stroked the dog between his ears as the older man stood looking on. "It's okay. He's just curious." The animal was a beauty, with one blue eye and one brown eye.

"Have you given any more thought to who may have driven that truck off your property the other night, Ben?" Evan asked casually once the man was settled in a chair.

"I've answered all of your officers' questions, chief. Multiple times. My answers haven't changed," the rancher replied without emotion.

Evan studied the man's weathered face. "I understand you've been trying to buy the Osborne farm."

"I tried to warn Chloe of the dangers of living on a farm alone. She should have listened to me."

"Did you have anything to do with the attack? Trying to scare her off?"

"The only thing I'm guilty of is offering advice to an old friend's daughter and trying to add to my acreage. And I will not sit here and be interrogated by you." The rancher pushed to his feet and walked over to the receptionist's desk, slamming his hand on the counter. "Cancel Max's appointment." Glaring at Evan, he added, "I'll take him to the vet in Cañon City for his shots."

Evan walked up to the counter. "Now, Ben, there's no need for that."

Ben harrumphed and led Max out the door, the Australian shepherd barking and straining at his leash when he spied a woman exiting her vehicle with a pet carrier.

Evan's cell phone rang, and he slipped it out of his pants' pocket. FBI Special Agent Randy Ingalls's number flashed on the screen.

Eight months ago, Agent Ingalls had approached Evan for his assistance. Working undercover, Ingalls had been trying to infiltrate an organization behind off-the-grid horse races in the county. Though the organizers always secured the appropriate permits for match races, Evan and Agent Ingalls both knew illegal activities such as substance abuse, including performance-enhancing drugs given to the animals, gambling, money laundering, and human trafficking were happening behind the scenes.

Evan had tried to reach the agent earlier. He

crossed to the receptionist's desk, pointed to Chloe's office and mouthed, *I'll be in there.*

Tina smiled. "Go ahead, dear."

Evan settled into the desk chair, making sure he'd still have a good view of the exam room door, and answered his phone. "Ingalls, thanks for returning my call."

"No problem. I'd like to hear more about these attacks and why you think they're connected to the match races."

Evan quickly filled the agent in on the events of the past thirty-six hours.

A sick feeling settled in the pit of Evan's stomach. If the changes in the reports Grace found weren't a clerical error, someone connected to Porter Animal Clinic was involved in the illegal activities, too. Most likely providing the drugs being used on the horses. But was that person behind the attacks? Would someone who worked at the clinic be willing to kill the sisters to keep their involvement a secret? As a law-enforcement officer, he knew that answer was yes. Anyone who felt trapped was capable of murder.

"I'm trying to go undercover as security at the next race," Ingalls said. "Send me photos of the clinic's staff. If any of them show up at the race, maybe we can narrow down your suspects."

"I'll get them to you as soon as I get to the office." Evan picked up the files from earlier and flipped through them. "I'll also send you a copy of the toxicology report on the horse that died."

"What are you doing here, James?" Grace's harsh tone drew Evan's attention to the open exam room door. She was facing her brother-in-law, whose back blocked the door to Chloe's office, obscuring Evan's view.

Had James seen him looking over the files? Evan ended his call and slid the folders into a drawer. He pushed away from the desk and stood, quietly listening. Ready to intervene if needed.

"I came to do my job," James stated matter-of-factly.

"Walking out yesterday was your choice. What right do you have to be here now?" Grace peered over James's shoulder, meeting Evan's gaze.

Noticing the tired, almost defeated look in her eyes, Evan offered her an encouraging smile and a nod.

James spun around and glared. "I should have known your bodyguard would be here."

"I take my job seriously. Protecting the citizens of Blackberry Falls, even those who have been away for a while, is my job." Evan measured his words, speaking in a soft, even tone as he walked toward the pair. Stopping in front of James, he added, "I believe Grace asked you what you're doing here."

"Like I told her, I'm here to do my job." James's shoulders slumped, and he gave a half shrug before looking at Grace. "You may not like me, but these animals have been my patients for the past four years. Since we were closed yesterday, I rescheduled two surgeries for today. I figured you'd like help. I can do the surgeries while you see the other patients."

Was James being sincere or was he playing a game to keep a close eye on the investigation?

"I don't know…" Grace looked at Evan questioningly.

He shrugged, unable to give her guidance on this matter. Not that Evan would take any chances where Grace was concerned. She would not be left unprotected with James on the premises.

"If you want me to leave, I will," James said.

"No. It's okay. You're right. Having you complete a surgery would be helpful. The ACL repair will take the longest, so start with it. I'll take care of the scheduled vaccinations and the walk-ins. If I get finished before you, I'll do the other surgery."

James nodded assent, turned and walked toward the door marked Operating Room 1, stopping to say something to Valerie on his way.

The vet tech laughed at whatever he'd said and glanced their way.

Grace turned back to Evan and whispered, "What do you make of James showing up today?"

He stepped back and motioned her into the office, closing the door after she'd entered. "I'm not sure. But I don't want you alone with him." He walked past her and crossed to the desk. "Officer Wilkes will need to be in close proximity of you at all times. Do you understand?"

"I'll make sure he has a seat with a clear view of the exam rooms."

Evan reached into the drawer and retrieved the folders. "I'm not sure if James saw me looking through these files or not, but I don't want to leave them where he might find them. Are you okay with me locking them in my car?"

"Normally, I wouldn't let medical records leave the clinic, but I don't see as we have any other choice at the moment." Grace hid a yawn behind her hand.

Up close, Evan could see the dark under-eye circles that she'd tried to conceal with makeup. He hated that she hadn't been able to sleep the night before. That made two nights with minimal sleep for her. If he accomplished nothing else today, he had to ensure she had a safe place to rest her head tonight.

When he'd called earlier to check on Chloe, he and Ryan had discussed the situation. The younger man had suggested Evan and Grace stay in the cabin overlooking the waterfall in the woods at the edge of his parents' property, the Flying V Ranch.

How would Grace take the suggestion? Like it or not, she wasn't staying at the clinic alone again. He'd also have to make arrangements for Camden to stay with his parents for the time being, but he wasn't worried about that. Cam would love getting to stay with Grammy and Poppy, fishing in the pond and eating Grammy's home cooking.

"Look, Grace, I think I have a safe place—"

"Dr. Porter?" Tina Layton poked her head around the door. "Your next patient is waiting in exam room three."

"I'll be right there." She turned back to him with an apologetic smile. "I've gotta go. Can we discuss this when you pick me up?"

"Sure. I'll be here by a quarter till." He followed her into the hall as he spoke. A dog barked in the waiting area, and Evan could see a golden Labrador retriever straining at his leash as Wilkes strolled down the hall toward them.

The officer nodded at Grace as she passed on her way to the exam room. Pride surged through

Evan at the willingness of his men to donate their free time to protect the Porter sisters.

It was nice knowing he wasn't alone in the quest to keep Grace alive, but he struggled to squelch the uneasy feeling settling into the pit of his stomach at the thought of not being the one there protecting her.

Grace knelt and handed the fluffy, white rabbit to his owner, a young brown-haired girl with freckles scattered across her face. "Here you go, Daisy. Marshmallow is perfectly healthy, and he's ready to go home."

Grace glanced at her watch. Eleven twenty. Forty minutes until closing time, and she had seen the last scheduled patient.

"Is Dr. Osborne still in surgery?" she asked Tina, who was in the waiting area straightening the magazines.

"Yes. He finished the ACL repair on the greyhound." Tina moved to the collars and leashes display and continued with her organizing. "He's operating on the Burmese cat now."

Grace picked up a paper coffee cup someone had left sitting on the floor beside one of the brown vinyl chairs and disposed of it. "What time did he get started?"

"Around eleven."

"Did he say how long he thought it would

take?" she asked as she reached to retrieve a chew toy that had fallen off the display on the counter.

"He expects to finish by noon." The older woman's smile reached all the way to her dark brown eyes, her brown hair styled in a short bob framed her face. "Go sit and rest a minute. I can finish straightening things. You've been on your feet all morning. I've left homemade blueberry muffins in the kitchenette, and there's a fresh pot of coffee."

The mention of food had Grace's stomach growling. She had forgotten to eat anything for breakfast. "Thank you, Tina. I'll be in Chloe's office if anyone needs me."

Officer Wilkes sat on a stool he'd placed at the end of the long reception desk. His vantage point gave him a clear view of the front door, the three exam rooms and the hall leading to the operating area.

"Come on," she said when she passed him. "Let's grab some coffee and muffins." Maybe nourishment would help erase the somber expression on the officer's face.

He followed her and soon they settled in chairs around the small table in the corner of her sister's office.

"Yum. That is probably the best blueberry muffin I've ever had," she said between bites.

"I could have told you that, ma'am. Ms. Tina always wins the blue ribbon at the fair for her baked goods."

Grace examined the man sitting across from her. Officer Wilkes had silver hair and blue eyes, his expression guarded. His wrinkled face was almost leathery, like a man who'd spent a lot of time outdoors. He seemed familiar, but she couldn't place him.

"Trying to figure out where you know me from?" he asked as if reading her mind.

"Actually, yes." No point trying to hide the fact that she couldn't remember all the people she'd known growing up, though most people would probably find it strange she didn't remember everyone since the population of the town was less than seven hundred.

"I guess you were about nine years old. You came with your daddy to make a house call at my place. I had a small farm—what people today would call a hobby farm—with a few goats, some chickens and some ducks. One of the goats had gotten his leg caught in some wire and needed stitches. I planned to load him up and bring him to the clinic, but when I called, Dr. Porter said it was closing time so he'd stop by on his way home." A smile lifted the corners of his mouth. "Your daddy always said it was less stressful for farm animals if he came to them, instead of them having to be brought to the clinic in trailers."

He met her eyes and the smile disappeared. "You were with your daddy that day. I think you had gone to the clinic after school. Anyway, you asked to see all the animals while he stitched up the goat."

"You gave me pellet food to feed the ducks," she interjected.

He nodded, a faraway expression on his weathered face. "I did."

A forgotten memory replayed in slow motion through her mind. "I tripped on a tree root and fell in the pond. You saved me."

"It was my fault for not watching you more closely."

The man's guilt at her carelessness saddened her. "You couldn't have known I'd fall in."

"I could have warned you and helped you avoid the accident." He placed his elbows on the table and leaned closer. "My advice for you, right now, to keep you from a disaster far worse than a dip in a pond, is to get in your vehicle and hightail it to Denver. And when your sister is released from the hospital, keep her there. Cut all ties with this town."

The hairs on her arms stood on end. Were his words a warning of concern or were they a threat?

Officer Wilkes smiled. "I'm sorry if that sounded mean, but I feel like I owe it to your daddy to step in and give fatherly advice since he's no longer around."

Before she could respond, Tina's voice sounded over Chloe's desk phone intercom. "Excuse me, Dr. Porter. Henry Green from Mountain View Ranch is on the line. His three-year-old Thoroughbred colt, Knight's Honor, is in distress."

She stood, dusted crumbs off her lap and crossed to the desk. "Thank you, I'll take the call in here."

"He's on line two."

Grace pushed a button, picked up the receiver and listened to Henry Green describe the horse's symptoms. Sweating profusely. Labored breathing. Listlessness. Mountain View Ranch? Henry and Olivia Green. They had been the owners listed on the necropsy report for Mountain Shadow.

"Mr. Green, are there any obvious signs of colic? Distended belly? Abdominal pain?"

"No. That was the first thing I checked."

Could Knight's Honor have been drugged, too? If so, the colt needed fluids to help flush the drugs out of his system.

She had to go with her gut. "Mr. Green, I'm on my way."

"Wouldn't you rather me bring him to you? That's how Dr. Osborne does things."

Grace bit back the retort that she wasn't Dr. Osborne. She was her father's daughter, and she'd treat the patients of Blackberry Falls the way he would have.

"No. I'll come to you." She met Officer Wilkes's gaze and smiled. "It'll be less stressful for Knight's Honor. In the meantime, see if you can get him to drink water. Don't give him anything else, just water. Got it?"

The gasp on the other end of the line had her questioning her decision. "If it's colic, water could rupture his stomach."

"And if my instincts are right, we're racing against time, and it could be the only thing that saves him." She hung up before he could respond and turned to the man standing at her elbow. "Officer Wilkes, I've got to make a house call."

"I don't think the chief would approve."

"That can't be helped. This is an emergency. If you want to come, that's fine, but I understand if you need to get home."

"No, ma'am. I'm not letting you out of my sight."

"You can call Evan while I gather what I need. Let's go." After informing Tina where she was going, she retrieved the keys to the clinic's rigged-out truck, equipped to handle most emergencies. Then she gathered a variety of IV bags and headed out the side door.

While Officer Wilkes tried to reach Evan, Grace stowed the supplies in one of the metal storage boxes along the side panel of the truck bed.

"The desk officer said the chief was on the phone and had left orders to not be disturbed unless it was an emergency. Since it's not, I asked the officer to give him a message telling him where we're headed."

She pulled out onto the highway and headed north. "Sounds like you did all you could do. I don't think he'll be too mad, though. It's not like I'm going off somewhere unprotected, you're with me."

The older gentleman frowned, as if he wasn't convinced Evan would be okay with the situation.

"Well, I trust you to take care of me. After all, you saved my life when I was nine."

Henry Green had truly sounded upset. She would not leave an animal to die because of her own fears.

Please, Lord, I pray I'm not driving into a trap.

"Take the next left. In about a mile, the entrance to Mountain View Ranch will be on the right. You'll see two large stone columns and a double wrought iron gate with horse silhouette cutouts."

Grace followed the instructions as Officer Wilkes directed, thankful for his guidance. The landscape had changed more than she had expected in the fifteen years since she'd left the area.

"This is it." Wilkes pointed to the gates that stood wide-open, awaiting their arrival.

Turning onto the asphalt drive lined with fenced pastures, she followed the road for a half mile, passing a two-story, lodge-style log home before ending at a massive post-and-beam barn.

Grace parked the truck next to the tall, open double doors. Other than the new entrance at the road, nothing about Mountain View Ranch had changed. With rolling hills and green pastures that looked like a postcard come to life, it was still one of the most beautiful places in Blackberry Falls.

A man in his early seventies strode out of the barn to meet them, a serious expression on his face. His hair had turned almost solid white and his face had a few more wrinkles than she remembered, but Grace would have recognized Henry Green anywhere.

His ranch had been one of the places she'd most loved going with her dad. As a child visiting the ranch, the Greens had allowed her to feed apples to the horses, skip rocks in the pond behind the main house, and climb the big oak tree that stood on the hill behind the horse barn. Nothing she'd ever done had upset Henry Green. Having married late in life, he and his wife, Olivia, had never had children. One might have expected he would have been like some of her father's other clients who didn't have patience for a curious child, but Henry had always been a laid-back person who didn't get riled easily.

The elderly man pulled her into a quick hug the moment she stepped out of her vehicle. "Grace Porter, it's good to have you home. Your daddy would be so proud that you're working at his clinic."

Her heart constricted at his words, and her throat tightened as tears stung her eyes. Her number one goal growing up had been to make her daddy proud, that was the main reason she'd followed him around begging to go on house calls the summer between third and fourth grade. The other reason had been her two-year-old sister at home, constantly following her around and getting into her things.

Henry moved back and commanded, "Now, grab your supplies and let's save my colt."

Grace quickly collected the items she'd brought with her as Officer Wilkes stood to the side talking to Henry. If the ranch owner wondered why she had an off-duty officer with her, he never let on. But why would he wonder when the gossip mill of Blackberry Falls had no doubt filled in every community member on the plight of the Porter sisters.

Her arms full, she nodded at the barn entrance. "Lead the way."

The interior aisle of the barn was more than a hundred feet long and lined with stalls on both sides. The lower half of each stall had been constructed of tiger wood, a strong hardwood that would be difficult for a spirited horse to kick and splinter. The upper half was constructed of a matte-black, powder-coated steel railing.

"It's awfully quiet around here," Wilkes commented.

"That's because we only use this barn for injured animals and foals. Got a bigger barn a little ways past this one. The ranch hands are out there now setting up a race between a couple of colts and a filly. You'll probably hear them in a bit, when they get started."

Henry paused outside a stall a third of the way down the aisle. Grace looked over the top railing and saw a magnificent chestnut colt with a white blaze lying listlessly in the corner, his labored breathing echoing in the small space.

"Did you give him water?" she asked as she followed the rancher into the stall. Officer Wilkes closed the door behind them and waited on the other side.

Henry nodded solemnly and patted the horse's shoulder. "He drank about half a gallon then collapsed here and hasn't moved again."

Grace examined the animal. No signs of trauma and no obvious signs of colic. His heart beat fast and erratically. She pulled a needle, a stabilizer and two Vacutainer blood collection vials from the equine medical bag she'd brought with her.

"Can you get on the other side and help hold him?" She waited for Henry to comply. Even though the horse was lethargic, she didn't want to risk his jerking upward and injuring himself or her.

Once the animal was secure, she pressed her thumb against the base of his long neck so the jugular vein would bulge. It took longer than it should have for the vein to fill with blood, an indication the Thoroughbred may be dehydrated. Inserting the needle, Grace drew two tubes of blood. After she'd completed that task, she started a one-liter bag of IV fluid. Slipping an S-hook through the small hole in the top of the bag, she handed it to the rancher to hook onto the hay feeder.

"Are you still ruling out colic?" Concern laced his voice.

She nodded and continued administering care to the distressed animal.

"What do you think it is?"

"I think he's had an overdose," she replied softly. "But we won't know if it's from the same drugs that killed Mountain Shadow until we get the labs back."

Grace met the ranch owner's gaze, anger burned in his hazel eyes. He didn't look like a man who had drugged his own horse.

"I was told Mountain Shadow died of a heart defect. Why that sorry, no-good, lying swindler!" Henry exploded.

"Who?"

"Never you mind. You concentrate on saving my horse." Pushing past Officer Wilkes, Henry exited the stall and headed down the aisle of the barn, his footsteps fading after he entered the office next to the tack room and slammed the door shut.

It was obvious Henry Green wasn't behind the drugging, but he knew who was. Grace looked at Wilkes and nodded toward the back of the barn. "Follow him and see if you can find out who he thinks did this."

"No way. The chief will have my hide if I let you out of my sight. I'll question Green when he gets back." The officer leaned against the stall door and crossed his booted feet at the ankles in a stubborn stance.

"You know, Wilkes, whoever drugged this horse is most likely the same person who attacked me. Finding out their name *is* the best way to protect me." She pushed to her feet and peered around him to look down the hall at the closed office door. "Go. Talk to him." When he raised an eyebrow and didn't budge, she added, "What could happen? You'll be less than fifty feet away."

EIGHT

Evan tapped a few keys on his laptop and hit Send.

"Okay, I emailed you the photos and bios of the employees of Porter Animal Clinic," he said into the phone.

"Great. I'll study them tonight, while I'm waiting for the phone call from the temp agency," Randy Ingalls replied.

Evan prayed the agent's plan to be hired as a security guard for the match race became a reality. "Do you know which ranches are taking part in the race tomorrow?"

"According to my source, there are a total of six. Two from Colorado Springs, one from Beulah Valley, one from Westcliffe, and two from Blackberry Falls…let me see." Evan heard papers rustle on the other end of the line. "Hamilton Thoroughbred Ranch and Mountain View Ranch."

"Hamilton Ranch was where Chloe Porter's

attacker jumped in a truck and lost Lieutenant Johnson. My men have been out there twice since the attack. The Hamiltons claim not to have seen anything, and neither they nor their hired hands could—or would—identify the truck or who it belonged to."

"Could you send someone in to work undercover?"

"Not likely. The downfall of running a police station in a small community is that everyone knows all the officers." Evan propped his elbows on the desk. "Of course, everyone knowing our officers can be an advantage, too, as it can lead some people to open up and tell us things. We'll continue to work on that. Let us know if you need our help with anything on your end."

"Sounds good. In the meantime, keep a close eye on Dr. Porter. If you're right and the evidence she found ties back to the group running the match races, the target on her back will only get bigger by the minute. These people don't play around, and they won't take a chance on losing what they've built here."

"Yeah, I know." Evan puffed out a breath and reached to shut down his computer.

He ended the conversation, asking the agent to keep him in the loop. It was noon, and he had promised Grace he'd be back at the clinic fifteen minutes ago. Pushing away from his desk, he headed out his office door.

"Chief!" Officer Lane Newman called out when Evan walked past the dispatch room. "I have a message for you from Wilkes."

Evan's steps faltered, and he did an about-face, striding over to the desk and accepting the piece of yellow memo paper the rookie held in the air.

For: Chief Bradshaw
From: Officer Tom Wilkes
Time: 11:32
Message: Headed to Mountain View Ranch with Dr. Porter for a house call.

Mountain View Ranch. Agent Ingalls's voice echoed in Evan's mind.

The message had been left thirty minutes earlier. "Why am I just now getting this? You should have notified me when the call came in."

The rookie shrugged. "You left orders not to be disturbed. I asked if it was an emergency. Officer Wilkes said it wasn't and to give you the message before you headed to the clinic."

"Get Wilkes—" He swallowed the rest of his command. Wilkes was off duty. He wouldn't have his radio. Evan's determination to keep his department from going over budget had put Grace in danger.

He pulled his cell phone out of his back pocket and hit a speed dial number. The call went straight to voice mail. "Wilkes, call in ASAP."

He disconnected and tried Grace's number. Voice mail.

Wadding up the yellow paper and tossing it on the desk, he turned and raced outside to his vehicle. What if his officer and Grace had been ambushed?

Grace pulled the earpieces from her ears, draped the stethoscope around her neck and ran her hand along the Thoroughbred's flank. His pulse had become less erratic and his breathing less labored. The fluids seemed to be working, and the toxins were being flushed out of his body. Still, she needed to contact Dr. Underwood at the Anderson Vaughn Equine Hospital in Pueblo West to let him know the animal would be transported to his hospital for further observation.

Grace slipped her cell out of her pocket. Ugh. No service. Another downside of small-town living. She'd have to find a spot with a stronger signal. Sliding her hand along the blaze that ran from Knight's Honor's forehead to his muzzle, she leaned in and whispered, "We're going to make you all better."

The colt neighed softly, and she kissed him, his hair tickling her nose. "I'll be right back, boy."

Slipping out of the stall, Grace headed for the main entrance. Her sneaker-clad feet barely made a sound on the concrete floor. The barn was eerily quiet except for the murmur of conversation coming from the office. She prayed Henry Green was opening up to Wilkes about who he suspected of drugging the horses and why.

Once outside, she checked her phone again. A weak signal but not nearly strong enough. She needed to hear Dr. Underwood, and he needed to hear her. Rounding the corner of the barn, she saw the oak tree still standing proud and tall on its hill overlooking the barn. Hmm. It couldn't hurt to see if a slightly higher elevation would improve cell reception.

"How's Knight's Honor?"

Grace jumped at the sound of a woman's voice behind her.

Turning, she saw Olivia Green headed in her direction, a wicker basket clutched in her perfectly manicured hand. In her mid-to late-sixties, wearing a royal blue pantsuit with her platinum blond hair perfectly coiffured, Olivia looked like she'd walked off a fashion runway. A socialite from New York who'd given up high society for small-town life when she married, Olivia Green had always been the most elegant woman in Blackberry Falls.

"He's stabilized." Grace lifted her phone. "I'm trying to call the equine hospital to let them know to expect him."

"Cell reception is horrible in this area. I've been after Henry for years to get some kind of booster antenna or something to help. But he said there's no point since we still have landlines." The older woman reached Grace's side and leaned in to kiss the air near her cheek. "Grace, it's so good to have you home."

"Thank you, Mrs. Green. It's nice to see you."

"Why don't you go back in and use the phone in Henry's office?"

Grace shrugged. "He and Officer Wilkes are in there talking. I didn't want to disturb them."

"Okay, dear. I understand." Olivia raised the basket she carried. "It's well past lunchtime, and I know Henry hasn't eaten a thing, so I brought you all some sandwiches and fruit."

"That was sweet of you."

"It was nothing. A woman likes to feel like she's contributing when there's a crisis, and I like to feed people." The woman waved her hand dismissively. "Now, go make your call.

I'll peek in on Knight's Honor before going back to the house. And I'll leave this basket on the bench outside his stall."

Grace hiked up the hill, taking in the view of the farm around her. She noticed the newer, larger barn farther back on the property. There was a large training area adjacent to it. Several onlookers watched as three horses with riders prepared to race inside the arena. It looked like the Greens had built a successful horse breeding and training business since she'd left Blackberry Falls.

A smile tugged at her lips. From the outside, Henry and Olivia Green seemed like an odd couple. He was a no-nonsense, down-to-earth man, most comfortable in blue jeans and boots. The total opposite of his wife. But they doted on each other and had always seemed to have a strong marriage.

A moment of sadness washed over her. Would she and Evan have had a marriage like the Greens' if she had stayed in Blackberry Falls instead of running like the scared woman-child she'd been? No sense fretting over it, since she'd never know.

Raising her phone, she checked the screen. Good, she had service. Clicking through her contacts, she moved closer to the tree to lean against the trunk. When she did so, she connected with something solid, but not hard like a tree. Startled, she whirled around and came face-to-face with the man who had attacked Chloe and wanted Grace dead.

A lost memory from long ago flashed in her mind's eye. She recognized him, but his name escaped her.

Grace stepped backward, stumbling on a root. She wobbled but somehow managed to maintain her footing while never breaking eye contact. A scream burned in her throat, begging for release, but when she opened her mouth, no sound came out. This couldn't be happening. It was broad daylight. There were people around. Someone had to see them on the hillside.

"Why are you so shocked to see me, Amazing Grace?" The man sneered. "I told you, you're next."

Like a starting pistol signaling the beginning of a race, his words spurred her into action. She turned and charged back down the hill, her screams drowned out by the crowd cheering the horses in the arena.

Evan activated the blinker and turned onto the private drive that wound through the Mountain View Ranch property. He had finally spoken with Officer Wilkes a few minutes ago. They were both in the barn. Grace was providing medical care for a horse that had possibly been drugged, and Wilkes was getting a list of suspects from Henry Green.

Grace was safe.

Still, the knot in Evan's stomach wouldn't loosen until he laid eyes on her.

Following the drive, he pulled around the main house to the original barn and slammed on his brakes. Grace was running down the hillside beyond the barn, a man pursuing her. The assailant grabbed her ponytail and dragged her back toward the trees.

Evan turned on the siren. Grace's captor spared him a quick glance and then tugged harder. Grace clawed at her attacker's hands. *Keep fighting, Gracie. Keep fighting.*

Evan pressed the accelerator, the SUV bouncing over the uneven terrain as he drove toward the pair. In the rearview mirror, he caught a glimpse of Wilkes running out of the barn. The Greens were close behind.

Shoving the gearshift into Park, Evan vaulted from the vehicle. The assailant slipped an arm around Grace's neck and held her like a shield.

Evan's hand hovered over his service revolver. The thought of using his weapon and possibly hitting Grace with a stray bullet made him hesitate. "Let her go!"

"Yeah, right." The man tightened his grip. Grace gasped for air, her face reddening.

Evan unsnapped his holster and stepped forward. "I said. Let. Her. Go."

Grace's attacker laughed and shoved her. She barreled into Evan. His arms instinctively went around her, but the power of the impact sent them both hurtling backward, tumbling down the incline. When they stopped, midway down the hill, he glanced back to the top. The man had vanished.

Officer Wilkes reached them. "Are you okay?"

"Yes. Go! Get him!" Evan commanded, his arm tightening around Grace, not wanting to let her go. Her face was buried in his chest.

"I'm sorry. I needed to call the animal hospital… Knight's Honor." She sobbed. "I thought I would be safe."

"Shh," he murmured. "It's okay. You're safe."

She pulled out of his arms, leaving him feeling suddenly empty.

"Because of you," she said. "You saved my life."

This time. But could he keep her alive?

Evan pushed to his feet, aware of the crowd gathered at the base of the hill. "Are you okay? Can you walk?"

She nodded. "I think so."

Taking her hand in his, he helped Grace to her feet and led her up the incline to his patrol vehicle, its engine still running. He settled her in the passenger seat. Closing the door, he leaned against the side of the SUV and radioed Dispatch for backup. When he finished, he contacted the county sheriff's office to request the K-9 unit be sent to help with the search.

Wilkes jogged up to the vehicle. "Sorry, Chief. He was gone before I entered the woods. I looked around but couldn't find his trail."

"How is that possible?" Evan demanded. "He couldn't have had more than a fifteen-second head start."

He studied his officer. Had the attacker really disappeared that quickly? Why had Wilkes left Grace alone? Was he working with the attacker? No. Evan squashed those thoughts. He trusted his officer with his life. He couldn't believe he'd be involved in anything that would harm Grace or Chloe.

Grace rolled down the window to listen to their conversation. Evan took in her pale complexion and the concern in her eyes. He hated to let her out of his sight, but he needed to work quickly to find her assailant before he came after her again. Attacking in broad daylight with other people around was a sign of desperation.

"I'm sorry, Grace. I never should have left your side," Wilkes apologized.

"You're right, you shouldn't have." Evan

turned on his officer. "If you ever put her in danger again, it will be your last day on the force. Do you understand?"

"Yes, sir," Wilkes replied, not breaking eye contact.

"It's not his fault. I'm the one who convinced him it was okay."

Evan took a deep breath. It did matter. His officer had been careless. He had to catch the guy. Puffing out the breath, he said, "Take Grace someplace safe. I don't care if it's the barn or the main house, as long as you guard her and keep the crowd away from her."

"What about you?" Grace asked, fear audible in her voice.

He turned to her. "I'll be there after I get the K-9 unit in the woods. We've got to find the man's trail."

"I know him!" Grace gasped and her eyes widened. "When I saw him, this time, I thought he looked familiar. His name is Avery Hebert."

"Are you sure?" Wilkes asked.

She nodded. "Yes. It's been over twenty years since I last saw him. That's why I didn't recognize him at first."

"Hebert?" Evan questioned. "Is he related to Ralph and Lydia Hebert?"

Evan knew the Heberts. Ralph had had to quit his job in construction after being diagnosed with Parkinson's a few months ago, leaving Lydia to support the family on her salary as a school lunchroom worker.

"Avery is their oldest son," Wilkes answered. "He was irresponsible when he was younger, in and out of trouble with the law on a regular basis." The officer scrunched his brow. "As I recall, after he graduated high school, he got a job at a farm in Rockvale, and he seemed to have straightened out his life. Then a couple of years later, he got arrested for a DUI while transporting a horse to auction. He lost his job, and then he took off. I heard he went to Wyoming."

"Well, he's back now," Grace said in a matter-of-fact tone.

"So you say," said Wilkes. "We haven't officially ID'd him."

"But I know it was him."

Evan squeezed her hand. "It's okay. We'll catch him." Turning back to Wilkes, he added, "Now, get her someplace safe."

"I really need to go to the barn to make sure Knight's Honor is ready to be transported to the hospital," Grace insisted.

"Fine. As long as you're not planning to be the one transporting him."

"Oh, no. Henry will transport. I just need to check the Thoroughbred once more to make sure he's stabilized."

"Okay. Wilkes, drive Grace to the barn in my vehicle and don't leave her side."

"Are you sure you wouldn't rather me stay and search and have someone else guard Dr. Porter?"

To be honest, after what happened, Evan would have preferred to have another officer guard Grace, but he didn't have a lot of options at the moment. Besides, he needed to be able to trust his officer. He opened his mouth to reply, but Grace beat him to it.

"What happened to me wasn't your fault. You told me not to leave the area." She frowned. "I was careless. I'm sorry."

Evan clapped Wilkes on the shoulder. "I trust you. But don't let her slip away from you again."

"No worries there," Grace assured him. "I'm not about to get out of his sight. I don't want another run-in with Avery."

Two Blackberry Falls police cruisers came up the drive with the county K-9 unit close behind, lights flashing.

Time to locate Grace's assailant. Assuming he was still on the ranch. If they couldn't find him, it would be time to hide Grace in a safe place. Evan hoped she wouldn't put up a fuss.

"I don't need to be driven back to the barn. It's a two-minute walk," Grace protested.

"My patrol car is right here. There's no need in you walking through the crowd to get back to the barn." Evan's tone was firm, indicating he wouldn't listen to any arguments.

He was right. The crowd watching the race had gathered when the commotion started.

Officer Wilkes drove her back to the barn, and Henry Green directed them to park inside, two employees closing the massive doors to stop prying eyes. Then, the rancher placed several of his men, armed with shotguns, at the various entrances to the barn.

If the armed guards on the outside weren't enough, Officer Wilkes stood less than ten feet from Grace, like a sentry guarding a fort, at full attention, observing the surroundings, his back to the stall.

Grace's hands shook as she worked, adrenaline still coursing through her veins from the recent attack. Taking a few steadying breaths, she worked to complete the task of unhooking the IV and prepping Knight's Honor for transfer. Once finished, she ran her hand the length of the colt's neck, leaned in and placed her cheek against his. "You will feel all better soon."

Stepping back, she called out, "Okay, Mr. Green. Knight's Honor is ready to go." She exited the stall as one of the ranch hands entered.

Grace handed the small zippered bag to

Henry. "These are the blood samples I drew when I first arrived. Dr. Underwood is expecting them. He said he'd have the results for us by Monday."

He accepted the bag, a look of concern on his face.

"Don't worry. Your colt's going to be okay. You did everything right, calling me as quickly as you did. And Dr. Underwood is one of the best."

"Thank you. For everything." The rancher looked down, unable to meet her eyes. "I'm sorry about Avery."

She sucked in a breath. "You knew he was the one who attacked Chloe? Is he the person you went to call?"

"I did try to call Avery, but I didn't know he attacked Chloe or was after you." Henry shook his head, and Officer Wilkes stepped closer, listening in. "One of my ranch hands saw you struggling on the hill with Avery and was headed to help you when Chief Bradshaw showed up. When you told me Mountain Shadow had been drugged and you thought Knight's Honor had been, too, I suspected Avery was the one who was responsible."

"Why would Avery Hebert drug your horses?" Evan asked, walking into the barn.

Henry moved the basket of uneaten food and

sat on the bench outside Knight's Honor's stall, his shoulders slumped. "Because I'm a sucker for a sob story, and I thought maybe he'd grown up and changed his ways."

"That tells me why you hired him, not why he'd give drugs to your horses. Was he planning to run this horse in the match race tomorrow?"

"Yes. At first, I was against it since Mountain Shadow died following the last race. But the necropsy report said he died of a heart defect. So, I let Avery talk me into allowing Knight's Honor to run tomorrow."

"So what exactly goes on at these races?"

Henry looked Evan in the eyes. "I don't know. I haven't attended one. When Mountain Shadow ran, I was in the hospital recovering from knee replacement surgery."

Grace had heard about the unsanctioned horse races taking place across the state. There had been many news reports about the horses being given performance-enhancing drugs, as well as the illegal gambling and human trafficking that went along with these races. She'd had no idea off-the-grid match races had invaded Freemont County.

"Why would you want a horse to run in an unsanctioned race?" she asked before she could stop herself, not meaning to take over Evan's questioning.

"That was my next question." Evan leaned against a post.

"I knew better. I read the news reports about the illegal activities surrounding them, though the races themselves aren't illegal. Avery convinced me it would be an opportunity to see how our colts competed against horses they hadn't trained with. I figured there was no harm. I knew I wouldn't let anyone drug my horses." Sadness seeped into the rancher's voice. "I can't believe I allowed it to happen twice. I knew in my gut Mountain Shadow had been drugged, but the necropsy report said otherwise."

"Someone falsified it." Grace hated to admit the second part of that truth, but she knew she had to be honest. "Someone at the clinic."

Henry jerked his head upward. "Who?"

"I don't know." Anger rose like bile burning inside her. If news spread about the falsified records, it could destroy the business her father had built. Grace could not let that happen. "But you have my word, I won't stop until I find out the truth."

NINE

After leaving Mountain View Ranch, Evan had followed Grace back to the clinic so she could return the truck and pack a few necessities for herself and Barkley. He'd tried to convince her to let someone else take care of the Great Dane for a few days, but she'd insisted that the animal had to stay with her. Evan had caved to her wishes because he understood her desire to do anything she could to feel like she was helping Chloe.

Now, hours later, Evan sat on a blanket beside the pond on his parents' property packing the remnants of the picnic his mom had provided for their dinner. Once finished, he placed everything in the cargo space of his SUV. He was forever thankful to live close to his family and to always have their support. When he'd called earlier to ask his parents if they could watch Camden, they hadn't questioned him or thought twice about disrupting their normal day-to-day lives to care for their six-year-old grandson for an indefinite period.

Evan prayed it wouldn't be more than a day or two, but until they captured Avery Hebert and the threat against Grace was over, he would devote his time to keeping her safe. And he couldn't have Camden in harm's way.

"That's it... Keep reeling... You've got it," Grace cheered for Camden as he worked to land the fish on his line. Barkley ran into the pond, barking at the fish splashing in the water.

Evan rushed to his son's side, and Grace got Barkley back onto the bank. Camden's little hand gripped the handle tightly as he spun it round and round. "Not so fast...that's it. You're doing great, son."

Finally, the fish was in the air. "Look at him, Dad! Isn't he a big one?"

"He sure is." Evan reached for the end of the line and pulled the largemouth bass in close, intent on setting him free.

"Hang on. Let me get a picture." Grace pulled her phone from her pocket.

Evan knelt beside Camden, and they both held the fishing line, the bass dangling between them, while Grace snapped a few pictures. He and Camden had been fishing together many times, but he'd never thought to take pictures. Evan was glad Grace had suggested it. He needed to do a better job of preserving memories with his son.

"How much do you think he weighs, Dad?"

"Hmm." Evan made a show of gauging its weight. "I'd say at least six pounds, seven ounces."

"You're silly, Dad." Camden giggled as Evan pretended to have difficulty lifting the fish.

"Time to set this little guy free." Evan gently removed the wiggling bass from the hook and lowered him back into the pond. He ruffled Camden's hair. "Okay, kiddo, I think it's time to load up and get you back to Grammy and Poppy's house."

"Can't we stay thirty more minutes?" Camden pleaded.

"Not today, son. It's already getting late. By the time I get you back to Grammy's and you get a bath, it'll be your bedtime."

"But, Dad, I want to spend more time with Barkley and Grace."

Evan lifted an eyebrow at his son's use of an adult's first name. He'd raised him to show respect to his elders.

She leaned in and whispered, "I told him he could call me Grace. I hope that's okay."

Evan hoped so, too. But he feared his son getting attached to her. When this was all over

and she walked out of their lives, he didn't want a brokenhearted child.

The sun setting on the horizon cast orange and purple streaks in the sky, illuminating the small log cabin overlooking a waterfall on the edge of the Flying V Ranch. Set back off the road, the original Vincent family homestead was the perfect place to hide from prying eyes, though Grace wasn't sure why Ryan and Bridget's parents were willing to let her stay on their property.

She doubted anyone could find her there, but she couldn't be sure her presence wouldn't bring harm to the Vincents or their property. "Are you sure this is a good idea?"

"Yes," Evan answered. "It's a secluded spot few people know about, which is hard to find in our little town."

"You're right." She lifted her suitcase out of the back of his Jeep Wrangler—secretly thankful he'd decided to switch from his police vehicle after dropping Camden off—and followed Evan into the cabin. He placed the large bag of dog food he'd carried in onto a kitchen chair before heading back outside.

Barkley sniffed his new surroundings then plopped down on the rug in front of the rock fireplace. The main room of the cabin had an

open-concept kitchen and living room. Leading off the living room, there was a short hallway with two doors. One was a small bedroom with a white, full-size, antique iron bed, an oak dresser and a matching side table with a lamp. The other door led to an updated bathroom with a claw-foot tub, a gray mosaic tile floor and a pedestal sink.

"What do you think?" Evan called from the main living area.

"I think it's very nice of Ryan's parents to allow us to use their cabin," Grace answered, retracing her steps down the hall. She looked at the duffel bag in his hand. "Do you really think it's necessary for you to stay here with me?"

Grace wasn't used to sharing living quarters with anyone. She'd lived alone since her junior year of college.

"I do." He tossed the duffel on the floor next to the sofa. "I'll sleep here, and you can have the bedroom."

The set of his jaw told her there would be no persuading him to change his mind. Wandering into the kitchen, Grace idly opened cabinet doors. The small pantry seemed well stocked, cans of homemade soups, vegetables and preserves lining the shelves. Opening the refrigerator, she noticed someone had stocked it with milk, eggs, fruit, cheese and a variety of lunch meat.

"Here's a note." Evan pulled a piece of paper from the thumbtack holding it in place on the corkboard attached to the side of the fridge. "'I tried to stock up on the necessities. If you can think of something I've left off the list or need anything at all, let me know, and I'll get it for you. We're praying for your safety and Chloe's healing. Mrs. V.'"

"That was thoughtful of her." Grace wasn't used to others doing so much for her. Back in Denver, she only knew the name of one of her neighbors.

"Yes, it was," Evan agreed, placing the note on the old butcher-block countertop. "It's getting late. Maybe you should go to bed. You've had a long day that started way too early."

"Actually, if you don't mind, I'd rather talk about Avery for a few minutes. I can't believe I've known who Chloe's attacker was this entire time."

"Technically, you didn't know this entire time. It took a specific event to jar your memory." He crossed the room and knelt in front of the fireplace. "Could you tell me what was different about today's attack that helped you remember?" he asked as he pulled kindling out of the metal bucket on the hearth and arranged it under the logs so he could start a fire.

Grace sat on the sofa and tucked her feet

under her. "I think it was the way he looked at me. When I was younger, he'd call me 'princess,' but he'd have such a look of disgust on his face I always knew he meant it as an insult. He had that same look today."

She shivered, whether from the topic they were discussing or the cool night air, she wasn't sure, but she would be glad once Evan had a roaring fire warming the place. Pulling a soft, blue throw off the back of the sofa, she tucked it around herself.

"Why do you think he would do that?" Evan asked.

"I always thought it was because his family was poor and he thought I was a spoiled kid. We weren't rich by any means, but we had nice things. The first time it happened, I was in the clinic parking lot, riding the new, lime-green, ten-speed bicycle I had gotten the day before for my birthday."

"What was he doing at the clinic?"

"Dad had given him a part-time job. I believe it was his senior year of high school. One night, I overheard Dad telling Mom that Avery was great with the animals, and if he'd let go of some of his anger at the world, he'd have a bright future."

"Wilkes mentioned Avery had a troubled childhood. Do you know what he meant?"

"Avery had several run-ins with the law. He liked to party, and that included abusing drugs and alcohol. After he went to work for Dad, he seemed to sober up. Then when he graduated high school, Dad helped him find a full-time job at a ranch working with horses. But like Wilkes said earlier, that didn't last.

"When Avery got out of jail, he came by the clinic. I was in the kennel playing with the puppies, and I heard him talking to Dad. He wanted his old job back, but Dad told him he wouldn't hire him unless he agreed to go to an AA meeting. Avery said he didn't need AA. Dad told him he couldn't have an alcoholic around his daughters."

"And you never saw him again?"

"Not until the night he pushed Chloe over the balcony and threatened me."

"Then seems to me, I need to do some digging to figure out what led him to that place at that moment in time."

"You mean besides wanting to murder my sister and me?"

The morning sun illuminated the kitchen enough for Evan to search for coffee and filters.

He opened a drawer beside the sink, but it held dishcloths and dish towels. When he opened the next drawer, a high-pitched squeak echoed in the quiet house. He carefully closed the drawer, praying the noise hadn't awakened Grace. It had been nearing midnight before she'd finally gone to bed, and he had no way of knowing if she'd drifted off to sleep as easily as he had, complete exhaustion claiming him once silence descended upon the cabin.

He located a tablespoon, placed a paper filter in the coffeemaker's basket and measured four heaping spoons of coffee grounds into it. He filled the reservoir with tap water and hit the power button.

Crossing over to the sofa, he folded the blanket he'd used the night before, stacking it and the pillow on the side table. Soon, the scent of coffee wafted into the air. The cabin was tiny, not more than five hundred square feet. Would the smell wake Grace? Maybe he should have held off on his morning caffeine fix.

Lisa used to laugh at him and his need for coffee as soon as his feet touched the floor each morning. They'd received one of those fancy coffeemakers that made one cup of coffee at a time as a wedding gift, but he'd never gotten use to making coffee that way. He preferred to make a pot of strong, black coffee he could pour multiple cups from. No fancy-flavored creamer, either. He liked a little heavy whipping cream in his coffee, nothing else.

Lisa had eventually sold the fancy coffee-maker at a yard sale and surprised him with one that made twelve cups at a time. It was programmable, so he could prep everything the night before and awaken to the smell of fresh-brewed coffee each morning.

He smiled at the memory, and his lip quivered. That had been ten months after they married, the same day she'd told him he was going to be a father. She'd laughed and told him he'd need the extra caffeine following the sleepless nights with a newborn.

The following year was one of the happiest times in his life. Lisa had been radiant, and they had enjoyed all the milestones together—the first ultrasound, the first kick, playfully arguing over names and finally the birth. The delivery had been difficult. After twenty-three hours of labor, Lisa's blood pressure had spiked and the doctor had to perform an emergency cesarean.

Camden had been beautiful and perfect, and Lisa had been a doting mother. Only, she had suffered from postpartum depression and had hidden it from everyone. If anyone asked how she felt, she would plaster a smile on her face and say, "Fine." When she looked tired, and he offered to hire someone to help her with the house and the baby, she'd insisted she could handle it herself. Being tired was normal when you had a newborn, she'd said.

He blamed himself for not knowing how much she was suffering. His only excuse was that he had been immersed in his job, working to achieve his goal of becoming chief of police when Chief Emerson retired. As a result he'd been unsuccessful at balancing his new family's responsibilities along with his work responsibilities.

Evan scrubbed a hand over his face. No point making excuses. He'd been a failure as a husband. He should have been more aware of his wife's feelings, insisting she seek help and ensuring she had time for herself—regular lunch dates with friends or time at the beauty salon to get her hair or nails done. Anything to give her time away from the stress of being a new mother.

Barkley whimpered, scratching at the bedroom door. "Shh, boy." Evan whispered as he hurried across the room and down the short hall to let him out. "Don't wake Grace."

The Great Dane quieted, and Evan slowly opened the door enough for the massive animal to squeeze out. A quick glance in the room showed a mound of covers in the center of the bed and a bare foot sticking out, dangling over the side. Grace was still asleep. Evan released a sigh of relief. He closed the door and tiptoed back to the kitchen.

Opening the cabinet where he'd seen dishes earlier, he found an oversize stoneware mug and poured himself a cup of coffee. Steaming mug in hand, he opened the front door and followed the Great Dane outside. There weren't any chairs on the small wooden porch, so Evan sat on the top step and watched as Barkley sniffed the perimeter of the cabin.

He took a sip of his coffee, closed his eyes and savored the moment, until his thoughts started to jumble and bump around in his brain.

They hadn't been able to locate Avery. Evan had known it was a long shot. The man wouldn't have tried to snatch Grace with so many people around if he hadn't had a planned escape route. Avery's parents insisted they hadn't seen him in four days. Evan was sure the man had gone into hiding, but he was also sure Avery wouldn't miss the unsanctioned match race today.

The only photo they'd been able to find of Avery had been a dated mug shot, one Grace said no longer provided an accurate representation of the man.

Agent Ingalls wanted Grace to attend the race to identify Avery, and Henry Green had agreed to let them have his tickets. That only left two problems. One, how could they get into the event without anyone identifying them? And two, how did he protect Grace in a crowded, open area?

Barkley ambled over to him and lay down at his feet. Evan guzzled the rest of his coffee and placed the mug on the wooden step beside him. He rested his elbows on his knees and propped his chin on his clasped hands, watching the sunrise.

Ribbons of orange and gold painted the horizon as the morning started to awaken. The sound of the waterfall added background music to the start of the day, acting as a balm for his soul.

"Lord, I've made many mistakes in my life, the greatest of which was turning from You after we lost Lisa. My eyes are fixed on You now, and that's where they will stay. Please, help me save Grace. I can't do it without You."

TEN

The cabin was quiet. Too quiet. The only sound was the faint roar of the waterfall that had lulled Grace to sleep last night. She pulled her hair through the elastic tie, securing the ponytail. How had she slept until nine o'clock? She hadn't slept past six in ten years or longer. Why hadn't Barkley woken her? His absence from the bedroom when she woke meant only one thing. Evan must have let him out. Heat warmed her cheeks at the thought of him in her bedroom while she slept. Had she been snoring? Or drooling?

She pulled a tube of sunscreen out of her bag, squirted a small amount into her palm and applied it to her face and neck. Okay, time to find Evan and Barkley. There was no way Evan would have left her there unguarded. He had to be around somewhere. Hopefully, he'd take her back to the clinic before they had to go to the race so she could call the hospital and check on Chloe. She'd tried to call last night but didn't have cell service at the cabin.

Walking into the living area, a sleepy Barkley raised his head to look at her before curling back up in front of the fireplace. It was obvious the fire had been out for a while since there were no embers. Of course, the temperatures during the daylight hours were much warmer than the nighttime.

The smell of coffee lured her into the kitchen area. The coffeemaker was still hot, but there wasn't much left in the pot. She emptied the contents into a mug and added two spoons of sugar and a dash of cream. Her stomach rumbled, so she snagged an apple out of the basket on the counter.

The door opened before she reached it, and Bridget entered carrying a pink, hard-sided makeup bag. Evan was close behind, a small suitcase in his hand.

"Bridget, what are you doing here? Don't tell me you're my new guard." Grace smiled, hoping the other woman would know she was teasing.

"Nope. I'm here to give you a makeover. Consider me your fairy godmother." The petite redhead smiled. "Except in this case, you're not being turned into a princess, so I guess it's more of a make-under."

"Seriously?"

"Yes, seriously." Evan placed the suitcase on the floor inside the door. "Since you've agreed to attend the race—against my wishes—and to ID Avery for Agent Ingalls, we need to change your looks. We don't want Avery to ID you."

"That's where I come in." Bridget placed the makeup case on the small kitchen table and opened it. Inside was an array of lipsticks, eye shadows, creams and things. "Did you know I'm a certified makeup artist? I took a six-week course a few years ago." As she chatted away, Bridget hefted the suitcase onto the table and opened it, revealing a multitude of wigs. "A bodyguard never knows when they may need to go undercover on a job."

Evan whistled. "Wow. You really take this stuff seriously, don't you?"

"Of course I do. Sometimes it's a matter of life or death," she replied.

Grace picked up a long, straight-haired black wig. She couldn't imagine wearing such a thing. With her pale complexion and freckles, it would be obvious the hair wasn't real.

"Oh, no, that won't do for you." Bridget took the wig and laid it on a chair. She dug into the suitcase and then held up a shoulder-length, brown, curly-haired wig. "I think this one will do nicely."

She straightened and turned back to Grace.

"Now, have a seat so I can get started. Getting both of you in disguises will take a couple of hours. And the match race starts at two."

"Did you figure out how you could get into the event with me?" Grace asked Evan as she sat in the hard, straight-back kitchen chair.

"Actually, I'm going to try to get away with using Henry's ticket."

"What? I thought he said the ticket wasn't transferable."

"Hold still," Bridget commanded, placing a hand under Grace's chin and lifting her face. "Close your eyes."

Grace did as instructed, acutely aware of Evan watching from across the room, a scowl on his face. "Tell me what you're thinking, Evan."

When they'd been younger, she wouldn't have had to ask what he was thinking, he would have told her or she would have instinctively known. She knew he was worried about keeping her safe, but she couldn't imagine how he planned to capture Avery.

"I don't want Henry at the race. It's too dangerous, and he's not as young as he used to be. I mean, I don't even want you there." She heard the frustration in his voice. "But if you insist on going along with Agent Ingalls's idea, then I'm going to be at your side."

"And if the people at the gate refuse to allow you to enter?"

"Then you don't enter, either," he said flatly.

She opened her eyes, turned and frowned at him. Grace knew he was right. She couldn't risk being at the race unprotected, but she needed to do what she could to help end the threat against her family.

Bridget pulled Grace's head back into position and started applying eyeliner. Having never been one to wear much makeup, Grace was afraid to see the outcome of this makeover. Did she have the right facial wash to remove all this goop at the end of the day?

"I don't think they'll refuse me entry," Evan said.

"Why is that?"

"You've heard the old saying 'money talks'? Well, I plan to throw a little money around to see if they're listening."

"You will pretend to be married high-rollers from Texas," Bridget chimed in. "Ryan and I used a similar disguise a few months ago, only we played the part of spoiled siblings from a rich New England family."

Bridget continued to tell about her and Ryan's adventure rescuing a woman from her abusive mobster husband, but Grace tuned her out, focusing on the notion she and Evan were going to pretend to be husband and wife. There was no way that would be awkward, right?

A look of despair washed over Grace's face. Was the idea of pretending to be Evan's wife so revolting? If so, could she pull it off? Or would she blow their cover? He wished he'd had time to come up with a better plan, but it was too late to make changes now.

The air in the room suddenly became unbearably stuffy. He got up and headed to the door. "Come on, Barkley. Let's get some air."

The dog followed him outside, and Evan closed the door behind him, not waiting to see if either woman had anything to say about his sudden departure.

Why had Grace's expression made him feel rejected all over again? He wasn't an eighteen-year-old kid with idyllic dreams anymore. He was a grown man, a father, and he knew better than to allow fanciful ideas to enter his head. He and Grace would never—could never—be anything more than friends. He'd put Avery behind bars, and then, once a new veterinarian had been hired to run the clinic, Grace would return to her life in Denver. And that was fine with him. Life would go back to the way it was meant to be. He'd raise his son to the best of his ability and continue to protect the citizens of Blackberry Falls.

Well, maybe one thing would change. He thought it might be time to let Camden have the dog he'd always wanted. Seeing his son interact with Barkley had made him realize his child needed a dog that would be his best friend. A pet he could play games with and would fill the void in his heart Evan feared would be there when Grace left.

He bent, picked up a stick and tossed it. Barkley looked at the stick, but didn't budge. "Guess you don't like playing fetch, huh? Wonder if I should consider a different breed for Camden. Maybe a golden retriever or an Australian shepherd." The dog moaned and covered his face with his paw. "Okay, I didn't mean to hurt your feelings. A Great Dane would be a great choice, too."

"Great Danes are wonderful dogs, but I'd suggest you make a list of the qualities you're looking for in a pet before making a final decision." Evan startled at the sound of Grace's voice behind him. He hadn't even heard the door open.

"That's what I—" His voice faltered.

Grace's face was forever imprinted in his mind, so much so, he imagined he could draw it blindfolded. The face staring back at him was not hers. Her freckles had been replaced with high cheekbones and a beauty mark just above full, red lips. Her silver-blue eyes were now a honey-brown color, emphasized with a few wrinkles at the corners—what his mom had always called laugh lines. To top off her new look, chestnut-colored hair framed her face, falling in a cascade of curls that brushed her shoulders. If he hadn't seen it with his own eyes, he never would have believed Grace was the woman standing before him.

"Aren't you going to say anything? What do you think?" She turned, showing off the designer jeans and pink, floral-print blouse. "Will anyone recognize me?"

"Um...uh...no."

"I think he's speechless!" Bridget beamed, pushing past Grace to grab his arm. "Okay, your turn." She marched him into the cabin, pushing him onto the chair where Grace sat earlier.

"Are you going to be able to make me as unrecognizable as Grace?"

"Of course, silly. You didn't think I was going to slap a pair of fake-nose-and-mustache glasses on you and call it done, did you?" Bridget giggled. "Give me more credit than that."

"I honestly didn't know what to expect," he said, not taking his eyes off Grace. "But one thing is for sure, I'll never doubt your ability as a disguise master again."

Grace's laughter mingled with Bridget's and his heart lifted. For the first time all day, Evan actually believed they might pull off Agent Ingalls's harebrained plan.

Evan captured Grace's hand in his own as they walked along the graveled parking area. Leaning in close, he whispered, "Stop fidgeting with your hair."

She frowned. "It's hot and itchy."

"I know. Mine is, too, but we don't want to blow our cover."

Evan honestly couldn't say whose transformation shocked him more, Grace's or his. When he'd looked into the mirror, he had truly been speechless. His ginger-colored hair had been replaced with a dark brown, short-hair wig. To complete the image, Bridget had attached facial hair with an adhesive she promised would come off with the remover she'd left behind, giving him thicker eyebrows and a close-cropped beard the same color as the wig. His appearance was so altered, he didn't think his parents or Camden would have been able to pick him out of a lineup.

Evan's gun pressed against the small of his back, offering a small amount of comfort. "Remember, let me do the talking."

She nodded. "I'll follow your lead."

They approached the guard at the gate. He had hoped Randy Ingalls would have been assigned to gate duty, guaranteeing their admittance, but he wasn't the one who greeted them. "Tickets?"

Evan handed over the tickets without saying a word. The guard, a tall, gangly ranch hand from the Hamilton ranch, glanced at the ticket, then back at Evan. "You're not Henry Green. How did you get these tickets?"

"Uncle Henry gave them to me. I'm Theodore Green the Third. Everyone calls me Trey." Evan held his breath, praying he'd disguised his voice well enough the man hadn't recognized it.

The guy looked him up and down. "I didn't know ol' Henry had a nephew."

"Actually, if you want to get technical, I'm his great-nephew. You see, he's my momma's daddy's baby brother."

"Well, *Trey*, your great-uncle Henry doesn't have the authority to give you these tickets. See right here." The man held the tickets under Evan's nose. "It says 'nontransferable.' Henry Green has to be here to use them."

"But, sir, Uncle Henry isn't coming. You might have heard, his colt, Knight's Honor, that was supposed to race today developed a bad case of colic. Anyway, Uncle Henry figured if his horse wasn't racing, there wasn't any need for him to be here. It's not like he's going to place a bet on a horse that isn't his, you know. But my wife here likes—"

"Look, Trey, I don't care what your wife likes." The man gestured to the line of people behind them. They looked annoyed. "I can't let you in. Now, kindly leave, before I have you escorted off the premises."

"I'm outta here." Grace huffed and turned on her heels, her red cowgirl boots kicking up dust. "You promised me I'd get to do some gambling on this trip. What was the point of me taking money out of the safe if I wouldn't get to have fun? I knew we should have gone to Vegas."

"What's going on here?" A big, burly man in his mid-to late-forties with thinning blond hair, wearing a tan Western suit and a Stetson hat, walked up to the gate from inside the event grounds.

"I'm sorry, Mr. Torres." The guard apologized. "These people were leaving."

Evan eyed the newcomer. The way the guard was acting, it was obvious this man was important, possibly even the person running the operation.

Putting his hand on the small of Grace's back, Evan spoke loudly. "It's okay, honey. I'll phone the pilot and tell him to get the jet fueled up and ready to go. We can be in Vegas in a few hours."

"Wait a minute." Torres motioned for them to come over to the fence, standing off to the side so others could enter. "Why don't you tell me who you are, and I'll decide if I allow you to enter or not?"

"Well, sir, like I tried to tell the man at the gate. I'm Theodore Green the Third, from Dallas. We're visiting my uncle, Henry Green, at Mountain View Ranch. Since his horse got colic—"

"Oh, good grief, Trey. Nobody cares about all that," Grace interrupted, talking in a syrupy-sweet Southern voice.

She turned to the burly man and smiled sweetly. "I'm Shelby Green." She nodded to Evan. "Trey's wife. You see, it's my birthday, which means I get to gamble. I only gamble twice a year, my birthday and New Year's Day. That way I don't get addicted, you know."

Evan bit back a smile. Grace was having fun weaving her tale, and Torres seemed to be buying it.

She got a serious look on her face, leaned in close, so only he and Torres could hear her. "What that means is my sweet man here gave me ten thousand dollars. I'm either going to gamble some, or all, of it here at your *little* horse race, or I'm headed to Vegas. The choice is yours."

"Is this a joke?"

Grace returned the man's stare, unblinking. "Oh, honey, I never joke about money."

"Cell phones must be turned off, and no cameras allowed. If you break the rules, you're outta here, and you forfeit all your bets." Torres looked to the guard and added, "Let them in."

Grace squealed and waltzed past the guard, Evan close on her heels.

Now the real test began. How many people in attendance knew Chief Evan Bradshaw and Dr. Grace Porter? Would he and Grace be able to stay in character without blowing their cover?

ELEVEN

Evan surveyed the area. A musty odor of hay, manure and horses surrounded them. The entire match race setup was crude. Horses were being held in a corral instead of a barn with stalls.

As Evan and Grace passed the holding area, a palomino colt neighed and reared on his hind legs. A handler fought to control the animal while another man stood to the side with a syringe.

When Grace's steps faltered, Evan slipped his arm around her waist and pulled her close. "Remember, don't react to anything you see."

She nodded and averted her eyes from the scene playing out in front of them, her jaw clenched.

The fact the men weren't even trying to hide what they were doing was alarming. Evan had no way of knowing what was in the syringe, but he seriously doubted it was full of vitamin supplements. He halted Grace and turned her to face him. Leaning in, he placed his lips near her cheek and whispered, "Time to take photos."

Pulling back, she met his eyes. Her lip quivered ever so slightly, but she smiled and reached up to grasp his silver-onyx bolo tie. Vanilla perfume assailed him. Her signature scent, bringing back memories of scented notes left in his locker and vanilla-lip-gloss kisses.

Mentally shaking himself, he took half a step to the right, providing a clear view for the camera hidden behind the fake stone. Grace's fingers slipped behind the oval slide, giving the appearance to onlookers she was adjusting the tie when in reality she was pressing the tiny button hidden on the back that activated the camera.

"I thought you were here to gamble." Torres walked over to them. "All you're doing is staring at your husband."

"Well, we haven't been married long, so sometimes I find myself looking at him wondering if it's real." Grace laughed. "But I'm glad you're here, Mr....Torres, was it?" She paused, but the man neither confirmed nor denied his name. "Can you tell me anything about the horses racing today? So I can pick one?"

"You'll find flyers at the betting booths listing the horses and their stats." He motioned to the four booths stationed around the three-quarter-mile oval track. A man, wearing a black T-shirt with Security written across the front, walked over and whispered in his ear.

When Torres turned, his jacket flapped open, revealing a holster. "The first race starts in fifteen minutes, so place your bets," he said over his shoulder as he walked away.

Once the man was out of earshot, Grace whispered, "Did you see the gun?"

"I did, but don't focus on that." Evan squeezed her hand. "You did great. Now, we need to go to one of the booths and look at the flyers."

Her eyes widened. "We're not really going to place a bet, are we?"

"No," he assured her. "But we have to make it look like we are."

Evan took Grace's elbow and guided her toward the booth. He pulled a flyer out of the holder on the small wood shelf under the ticket window then leaned both elbows on the shelf as he pretended to study the form.

"Which horse would you like to bet on?" the woman behind the window asked.

"Not sure yet. We need to study the stats first." He pulled Grace aside and motioned for the next person in line to go ahead of them. They slowly eased away from the booth, trying not to draw attention to themselves.

Dressed in a black Security shirt, with a baseball cap pulled low to obscure his face, Agent Ingalls walked up and leaned on the metal fence railing beside them, his back to the track as he scanned the crowd.

"Don't acknowledge me. Just listen. You will find fake betting tickets stuffed inside the toilet paper roll in the last Porta Potty." He briefly made eye contact. "Nice disguises. Wouldn't have recognized you without the photo you sent earlier." And then he was gone.

Grace had clutched Evan's hand when Randy Ingalls appeared, and her nails bit into his skin. He pried his hand free. "I'm sorry," she gasped.

"It's okay." He laced his fingers through hers and smiled. "Now, let's get those tickets."

They walked to the row of Porta Potties and got in line for the one on the end. Finally, it was his turn.

"I want you to stand right outside the door," Evan said. "If you need me, yell."

"Believe me, I will." She smiled. "Loudly."

He entered the small, plastic water closet, holding his breath as he worked to quickly remove the roll of toilet paper from the holder. The tickets were exactly where Ingalls had said they would be. There were tickets for each horse in each race—smart thinking on the agent's part. This way, no matter who won the race,

Evan and Grace could pretend to lose. Dividing the tickets, he slipped them into his pocket.

There was a knock on the door. "Honey. The race is about to start."

Something must have startled Grace. She wouldn't have knocked otherwise. He put the roll of paper on top of the holder and then slipped outside, taking a deep breath of fresh air.

He put his arm around her shoulders and turned her toward the track. "Everything okay?"

"I saw someone who resembled Avery's coloring and build, but I couldn't see his face."

Excitement charged through him. Avery Hebert had showed up. "Which way?"

"Over close to the corral."

Evan turned in that direction. "Well then, lets make our way over there."

They wove their way through the crowd. The first of three match races was about to start, so most of the people were vying for places to stand with the best views of the track. Evan would estimate there were close to five hundred people in attendance.

They were less than twenty feet from their destination when he saw him. But it was the person with Avery that had Evan stopping short. He looked at Grace to see if she'd noticed. Her facial expression told him she had.

"Val—"

He pulled her into his arms and claimed her lips, silencing her words. The action had been impulsive, intended to protect their cover, but in that instant, Evan knew he was in trouble. Her kiss was as sweet as he remembered, but it was an indulgence he couldn't afford.

"I'm starting to regret letting you two in here today," Torres's voice boomed behind them.

Evan pulled back, avoiding eye contact with Grace.

"A kiss for luck, that's all," Grace said, her voice husky.

Had the kiss affected her as much as it had him, Evan wondered, or was she simply embarrassed at being caught?

Whatever was the case, it didn't matter. Right now the only thing that mattered was catching Avery. Nothing else.

Grace's heart fluttered in her chest, as if it were a hummingbird searching to escape its cage. She took a few steadying breaths, willing her nerves to calm. Whatever had possessed Evan to kiss her, here of all places, in front of so many people?

She looked around, getting her bearings. Torres huffed and walked over to Avery, who now stood at the metal fence, observing the track, Valerie at his side.

Oh. Grace touched her lips, the warmth of Evan's kiss still on them. That's why he'd kissed her. She'd almost blown their cover. Shelby Green from Dallas, Texas, wouldn't know a veterinary technician from Blackberry Falls, Colorado.

"I'm sorry. I did the first thing I could think of—"

"To shut me up." She forced a smile, but her heart felt like it was sinking in quicksand. "It's okay. Let's finish what we started. I won't mess up again."

"Are you sure being here, pretending to be someone else, isn't too hard for you?" Concern laced Evan's voice.

She nodded, and he clasped her hand. "Okay, hang on tight. I don't want to lose you in this crowd."

Evan pushed through the throng, stopping to whisper something to Ingalls before nudging his way over to where Avery stood.

When the starting pistol sounded, Grace found herself standing right beside her employee. Was this woman whom she thought of as family involved in the attacks on her and Chloe?

While the crowd around them cheered, urging the two riders to the finish line, Grace observed Avery and Valerie. They laughed and cheered with the onlookers, Avery's hand on her back. Grace couldn't believe their beloved employee was mixed up with Avery and his illegal dealings. Valerie's words came back to her. *You saw the attacker's face. Can you identify him?* It all started to make sense. Though she hated to believe her friend would betray her, Grace knew Valerie would have had the opportunity and skills to falsify the medical reports.

Evan nudged her, nodding at the track. She'd been staring. Ugh. She needed to focus and not let her emotions rule her actions. If she blew their cover, it could mean their lives.

The horses were coming around the last turn, and Evan cheered beside her as if his life depended on it.

"Come on, boy! Faster!" Grace yelled, purposely omitting the horse's name.

Evan had warned her before they'd arrived not to yell out the name of a horse when cheering, because if the horse won, people would wonder why they didn't claim their "winnings." If anyone asked which horse they had placed a bet on, they'd dodge the question by replying they didn't want to jinx themselves by saying. Instead, they would wait until the race was over to announce their pick and act disappointed because they had lost.

As the horses crossed the finish line, the

crowd erupted in a chorus of cheers and boos. Avery swept a giggling Valerie into a big hug. "See, darlin', I told you Freckled Charmer was a winner. Now let's go get our winnings so I can take you out for a nice dinner."

Valerie looped her arm through Avery's and said, "Let's go." The pair headed to the nearest booth, walking past Evan and Grace without recognizing them.

Whew. Grace released her breath. Bridget's disguises had worked.

Torres turned to them. "Well, how did you do, birthday girl?"

Grace frowned. "I lost."

Evan made a show of pulling the fake betting tickets out of his pocket and tearing them up. "Well, Shelby, looks like we're done here."

The burly man smirked. "Too bad. But there are still two more races. Better luck next time."

"No next time today." Grace sighed and turned to Evan. "You told me not to bet it all on the first race."

"You bet all ten thousand on the first race?" Torres questioned.

"I really thought we'd win."

The man's smirk turned to a full belly laugh. "Looks like your birthday ain't so lucky, after all." Torres walked away, headed to the betting booth.

"Let's get out of here, before he finds out we didn't place a bet."

"What about Avery and Valerie?" She twisted to look behind them. The pair had stopped to talk to Torres. Avery had a wad of money in his hand.

"The way he was talking, I have a feeling they aren't sticking around for all the races, either." Evan steered her toward the entrance. "Even if they do, Ingalls saw him. I'm sure he's notified his partner who's stationed outside the entrance to follow them when they leave."

Grace didn't want to have gotten this close to capturing the man after her just to lose him again. Evan had warned her that no matter what they saw at the race today, he couldn't make any arrests because they were outside his jurisdiction. It was up to Agent Ingalls and his partner to determine which arrests—if any—they could make.

"What if he gives them the slip?"

Evan laughed. "There you go, trying to sound like a movie detective again."

"Ev—" She took a deep breath. "Trey. I'm serious."

"I know you are. I am, too. Your safety is my top priority."

They walked past the guard who'd tried to

deny them admittance and headed for the parking area.

"Hey! Greg, stop them!" Torres yelled, running in their direction.

"Keep walking, but don't run. He may not mean us," Evan instructed her.

Darting a glance over her shoulder, Grace saw that Avery and Valerie had reached the gate. The man, Greg, stepped in front of them.

"Not them! Stop Mr. and Mrs. Texas!"

Greg spun and sprinted in their direction.

"Run!" Evan commanded.

They raced to the rental truck, a black extended-cab GMC, parked two rows over. The doors beeped as he hit the unlock button on the remote.

Greg was closing in on them when a white SUV sped out of nowhere, blocking his path. He hit the hood with his fist and yelled. The female driver laid on the horn and pulled forward as Greg tried to go around the front of her vehicle, encouraging him to yell louder while enabling them to reach the safety of the truck.

Grace climbed into the passenger seat as Evan started the engine. "Go. Go. Go!" she urged, twisting in her seat to see Greg and Torres standing in the middle of the parking lot staring after their fleeing vehicle.

Grace settled back into her seat and fastened

the seat belt. "Wow, that was perfect timing the vehicle showed up when it did."

"Yes, wasn't it," he said more as a statement than a question.

"What are you not telling me?"

"Randy Ingalls's partner, Agent Katherine Lewis, was driving that vehicle." He merged onto US-50, heading toward Penrose.

"Why do you think Torres chased us?"

"I think he went to verify we placed a large bet. Found out we didn't and realized he'd been tricked."

"Could he have figured out who we were?"

"If anyone could have recognized us, it would have been Valerie. She looked straight at us when they walked by on their way to collect their winnings and didn't even blink."

"Do you think she could be the one who stole the drugs and altered the records?" Grace felt disloyal even letting the thought enter her head, but she had to ask.

"We definitely can't rule her out yet."

Grace thought of the things she'd witnessed at the race, especially the injections being given to the horses. To her knowledge, there hadn't been a veterinarian on duty like there would have been at a sanctioned race. Anger welled inside her at the thought of an employee of Porter Animal Clinic being involved in illegal activities involving animals. How could anyone who worked in a veterinary clinic take part in such an event?

Evan put his Jeep into Reverse and backed out of the space in the Denver Memorial parking deck. He hadn't planned on making the trip to Denver tonight, but after seeing Grace's disappointment over discovering Valerie with Avery, he'd wanted to do something nice for her. So, after returning the rental and retrieving his personal vehicle, he'd taken her to visit Chloe.

He glanced at Grace, sitting beside him. Though he'd only been able to remove his contacts and wig, she had erased all traces of Shelby Green before entering Chloe's hospital room. "Are you hungry? We could go through a drive-through if you'd like."

"How about we eat in Monument? There's a burger joint I like to stop at when I make this drive. It's almost halfway, and a perfect spot to stop and stretch. Plus, they make the best burgers and onion rings."

"Sounds good to me." He pulled to a stop and put tokens into the slot so the mechanical arm would rise, allowing them to exit the parking deck.

"Thank you for taking me to see Chloe tonight. I know you hadn't planned on making the trip, but I appreciate it."

"Did you enjoy your time with your sister?"

"Oh, yes. Dr. Carson seems completely satisfied with her progress." She smiled. "The swelling has gone down, and he's optimistic she'll make a full recovery."

She continued, happily rattling on, filling him in on the changes in Chloe's condition, and all the things she wanted to do with her sister once she had fully recovered. The time with her sister, even if the conversation had been one-sided, had done her good.

Evan wished he had witnessed Grace's special time with Chloe, but he'd stayed outside the room, talking to Lieutenant Johnson, who was waiting on Ryan to arrive and take over the night-shift guard duty.

"Did the doctor say when he planned to bring her out of the coma?"

"He said there's no way to know for sure. It could be tomorrow or it could be several more days." She sighed. "He promised to call me when they start the process to wake her. I really want to be there. To be the first person she sees."

"I'll do everything I can to make that happen."

"I know you will. It's the kind of person you are. You have a servant's heart, and you take care of the people in your life. That's what makes you so good at your job."

Her words jolted him. When Evan had been

in high school, his main goal in everything he did had been to make Grace proud of him. She wouldn't be so proud if she knew how he'd failed Lisa. Maybe it was time to come clean.

"I'm not perfect. There have been plenty of times when I've not taken care of the people in my life. Lisa for one." His voice cracked, and he fought to tamp down the pain.

He turned onto the interstate access road and built up speed to merge onto I-225. The traffic was thick even for nine o'clock on a Sunday night.

"Do you want to talk about it?" Grace asked softly.

Did he want to? No. But he needed to tell her his secret. She had to understand so she wouldn't have too high an opinion of his abilities.

"After Lisa had Camden, she became withdrawn. She had a difficult labor. At first, I thought the trauma of the labor combined with the demands of a newborn were the reasons she seemed so tired and withdrawn. I offered to hire a nanny to help, but that infuriated her."

A pang of guilt stabbed at him for talking about his deceased wife and revealing her secrets to his first love, but he couldn't tell his story without revealing Lisa's, too.

Lord, forgive me. I'm not meaning to gossip.

A bolt of lightning lit the sky, followed immediately by a loud clap of thunder. Big, fat rain-drops began to fall from the sky, obscuring his view. He turned on the wipers, but they were of little use in this downpour. Putting on the flash-ers, he pulled onto the shoulder of the highway.

He turned to face Grace. It was time she knew she'd made the right decision to build a life somewhere else, away from him.

"Lisa thought I was implying she wasn't ca-pable of taking care of our son." He shook his head. "That wasn't what I meant at all."

"Of course, it wasn't," Grace insisted.

Sweet Grace, she still didn't get it. "I could have handled things better. If, instead of trying to throw money at the situation, I had paid at-tention and been there for my wife, I may have realized she was suffering from postpartum de-pression. And maybe she'd be alive today."

Grace gasped. "You don't mean she…"

"Harmed herself?" He definitely hadn't meant to imply anything like that. "No. But two weeks after we found out we were having a daughter, Lisa suffered a miscarriage and her depression deepened. She was sleeping all the time and not eating. Her appearance became very gaunt. I tried to get her to see a counselor, but she refused. Her ob-gyn prescribed a mild antidepressant, but she wouldn't take it."

Lightning danced in the night sky, and he

studied it as he tried to choose his next words. Grace sat quietly. Evan knew she would wait indefinitely for him to continue, and if he didn't, she would be okay with that, too. She'd never been pushy about needing to know everything. Even when she'd been younger, she'd seemed to instinctively know there were times people needed to keep things to themselves. It was one of the qualities he'd always admired in her.

The downpour eased enough that he could see again. So he merged back onto the interstate, driving in silence, his mind a jumble of thoughts as he waged an internal war with himself, struggling with his guilt for talking about Lisa when she wasn't there and his need to be honest. Mostly with himself, for the first time since the accident.

After he worked his way through the I-25 interchange and they were headed south, his need to be honest with Grace won. "Four months after the miscarriage, we were nearing our third wedding anniversary. I thought a change of scenery—a weekend getaway to Denver— would be good for her. For us."

Grace shifted in her seat, tucking her foot under her leg as she always did when listening intently.

"Lisa's parents had agreed to watch Camden," Evan continued. "He was twenty months old, and we'd never left him to go on a trip. I booked two nights in a nice hotel two blocks from the theater district. I had the entire trip planned, a morning of pampering in the spa for Lisa, followed by shopping, a romantic dinner and a play."

"That was thoughtful," Grace said.

Unfortunately, Lisa hadn't seen it that way. She'd accused him of being controlling and said he shouldn't have planned such a trip without checking with her first. It hadn't mattered what he'd said, she'd been looking for a fight. His second biggest regret from that weekend, besides planning it in the first place, was that he hadn't taken her straight back to Blackberry Falls when she'd first complained.

The exit for Monument came into view.

"Where's the burger joint?" he asked.

She directed him to a small all-night diner.

There were half a dozen cars in the parking lot. He pulled into an empty space about twenty feet from the door. The rain had become a torrential downfall. They were going to get soaked. Evan opened the center console, pulled out a blue compact umbrella and held it out to her. "Here. You use this."

She accepted the offering but didn't move. "What happened that weekend?"

Grace was waiting for him to finish telling her about Lisa. Hmm. Maybe she had changed when it came to fulfilling her curiosity. Oh, well. Since he was the one who had brought up the topic and insisted on baring his soul, he'd finish.

"She hated the entire trip and refused to leave the room." A clap of thunder shook the vehicle. "I finally convinced her to go to dinner and the play…it was one she'd wanted to see for a while. I promised her if she'd do that much, we'd cut our trip short. After the play, we'd go straight back to the hotel, check out and head home, but—" His voice cracked. "We never made it back to the hotel."

Grace reached across the seat and clasped his hand. Her touch burned like a brand.

"I'm sorry. I heard about the drive-by shooting. I didn't know it was an anniversary trip, or that Lisa had suffered from postpartum."

"It wasn't something we announced." Evan pulled his hand free of her grasp, opened his door and ran for the awning covering the diner's door, ignoring the rain pelting his body.

He didn't want Grace's pity. He simply needed her to understand she'd made the right choice in walking away. And she needed to remember that, since he could never give his heart away again. Not to anyone. Even her.

TWELVE

Evan had just run through the rain to the diner, away from her. Shame washed over Grace. She hadn't meant to seem insensitive with her comment. Of course, they hadn't announced Lisa's postpartum depression, but it was Blackberry Falls where everyone knew everything. She was impressed he'd been able to keep it a secret.

But why had he told her? Had being in Denver twice in the past few days brought all the memories crashing down on him? His pain was evident, and it made her heart ache.

She'd been happy Evan had found someone to spend his life with, and she hated that he and Camden had to live without Lisa in their lives any longer. Grace owed him an apology. Whether or not he'd accept it, she didn't know, but she'd have to try.

The rain beat against the windows. She looked at the compact umbrella. Even if it could offer enough protection from the downpour, once she opened the door and stuck the umbrella out to open it, she'd be soaking wet.

Tossing the umbrella back into the center console, Grace plucked her oversize leather messenger bag off the floorboard, opened her door and dashed across the parking lot to Evan's side.

"Why didn't you use the umbrella?"

She shrugged. "The way the rain is blowing, I didn't think an umbrella would do much good." Tugging the door open, she added, "Come on, I'm starved."

The moment she entered the diner, the smell of greasy burgers and salty fries assaulted her. The interior of the restaurant was a nod to a fifties diner without coming off as a cheesy imitation. The floors were black-and-white vinyl tiles laid in a checkerboard pattern. The tables were red Formica, and the booth seats were covered in red-and-white vinyl. That was where the similarity ended.

Instead of a jukebox full of rock 'n' roll songs, country music played through surround-sound speakers, and instead of a dress with an apron, the waitress wore blue jeans and a red, polo-style shirt.

Grace slid into a booth next to the front window and pulled out a laminated menu, even though she knew exactly what she would order. It kept her hands busy.

Evan slid into the seat across from her. "This place is…interesting."

"Kind of old meets new, wouldn't you say?"

"Exactly." He rubbed his hand over his fake beard. "You know, I'm regretting we didn't bring a change of clothes."

She smiled. "It sure was funny seeing Lieutenant Johnson's face when he finally realized we were telling the truth about who we were."

"He didn't believe it until we took out our contacts and pulled off the wigs." He scratched at the beard again. "This thing is itching. I wish I'd brought the adhesive dissolvent."

"Oh. Why didn't I think of this sooner? I might have something that would work." She dug into her purse and took out a small blue makeup bag with a hummingbird-print design. Unzipping the bag, she pulled out a rectangular tin, a small plastic bottle and an individually wrapped nail polish remover pad.

Evan leaned over the table for a better view. "What is all this stuff?"

She held up the tin. "Cotton swabs." Then she picked up the bottle. "Baby oil."

He reached across and picked up the small pink square packet. "An acetone nail polish remover pad?"

"That is a last resort," she laughed, handing him the supplies. "I'm pretty sure, if you apply

the baby oil and wait a minute or two, the adhesive will break down and you'll be able to remove the beard. You already took off the wig,
and not to be mean or anything, you kinda look
funny with red hair and a dark brown beard and
eyebrows."

He pointed to his face and wiggled his eyebrows. "Really? You think this looks funny."

Grace choked back laughter as the waitress walked up to their table and set down two
glasses of water.

"Hi, my name is Kenzie. I'll be taking your
order. What can I get you to drink?" The woman
looked like she should be performing with a
rock band instead of working in a diner. In her
early twenties, she had short black hair, several
piercings, including a nose ring, and an intri-
cate dogwood-flowers tattoo covering most of
her right arm.

Evan motioned for Grace to go first.

"I'd like coffee, please. And if you don't
mind, could we go ahead and place our food
order, too?"

"Sure, no problem," Kenzie replied.

"Great, I'd like a cheeseburger, all the way,
and an order of onion rings," she said, putting
the unopened menu back in its table holder.

The girl wrote everything on her order pad.
Then she turned to Evan. "And for you, sir?"

"I'll have the same."

"Okay. I'll be right back with your coffee." She took a few steps then stopped and turned back to Evan. "You know, if you're going to wear a fake beard and mustache, you should get a good quality one that matches your natural hair."

Grace exploded in laughter as Kenzie walked away.

Evan held up both hands, palms forward in mock surrender. "Okay. Okay. I'll go take off the facial hair. I'm tired of itching." He slid out of the booth and then removed the bolo tie. Slipping it into his inside jacket pocket, he removed the jacket and folded it before holding it out to her. "Do you mind hanging on to this while I'm gone?"

"No problem." She accepted the jacket, placing it under her purse beside her on the seat.

Evan held up his phone. "I'll be as quick as possible, but if anything happens, call."

She nodded, and he headed to the restroom at the back of the diner.

Kenzie brought two large mugs of coffee to the table along with a red-plastic food basket full of small tubs of individual servings of cream. As she took the items off the tray and placed them on the table, a small wolf tattoo on her inner wrist triggered a flash memory—of a different wolf tattoo on the forearm of the intruder who'd attacked Grace two nights earlier in the clinic.

Grace's breath caught, and the girl looked at her quizzically.

"Sorry. Your, um, wolf tattoo reminded me of someone."

After the girl walked away, Grace emptied the contents of two tubs of creamer into her cup and stirred. Lifting the mug with shaking hands, she took a sip, willing the coffee's warmth to chase away the sudden chill in the air and, hopefully, to evaporate the stress of this very trying day.

Her gaze drifted to the parking lot. The rain had slowed to a drizzle. With any luck, it would stop before they left the diner.

A vehicle pulled into the lot, and she watched as Mr. Torres and Greg the guard got out. What were they doing here?

Grace's heart slammed against her chest. With a trembling hand, she placed the mug on the table, creamy, brown liquid sloshing out. Pulling three or four napkins from the silver dispenser on the table, she mopped up the spill.

What should she do? Would they recognize her? The only thing to give her away was her clothes. Think fast. Opening her messenger bag, she pulled out a lightweight beige sweater she'd stuffed inside on a whim when leaving the cabin earlier. She quickly pushed her arms though the sweater's sleeves and buttoned it all the way to the top. She then tucked the collar of her pink-floral blouse inside so the fabric wouldn't show.

Slipping her phone out of her purse, she started to call Evan, but hesitated for fear of being overheard. She quickly sent him a text instead. Torres and Greg are here.

The bell over the door sounded as the men entered the diner. They looked around and then headed in her direction. Glancing down, she closed the text screen, pulled up a word game and pretended to be absorbed in her phone.

"Well, well, well, if it ain't Dr. Porter. What are you doing so far from Blackberry Falls?" The two men slipped into the booth, uninvited, and sat across from her.

Torres snapped his fingers. "Oh, right. I heard about the attack on your sister. I guess you've been to visit her. How's she doing?"

Do not register a reaction. Remember, you've never met them before. Don't act like you know them.

Grace looked at the man and tilted her head. "I'm sorry? Have we met?"

"I guess not. Let me introduce myself." He smiled and held out his hand "My name is Antonio Torres."

She ignored his offer of a handshake, and

Greg snickered. Torres shot his goon a look, and the man choked down the laugh.

Dropping his elbows on the table, Torres clasped his hands together and rested his chin on top of them. "I truly was sorry to hear about Dr. Osborne's wife. Do they know who attacked her? Is she going to be okay?"

Where was Evan?

She glanced toward the back of the diner. The men's room door opened, and he stepped out, looking like his old self. He still sported the white dress shirt and the suit pants he'd worn to the race, but without the bolo and the jacket, he didn't resemble his alter ego Trey. Evan met her gaze and winked. Relief surged through her.

Turning back to Torres she replied, "Thank you for your concern, but I'd rather not discuss my personal business."

Torres leaned back, a look of shock on his face. "No need to get defensive. I was only being neighborly."

"Excuse me, but you're in my seat," Evan said, stopping to stand beside her.

"Chief Bradshaw. I didn't know you were here, too," Torres said, not moving.

"Now you do. Like I said, you're in my seat, Mr. Torres."

The man raised an eyebrow, shock evident on his face.

"Don't look so surprised. I always make it a habit to know newcomers to the area."

Torres jerked his head for Greg to get up and then slid out of the booth behind him. Evan slid into the vacated spot, reached across the table and took her hand.

At his touch, a jolt of awareness shook her. Had Evan felt it, too? His thumb massaged the back of her hand, and the anxiety she'd felt when Torres and Greg entered the diner evaporated.

Grace plastered on a smile and looked up at Antonio Torres, who stood, seemingly rooted to the spot, staring at them. "If you'll excuse us, it looks like our waitress is headed this way with our food."

"Sure," he said, looking from her to Evan. "Enjoy your meal."

After he'd walked away, Evan gave her hand a gentle squeeze, his smile warming her in a way coffee never could.

The waitress delivered their meal. Suddenly the thought of eating the greasy food she had craved made Grace feel nauseous. She wondered if she'd be able to swallow even one bite with the two men sitting a few booths away.

Torres and Greg sat in the corner booth two tables away. Far enough away to look like they were leaving Evan and Grace alone, but close enough to overhear each other's conversation. At least they had sat where Evan had a clear view of them and Grace didn't, though he doubted she'd forget the men were near.

"Let's give thanks." Evan leaned in close, still holding Grace's hand tightly in his, and prayed.

"Amen," she echoed as he finished, offering him a lopsided smile.

Suddenly he wanted nothing more than to load her, Camden and Barkley into his vehicle and get far away from the danger lurking around her.

"Thank you," she said as she pulled her hand free. "Living alone, it's been a while since I've had someone else to pray over a meal for me."

"My pleasure," he replied, swallowing the sorrow rising within him at the thought of all the meals they could have shared if things had been different. Only, if things had been different, he wouldn't have Camden, and he could never imagine his life without his son. Though he'd forever regret failing her when she'd needed him most, he'd never regret loving Lisa.

Shaking the cobwebs of memory from his mind, he poured a blob of ketchup onto his plate and dipped an onion ring into the condiment before taking a bite and forcing the food past the lump in his throat. "Yu-um You were right. These are delicious."

Grace looked as if she needed to tell him something, but he sensed this wasn't the time or place. "Later," he whispered and nodded to her plate. "Eat."

She picked up her burger, took a bite, chewed and swallowed. Then she smiled and took a bigger bite. Good. He'd been afraid Grace's rattled nerves wouldn't allow her to eat, and she hadn't eaten much the past few days, her already slim frame starting to look gaunt.

When both of their plates were empty, Evan motioned to the waitress to bring their check. Food had just been delivered to Torres's table, and though Evan had no way of knowing if the man was a threat to Grace, he'd feel better getting out of the area ahead of him and his goon.

Kenzie brought their bill, and he handed her more than enough cash to cover the total plus leave her with a generous tip.

In the meantime, Grace rolled his jacket into a tight ball and stuffed it into her purse. He'd wondered why she'd carried such a large bag, now he knew. It was so she could hide things in it.

They stepped out into the cool night air. The rain had stopped, leaving a sweet, fresh scent in its wake.

Evan guided Grace to his Jeep, opening the passenger-side door for her. "I couldn't say it earlier—too many listening ears—but you did great in there. Actually, you've been great all day, the way you slipped into character as Shelby and all."

She laughed. "I guess watching those who-dunit movies paid off."

"I guess so," he smiled and closed the door.

Rounding the vehicle, he quickly slid behind the wheel and started the engine. Evan cast one last glance at the diner and his smile evaporated, the hairs on the nape of his neck tingling. Torres was staring in his direction, a cell phone to his ear.

Putting the vehicle in Reverse, he exited the parking lot. Time to get Grace back to the safety of the cabin.

"You missed the on-ramp," Grace noted as he sped past the interstate and turned right onto 2nd Street.

"I know. I think we'll stick to back roads to-night."

"You think they'll follow us, don't you?"

"I'm not sure. But they'll expect us to take the interstate, so the back roads should be safer."

"When you say 'back roads,' you don't mean an off-road trail as in the dirt-and-gravel road that goes over the mountain, do you?"

Was Evan imagining the sound of fear in her voice? Had his honesty about how he'd failed

Lisa caused Grace to doubt his ability to protect her?

"Yes. But I'll also call Agent Ingalls and make him aware of the situation." He gave her a reassuring smile. "It's going to be okay. I promise."

"Do you realize how many times you've said 'I promise' to me in the past three days?"

Had he said it a lot? He had no idea. "I take it I've said it several times. Doesn't mean I'm any less sincere."

"I know. You wouldn't make a promise unless you meant to keep it, but don't make promises that are out of your control. Whether or not everything is okay isn't up to you." Her voice softened. "All you can do is try to make the best choices in any given situation and know the rest is in God's hands."

Evan processed her words as he turned onto Mt. Herman Road—as Grace had said, a dirt-and-gravel road. A trail favorite of mountain bikers, it wasn't ideal for automobile travel, especially on a dark and stormy night. Nonetheless, it would help carry them across the mountain where, after several turns, they'd follow County Road 11 south to Blackberry Falls, adding an extra hour of travel.

Grace shifted in her seat and stared at him, waiting for a reply. She was right. No matter the outcome, God was in control.

"Pray more, worry less. That's what my mom always said to me when I was growing up. Okay, I won't make promises of things I have no power over." He swallowed. Why had it taken him so long to learn that lesson? He'd made promises to Lisa the last night of her life, but he hadn't been able to fulfill them.

"I'm not worried. I trust you," she replied.

He pressed the voice command on the steering wheel to put a call into Agent Ingalls, but the call wouldn't go through. No cell signal. Why hadn't he tried before turning onto the rutted-out old dirt road?

Dear Lord, it's too late to change the route now. I pray I made the right choice. Please, keep us safe.

The road was narrow, and on a good day, when the sun was shining, it took about an hour to drive across. Unfortunately, today wasn't a good day. It was a dark, moonless night, and the road was muddy.

"It seemed like there was something you wanted to tell me back at the diner. What was it?" he asked Grace.

"Oh, yeah." She turned in her seat to look at him as she often did when talking. "Kenzie, our waitress, had a wolf tattoo. When I saw it, I remembered the guy who attacked me at the clinic had one."

"Identical to hers?"

"No. His was a wolf's head inside a triangle, on the inside of his forearm. I'm sorry I didn't remember it sooner."

"No need to be sorry. Memories can't be forced, sometimes they have to happen organically."

"I guess. Do you think it will help us catch the guy?"

"Possibly. When we get back to the cabin, I'll have you draw a rough sketch of what you saw. Then I can send it out to the tattoo parlors in the area to see if anyone remembers doing the work."

Evan rounded a bend a little too fast and the Jeep fishtailed, the nose coming to a stop too close to the edge of the road and a steep drop.

"Well, that was like a ride at a theme park, only not as much fun." Grace laughed nervously.

"I underestimated how slick this road would be after the heavy rainfall. Sorry," he replied as he shifted the vehicle into four-wheel drive. He needed to put as many miles between them and Torres as possible, but he couldn't be careless in the process.

They continued the ride in silence. Evan drove slow and steady, his nerves tautening with each passing mile. If Grace was nervous, she didn't say anything. Maybe she was afraid of distracting him while they were on this road.

They finally reached the other side of the mountain, and it had only taken them twenty minutes longer than normal.

Being back in cell service range, Evan tried to reach Randy Ingalls again, but the call went to voice mail. He left a message, asking the agent to call, and then he turned onto County Road 11, headed south toward Blackberry Falls. They would arrive at the cabin in forty-five minutes, a little before midnight.

"Do you think Torres being at the diner was a coincidence?" Grace asked the question he'd been pondering ever since he'd received her text while removing Trey Green's persona in the men's room.

Touching the tips of his fingers to his brow line, Evan was reassured to know he did, indeed, still have eyebrows. The beard and mustache had been removed using the nail polish remover, but when Grace's text arrived, he'd been struggling to get the fake eyebrows off. In the end, he'd pulled them off in one quick, painful tug.

"I've been thinking about that." He sighed. "Unless they followed us from the hospital, I can't imagine them knowing we were at the diner. I took every precaution and didn't see anyone tailing us. And I don't believe Torres would have left the match race until all the races were over and all the money counted, which would have given us at least a two-hour head start."

"So, you're saying it was a coincidence?"

"Yes, but that doesn't mean Torres isn't a threat. The fact he made a point of talking to you concerns me."

"Yeah, it concerned me, too." Grace pulled her sweater tighter.

Evan didn't know if she was chilled from the cool night or if it was nerves. He reached over and turned up the heat, adjusting the vents so the air would warm her.

A truck came speeding up behind them. He couldn't be sure because they were out in the country and there weren't any streetlights, but it looked a lot like the truck that had tried to push them into the oncoming train the night Chloe had been attacked. Evan sped up. He had to lose them before they reached the turnoff to the cabin.

Grace twisted in her seat to look out the rear window, but didn't say a word.

Evan's phone rang. He hit the answer button on the steering wheel. "Chief Bradshaw here."

"We lost Avery Hebert." Agent Ingalls's voice sounded over the speaker.

Evan glanced at Grace, her eyes still focused on the vehicle tailing them. "I think we found him."

"Where are you?" Ingalls asked.

"County Road 11. About fifteen miles north of the Flying V Ranch."

Grace screamed, "He's going to hit us!" She twisted around in her seat, facing the front as the truck rammed into the back of Evan's vehicle. Metal crunched against metal, and his tires skidded on the wet pavement.

"Bradshaw, what's happening?" Ingalls asked urgently.

"He's trying to make us crash." Tightening his grip on the steering wheel, Evan spared a brief glance at Grace. "Are you okay?"

"I'm fine. But how are we going to stop him?" She looked over her shoulder and then back to him again. "Can I hold the steering wheel, and you shoot his tires or something?"

"Don't do anything reckless," Ingalls yelled across the speakers. "We've notified the sheriff's office, and I'm on my way." The call went silent.

Evan sped up, putting a little distance between him and the truck, but the other driver soon closed the gap, ramming into them again. This time the impact shattered the back window, but Evan had been able to hold the Jeep steady without skidding.

Evan raced away again, driving dangerously fast on the wet road. His headlights flashed on a bright yellow diamond-shaped road sign, and an eerie, sinking feeling settled in the pit of his stomach. A quick glance in the rearview mirror showed the truck was still barreling down on them—and they were fast approaching the Hangman's Noose curve.

His analytical brain immediately pulled up the stats. No less than ten accidents occurred on that curve per year and, on average, two fatalities annually. It was little surprise they hadn't passed one vehicle since ending up on this stretch of road, most of the locals knew to avoid this area at night, especially following a thunderstorm when the road would be slick.

Evan could only see one option if he hoped to avoid crashing in the curve. Thankfully, there wasn't any oncoming traffic. "Looks like we will have to try a stuntman maneuver from one of your whodunit shows. Hold on tight."

Grace gripped the armrest and prayed in a muffled whisper.

Evan inhaled. Took his foot off the gas and allowed the other vehicle to almost kiss his bumper. Tightening his grip on the steering wheel, he darted into the other lane. And slammed on his brakes. The truck came alongside him. The other driver swerved into them, clipping the front of the Jeep. Metal clashing with metal, sparks flying like fireflies. Evan struggled to control the spin. His vehicle did doughnuts on the pavement then slid off the road, sideswiping a tree before landing with the rear wheels wedged in the ditch. Thankfully, the impact wasn't hard enough for the airbags to deploy.

"Are you hurt?" he asked Grace.

"I don't think so," she replied.

Evan tried to push open his door. Stuck. He twisted enough to get a booted foot against the door and kicked, hard. After the third try, the door popped open. "Call nine-one-one. Tell them there's been an accident."

"Where are you going?" she asked, fear evident in her voice.

"I've got to check on the other vehicle. I'm pretty sure it was Avery driving. But I was so focused on trying to keep us alive that I didn't see if he got away or if he crashed, too." He took her hand in his. "Are you sure you're okay?"

"Yes. Just a little shaken."

He put his hand on the side of her head. Burying his fingers in her hair, he leaned in and claimed her lips. Not a kiss to stop her from talking, like the one earlier that afternoon, but a kiss of need. One to satisfy his mind that she was okay. That he was okay. And they would get through this. His heart soared, a new energy running through his veins. He felt a heightened sense of awareness, like he had been asleep and had just awakened and could accomplish anything. Right now he needed to conquer their attacker.

Reluctantly pulling back, his eyes connected with hers. "Stay here. If the doors will lock, lock them. Don't open them until I get back. I'll be as quick as I can."

She nodded, searching his face in silent assessment. He didn't regret the kiss—he had needed it at that moment, as surely as his body needed oxygen to live, though he knew he'd have to answer for it later.

Opening the console, he took out his Glock and a flashlight, stepped out of the vehicle and closed the door. Time to make sure Avery wasn't circling back around to attack again.

THIRTEEN

The clouds parted, allowing the full, bright moon to shine through, providing a minimal amount of light. Evan scrambled up the bank. When he reached the pavement, he clicked on the flashlight, sweeping the beam in an arc from one side of the road to the other. Black tire marks on the asphalt showed the location where his vehicle had spun and skidded. Approximately fifty feet away, a series of yellow road signs with black arrows marked the start of the curve. They had barely escaped the Hangman's Noose.

The low hum of an idling engine drew his attention. He picked up the pace, running down the incline of the curve, one hand holding the flashlight and the other hovering near his gun.

The flashlight beam illuminated a man in the ditch, lying stomach-down, his face turned heavenward. Evan squatted beside him. No pulse. Avery Hebert was dead; his neck had been broken.

The truck had come to rest against a big oak tree roughly ten yards away from the victim, the driver's door hung open. Evan crossed to it, reached in and turned the engine off. Avery must not have been wearing his seat belt.

Evan needed to call for the coroner. He reached in his back pocket for his phone. It wasn't there. Ugh. Frustration soared through him as he started walking back to the spot where his vehicle sat in a ditch, the steep slope of the curve making going up much more difficult than coming down had been.

Evan had wanted to stop Avery from killing him and Grace, but he hadn't wanted the man dead. He had needed answers from Avery, namely had he acted alone or had he been working for someone.

Was Grace safe now that Avery was dead, or was she in greater danger from an unknown threat?

Grace may have been cold earlier, but not anymore. The inside of the SUV was stifling. Her heart raced and sweat beaded on her forehead. She'd love nothing more than to step outside the vehicle and allow the night air to cool her, but she dared not get out until Evan returned.

Every event of the day had seemed more escalated than the previous one. To top it off, she had no idea how to interpret Evan's kiss. He'd kissed her at the match race because she'd been about to blow their cover, but why had he kissed her just now like a warrior going off to battle?

And what a kiss it had been. Grace hadn't been kissed like that in…well…fifteen years. Evan had always been the only man who could churn up her emotions like that. Lifting her hair off her neck, she fanned herself with her free hand.

What was taking Evan so long? Had Avery crashed in the curve and been injured? She couldn't imagine Avery escaping unscathed driving at such a high speed on a wet road. He had to have known he was putting himself at risk, not only her.

A shudder ran the length of her body. He hadn't only targeted her, but Avery would have killed Evan, too, leaving Camden an orphan.

Sirens pierced the silence, pulling Grace from her thoughts. Help had arrived. She craned her neck as red, blue and yellow lights strobed across the front windshield. Car doors slammed, and she heard the pounding of feet headed in her direction. There was a rap on the driver's-side window.

"Ma'am. Are you okay?" A man, shrouded in darkness, peered inside.

She reached forward and then paused, her hand hovering over the handle. Evan had made her promise not to exit the vehicle until he returned. She thought the man on the other side of the door was a police officer, but she couldn't make out his uniform or his badge.

A beam of light bounced along the windshield as the man went around the vehicle to her side. He rattled the door handle. "Ma'am. Open the door."

She shook her head. He took a step back, his eyes never leaving hers. He must think she'd addled her brain in the accident.

He touched his shoulder, and she heard the static sound of a radio. "Where's the ambulance?"

After a moment of silence, the dispatcher replied, "ETA three minutes. Are you able to assess the injuries?"

"Negative. There's a female victim. Age thirty, thirty-five. She doesn't appear to be injured, but she refuses to exit the vehicle. Do the responding EMTs know sign language?"

Grace fought to suppress the hysterical giggle tickling the back of her throat. The man *was* a

sheriff's deputy. She couldn't have him thinking she was deaf.

Opening the door, she slid out of the Jeep.
Surely, Evan wouldn't be upset with her for getting out since a police officer was here.

"I'm sorry, Officer——" she leaned close to
read his badge "——Rice." Seeing his surprised
expression, she quickly added, "No, I'm not
deaf... I guess I was still stunned from the accident."

"Understandable." The officer grasped her
elbow and steadied her. "What's your name,
ma'am?"

"Grace Porter."

"Are you hurt anywhere, Ms. Porter?"

She shook her head.

"Was someone else with you? Who was driving?"

"Police Chief Evan Bradshaw. He went to
check on the driver of the other vehicle."

"Okay." Officer Rice nodded as he guided
her up the slight incline of the ditch. "My partner went to check out the curve, so they should
see each other."

They reached the top of the embankment, and
Evan raced toward them. He immediately pulled
out his wallet and displayed his badge. "Officer Hooper is putting out flares. I don't expect
we'll see much traffic, but we'll need another

officer to help direct just in case." He paused and flicked a glance at her before turning back to Officer Rice. "We'll also need the coroner. There's one fatality in the curve."

She gasped. "Is it Avery?"

Evan nodded.

The man who had injured Chloe and tormented Grace was dead? Bile rose in her throat and a wave of dizziness assaulted her.

Evan put a hand on her lower back and led her to a boulder on the side of the road. "Sit here until the ambulance arrives." He knelt beside her, holding his flashlight off to the side where it would cast a glow across her face. "Are you okay? Did you hit your head when we wrecked?"

"No. And I don't have a concussion."

Officer Rice stood a few feet away talking to Dispatch.

Evan lifted her chin and searched her eyes. She knew he was looking to see if her pupils were dilated.

"I'm fine," she whispered. "Is Avery really dead?"

"Yes."

"Does this mean it's over? My sister and I can live our lives in peace?" She felt like a horrible person because her first thought was of her and her sister's safety and not of the sadness Avery's family would endure at his loss.

He shrugged. "I don't know."

Grace wanted to ask what he knew, but she swallowed the question. Evan had always been honest with her. If he had more information, he'd tell her. Hounding him wouldn't help.

An ambulance arrived on the scene, followed close behind by a large, black SUV with tinted windows.

Randy Ingalls stepped out of the SUV and headed their way. "Are you both okay?"

"We're fine." Evan stood and turned toward the agent. "Avery Hebert is dead. He crashed in the curve."

The EMT pushed his way past Evan and Ingalls and came to her side. "Do you hurt anywhere, Dr. Porter?"

"I'm fine," she answered, looking at the man's badge. Patterson. "You're one of the first responders who helped my sister the other night."

"Yes, ma'am." He held up a penlight and checked her pupils. "Can you walk?"

"Yes." She sighed. "I really am fine. I was wearing my seat belt. My shoulder will be sore and bruised in the morning. Other than that, I don't have any injuries."

Patterson smiled. "Good. I'm glad you had on your seat belt. Now, let's walk over to the ambulance. I'll check your blood pressure and oxygen levels and make sure you really are fine."

Standing to the side talking to Randy Ingalls, Evan gave her a stern look and jerked his head toward the ambulance. He then turned his attention back to the agent. If his and the agent's animated discussion was an indicator, Evan would be tied up awhile.

She was tired. All she wanted was to go home—or back to the cabin—make sure Barkley was okay, and go to sleep. Reluctantly, she allowed Patterson to help her to her feet and guide her to the ambulance. Maybe, if she permitted the EMTs to check her out, she could convince Evan to have one of the officers drive her to the Vincents' cabin.

Evan lifted the cup to his mouth and drained it. The coffee was strong and bitter, but he needed the caffeine boost before making the drive from the station to the cabin. He'd never intended to be away from Grace for this long, but it had been a long night. First, he'd had to complete the paperwork. Then, he'd had to go out to Ralph and Lydia Hebert's home to tell them their son was dead. As a parent himself, that was always one of the hardest parts of his job; no parent should ever have to bury their child. No matter what evil things Avery had done, his parents loved him.

He placed the mug on his desk and stood. Time to go to the cabin and see Grace. He needed to let her know they hadn't been able to confirm whether Avery was working with someone or alone. Valerie had been brought in for questioning, but she had seemed genuinely shocked that Avery had been the man who'd attacked Chloe and tried to kill Grace. She insisted she and Avery hadn't been dating long. As a matter of fact, the match race had only been their second date. Evan had no evidence to tie her to the attacks, and in his gut, he believed she was innocent.

Lifting a hand in farewell to Lieutenant Johnson, Evan stepped out of the station. The sun had begun to rise, casting the morning in a beautiful golden light. The beauty of the day brought joy to his heart, and he was suddenly in a great hurry to get to Grace.

A woman of medium height with shoulder-length black hair and unnaturally violet eyes blocked his path. Marcia O'Neal. What could have brought her to the station so early in the morning?

All of his senses instantly went on high alert. "Can I help you?"

"Chief Bradshaw, I..." She swallowed and

then blurted, "James Osborne is behind the attack on Chloe."

Evan's pulse quickened. Did James's mistress hold the evidence they had been searching for?

"Let's step inside and talk." He retraced his steps, holding the door open for her to precede him inside. Upon entering the building, he motioned to Johnson to follow them into his office.

Once the door was closed and Evan was seated at his desk with Marcia in the faux-leather guest chair facing him and Johnson standing to the side, Evan turned to Marcia. "Ms. O'Neal, would you mind repeating what you said outside?"

She looked at Johnson and said, "I have reason to believe James Osborne is behind the attack on Chloe."

Lieutenant Johnson leaned on the corner of the desk. "What led you to that conclusion?"

Marcia pulled a tissue out of the box on the desk. "I'm sure you've heard James and I, um, that we…"

"Have been dating?" Evan asked softly.

She nodded, absently shredding the tissue in her hands. "I'm not a home-wrecker you know. James told me the marriage was over. He moved out and was working toward getting his divorce."

"Marcia, what evidence do you have James is

behind the attacks?" Evan was tired and didn't have the patience needed to sit and listen to her rationale for taking up with a married man.

"I overheard a phone conversation last night." She took a deep breath, her eyes focused on destroying the tissue.

"I'm curious." He leaned forward, his elbows on his desk. "Why would James have such a conversation in your presence?"

Marcia met his gaze, unwavering. "He didn't know I was there. I thought I'd surprise him with a home-cooked meal. I made a lasagna." She looked back down at her hands, the tissue nothing more than confetti now. "When I went up the steps to the porch, I heard him on the phone. The windows were open. I peeked in the window to his office, thinking I'd get his attention so he could let me in, then I could go into the kitchen and set the meal up."

"But?" Johnson prompted. His focus zeroed in on the young woman, and Evan knew his lieutenant was reading her body language.

"James sounded furious. I heard him tell the person on the other end of the line they better not mess up the job like they bungled the last one." Marcia looked from Evan to Johnson and back again. "I don't know what *job* he was talking about."

"It's okay. I do." Evan's gut tightened. Instinct

told him James had been talking to Avery, and the job had been to kill him and Grace. "Did you hear anything else?"

"He told the person if they had…" Marcia shuddered and tears started streaming down her face. "Had…killed Chloe like they were paid to do, there wouldn't be a mess to clean up now."

Evan met Johnson's eyes. His lieutenant inclined his head in a subtle nod. He believed Marcia was telling the truth. So did Evan.

Reaching for his desk phone, Evan buzzed Reba Franklin and ordered the dispatcher to send an officer to pick up Dr. James Osborne and bring him in for questioning.

Johnson put a hand on Marcia's shoulder. "Is there any way James could know you overheard his conversation?"

She shook her head. "I left without him seeing me."

There was one more detail Evan had to know. "You said this was last night?"

"Yes. Around six o'clock."

Over five hours before he and Grace had landed in the ditch and Avery had been killed. He bit back an exclamation and took a deep breath, releasing it slowly. "May I ask why it took you twelve hours to report this?"

"I was in shock. I thought maybe I'd misheard the conversation." Her eyes pleaded with him to understand. "I couldn't reconcile that the man I knew would be capable of something like this."

"What changed your mind?"

"I heard about what happened last night. You and Dr. Porter. And Avery." Her voice cracked. "I got to thinking about how Dr. Porter was the one who saved her sister from the intruder, and it made me wonder if she was the *mess* James wanted *cleaned up.*"

Marcia wailed, "It's my fault. A man's dead. And you and Dr. Porter could have been hurt." She jumped out of her seat, the shredded tissue tumbling off her lap and onto the floor like snow. "I'm sorry I didn't come in last night. I wasn't trying to obstruct justice."

"It's okay. You came in. That's the important thing," Lieutenant Johnson said, pulling additional tissues from the box and pressing them into her hand.

Marcia settled back onto the chair, wiping her face and sniffling.

The phone on Evan's desk buzzed, and he picked up the receiver. "Yes?"

"Sir, we haven't been able to locate Dr. Osborne. He isn't at his house or the clinic."

"Okay, put an APB out on his vehicle. A black Por—"

"Excuse me, Chief Bradshaw," Marcia interrupted. "James told me he had to take his vehicle in for service Saturday afternoon and it would be in the shop for a few days."

"Do you know what he's driving in the meantime?"

"I know he got a rental. Last night, I noticed there was a white sedan in the drive. But I don't know the make or model. I'm sorry." She appeared deeply concerned she couldn't provide additional information.

"It's okay. You've given us a lot of important information." He reached out his hand. "Thank you for coming in."

Turning to his lieutenant, he added, "Take Ms. O'Neal to your office and write up her statement, then see she gets home safely."

Speaking into the phone, he relayed the new information and instructed Reba to have an officer check out the rental car places and dealerships within a thirty mile radius.

Time to get to the cabin and ensure Grace stayed safe. He exited the building at an almost full-on sprint, thankful he'd had enough sense to have an officer pick up his police SUV from his home and deliver it to the station after the accident last night.

Lord, please don't let James get to her. I just got her back in my life, and I'd really like to keep her there.

As friends. Or more, if she were willing.

FOURTEEN

A loud pounding rattled the cabin, and Grace bolted upright in bed. Barkley plodded to the bedroom door, barking. She picked her phone up off the bedside table and checked the time— 6:23 a.m. She had only slept about four hours. When Deputy Rice escorted her to the cabin a little before two, she'd found a note from Bridget's father, George Vincent, saying he'd stopped by and walked Barkley earlier, so she'd gone straight to bed.

The loud knocking came again. Jumping out of the bed, she quickly put her phone down and pulled on a long-sleeved Denver Broncos T-shirt and a pair of denim shorts.

Easing open the bedroom door, she started to tiptoe down the short hall. Then Barkley plowed into her, slamming her into the wall on his quest to get to the front door first.

"Ouch," she whispered as she rubbed the shoulder that had taken the brunt of the hit. She hoped whoever was at the door hadn't heard the bang.

Leaving all the lights off, she crept into the main living area and peeked out the curtain covering the window over the dining table. There was a white sedan parked in the drive. Who could it be? Her position didn't offer a clear view of the porch, but she could make out a man's silhouette.

"Open up, Grace," James's voice demanded through the door as he continued to pound on the solid wood surface.

Evan had only allowed her to return to the cabin alone because she had promised to stay inside and not open the door for anyone.

Barkley ran around and around in a circle, barking. He definitely wasn't good at being stealthy. The Great Dane's presence at the cabin didn't necessarily imply anyone else was there. Maybe James would leave.

She needed to call Evan. Quietly making her way back to the bedroom, Grace picked up her cell phone. No service.

The banging stopped, and James yelled, "Barkley! Down."

Barkley quieted. Grace inched back down the hall, pausing in the opening to the living area. The Great Dane lay down in front of the door, listening, his head tilted to the side.

"Grace, I know you're in there," James said into the silence. "If you can hear me, the hospital called. They couldn't reach you. Chloe—"

Grace flew across the room and fumbled with the lock, cutting off his words. Finally, she jerked the door open. James stood on the porch wearing a pair of black jeans, a white-and-gray-striped T-shirt and a lightweight gray jacket. He looked disheveled, his hair uncombed and his clothes wrinkled.

"What? What did the hospital say?"

James smiled. "Chloe is awake. She's asking for you."

"Why'd they call you? Why didn't they call me? Or Evan?" She eyed him suspiciously.

"They couldn't reach you." He arched an eyebrow. "I imagine you don't have the best cell service out here."

"Doesn't explain why they didn't call Evan." She looked at her phone. One bar. Not enough service to get a call out.

"Look. I don't know why they didn't call Evan. Maybe they tried, but he was busy. I don't know." James sounded aggravated, and he shoved a hand through his hair. "All I know is a nurse called and said Chloe was awake and asking for you."

"But why did they call you?"

He shrugged. "I guess Chloe never got around

to changing her medical records, and I'm still listed as someone who's allowed to have access to her health information." Turning and heading off the porch, he added, "Look, I don't need the third degree. I came to take you to your sister. I thought it was one last act of kindness I could do before the divorce is finalized and I'm no longer a member of the family."

He reached the new, white sedan and opened the door.

"Wait!" There was no way of knowing how long Evan would be tied up at the station, and she didn't have a vehicle at the cabin. If Chloe was awake, Grace needed to get to her as soon as possible.

"Let me put my shoes on and take care of Barkley. I'll be right back."

Closing the door and locking it, she hurried to the bedroom, put on her sneakers and grabbed her bag. Then she rushed back into the living room and quickly filled Barkley's water and food bowls. "Be good, boy. I'll make sure Evan or someone comes by soon to let you out. Okay?" She rubbed him between the ears.

Time to leave Evan a note. Opening kitchen drawers, she hunted down a notepad and a pen. Bingo. The third drawer had a yellow legal pad and an assortment of pens and pencils. Grace removed what she needed and started to close the drawer when her eyes fell on a small cylinder. Mace. She bit her lower lip. It couldn't hurt to have some form of protection. What if they ran into Torres or his goon?

The door handle rattled. "Why did you lock the door? Let me in." James roared, rattling it even harder.

"Sorry. I'll be right there," she yelled.

Slipping the Mace into the front pocket of her shorts, she pulled the loose T-shirt down over it, concealing the weapon. Then, she quickly jotted a note for Evan.

> James came to get me. Chloe woke up. We're headed to the hospital. Please take care of Barkley until I return.

She paused. She'd almost written *Love, Grace*. Out of habit? Or because she had fallen for him again?

Her hand hovered in the air, her heart racing.

No need to sign the note, he'd know it was from her. But it seemed incomplete without a closing, so she wrote the date and time and her initials, like she would on a medical record.

Grace dropped the pen onto the table. Looping the bag over her shoulder, she headed out of the cabin, bumping into James, who stood glaring at her. "Why did you lock the door?"

"Habit, I guess." She shrugged and headed down the porch steps to the sedan.

"Where's your sports car? Did you trade it?" she asked as he held the passenger door open for her. She settled onto the leather seat, taking in the new car smell.

"Oh, um. No." He closed the door and jogged around the front of the vehicle to the driver's side.

Grace knew how much James loved his sports car. Chloe had said it was his most prized possession. "If you didn't trade your car, why are you driving this one?"

"The dealership loaned it to me. Uh, my car is in the shop." He shifted into gear and pulled around the cabin, taking an old, rutted logging trail, tree limbs scraping against the new vehicle.

"Why are you going this way? It's smoother to go out past the main house and down the drive." Was he trying to keep her departure a secret?

"This way is shorter." He glared at her. "Aren't you in a hurry to get to your sister?"

"Of course." She fought to keep alarm out of her voice. "I'd hate for you to get the loaner scratched on my account."

"Don't worry about it. I'll cover any damages," he snickered. "Getting to the hospital fast is the most important thing right now."

He barely slowed down when he reached the

road, the tires spinning as he pulled onto the asphalt and sped away from Blackberry Falls, far exceeding the speed limit.

His behavior seemed reckless. The need to call or text Evan engulfed her. Slipping her phone out of her purse, she punched in his number. Nothing. *Don't panic.*

"Is your phone not working?" James nodded at the cup holder where his phone rested. "Use mine if you'd like."

Whew. He wasn't trying to isolate her or to keep her from telling anyone she was with him.

"Thank you." She picked up his phone and tried again. Nothing. What was going on?

"The cell towers could be experiencing an outage," James said as if he could read her mind.

"Maybe." She furrowed her brow. What were the odds of the cell service going out today of all days?

Evan wadded up the note. How had James found Grace? She should have been safe at the cabin. Had someone at the scene last night overheard him asking Deputy Rice to drop her off here? It would have only taken one person telling another where Grace was staying for news to spread quickly around town and into the ears of the one person they were fighting to protect her from. Once again, he'd failed a woman he loved. He slammed his fist on the table, causing the pen to bounce and roll onto the floor. Barkley yelped and took off to the bedroom to hide.

"Sorry, boy," he apologized to the Great Dane's retreating back.

Picking up the paper, he smoothed out the wrinkled note and reread Grace's message. According to the time she'd written, James had about a thirty-minute head start.

Evan barged out the door and hurried down the steps.

Wait a minute. How had James accessed the ranch unnoticed? The Vincents would have noticed an unauthorized vehicle entering and exiting through the main drive. A broken tree limb caught his attention.

Walking over to the area where the tree stood, he spotted tire tracks on an old, overgrown logging road. So that was how he'd done it.

Evan sprinted to his vehicle and followed the trail, his SUV bouncing over the uneven terrain. James must have been desperate to drive a rented sedan over a rutted-out logging trail. There was no way the vehicle wouldn't suffer some amount of body damage.

In his rush to leave the cabin, Evan had failed to check the guard duty roster to see which officer was at the hospital. He didn't want to stop long enough to pull up the email on his cell. Exiting the ranch onto the paved road, he hit the voice command button on the steering wheel and instructed the automated assistant to call Ryan.

His friend answered on the third ring. "Hi, Evan. What's up?"

"I'm driving and can't access my email. I need to know who's on guard duty at the hospital."

"The email wouldn't have helped you," Ryan replied. "Officer Nolan was supposed to be on duty, but he had car trouble, so Officer Wilkes came in his place."

"Okay, thanks—"

"Wait!" Ryan yelled before Evan disconnected. "What's going on? Did something happen?"

Evan quickly filled him in on the situation, including the information Marcia had shared with him. "If Chloe were awake, the hospital would have called me. They have strict orders to contact me if they can't reach Grace."

"I agree. It sounds like James used the only thing he could to lure Grace away from the cabin."

A new wave of guilt washed over him. "We must stop James before he reaches Chloe, but we've also got to keep him from hurting Grace."

"Uh…" Ryan paused for a second, as if struggling to find the right words. "Are you sure James is headed to the hospital? I mean Chloe's in a coma, and it's still unclear if she'll completely recover. Why risk going to the hospital at this point?"

Evan had been asking himself that same question since he'd first read the note, but it wasn't until this very moment that he figured out the answer. "Because he's meticulous and doesn't like losing. The person he relied on to take care of the situation failed. Then died. Now it's up to James to fix everything. Kind of like the adage, 'if you want something done right, do it yourself.' James's personality won't allow loose ends."

Muffled sounds echoed across the line, followed by the slam of a car door. "I'm headed to the hospital. I'll make sure a plan is in place. You just concentrate on getting here as quickly as possible."

"Are you sure? You can't have been home long after guarding Chloe last night."

"I'm sure. I'm only fifteen minutes away. Besides, there's no way I'd sleep knowing what was happening."

The weight on Evan's chest lifted ever so slightly, even though a panicked feeling of doom still lingered.

"Don't worry about things on this end," Ryan added when Evan remained silent. "If your timeline is correct, we have close to ninety minutes to head James off."

"Thanks, Ryan. Keep me posted."

"Will do." The line went dead.

Evan merged onto the interstate and accelerated well above the speed limit, racing to chisel away at the lead James had on him.

An hour later, there were only twenty miles between him and the hospital, and hopefully less between him and Grace. He couldn't imagine James would risk being stopped for speeding.

Evan itched to call Ryan but knew his friend was busy working out the security details and would call when he had a chance.

Traffic slowed ahead and then came to a halt. There was no sign of an accident, so he had no idea what had caused the standstill. Most likely it was a typical Denver traffic jam. He took a few deep breaths. Getting angry wouldn't help anything at the moment.

His cell phone rang, Ryan's number flashing on the display screen. He pressed the answer button on the steering column.

"What's happening?" Evan demanded, unable to conceal the fear in his voice.

"As soon as we hung up, I called in a favor with Denver Memorial's CEO. He met me at the hospital, and we've spent the past hour putting a plan into place."

"Please tell me the hospital isn't surrounded with police cars and flashing lights. James will bolt if he suspects his plan has been jeopardized, and then we could lose Grace forever."

"Come on, give me more credit than that. I know we've not stayed in close contact in recent years, but I am good at my job," Ryan reprimanded him.

He dragged a hand over his face. "You're right. I'm sorry. It's so hard not being there, and now traffic is at a standstill."

"Where are you?"

Evan supplied the number for the exit less than half a mile away.

"Are you in the right-hand lane? Can you take the exit?"

"Yes." Turning on his lights and siren, Evan merged onto the shoulder and exited the interstate.

Following Ryan's directions, Evan was soon on a new route to the hospital. "Okay, fill me in on the plan."

"Well, like you pointed out, we don't want to alarm James or force a showdown in a crowded area, especially since we don't know if he's armed or not. Instead, security will alert us to his presence. Then when they arrive at the Neuro ICU, an undercover officer posing as a nurse will tell them Chloe was moved to a new room after she woke up. They'll be directed to a room on another floor where we'll be waiting."

"Sounds like you've got everything covered."

"We can't plan for every contingency, but we'll do our best to control the situation."

"Okay, well tell Wilkes to keep me posted." At least he had one officer on scene.

He needed to get to Denver Memorial to ensure Ryan's plan was carried out flawlessly. If it failed, Evan didn't know if his heart would ever fully recover. He pressed down harder on the accelerator, praying James and Grace were stalled in the gridlock on the interstate.

Grace checked her cell for what seemed like the hundredth time. Still no service. She sighed and dropped the mobile back into her bag. Stuck in a traffic jam on I-25, they had moved less than a hundred yards in the last twenty minutes.

Even though James was becoming more agitated by the minute, muttering under his breath and striking his hand against the steering wheel, for the first time in her life, Grace understood the term "deafening silence." There had been very few words passed between her and James since they'd left Blackberry Falls. She had tried to start a conversation a few times, but only received curt replies in response. James had never been one for small talk. Before long, the silence in the vehicle had zoomed right past uncomfortable to complete awkwardness.

What did one say to their sister's estranged husband?

Now that she thought about it, Grace couldn't recall a single time in the three years of her sister's marriage where she'd had a conversation of any substance with her brother-in-law.

Since he didn't seem to want to talk, Grace used the time to have a lengthy conversation with God. First, she thanked Him for allowing Chloe to wake up, and asked for her sister's continued healing. Next she prayed for Evan and his emotional healing, from the trauma of his wife's murder and from his guilt for feeling like he'd let her down as a husband.

Dear Lord, Evan's a good man. Please, let him find love again. I know he'd be a good, caring husband, and he needs to realize it, too. And Camden needs siblings. He'd be such a good big brother.

A longing to be Camden's mom filled her. How had that little boy stolen her heart in such a short time? Because he was his father's child. A sharp pain stabbed her heart, and she caught her breath.

She loved Evan. Always had, always would.

If she had the slightest inkling he would give her a second chance, she'd move back to Blackberry Falls and take over the clinic. She could bear anything—even small-town living where everyone knew everyone else's business—to be with him. Only, small-town living hadn't seemed as much of a burden the past few days as she had believed it to be as a teenager. After hers and Chloe's attacks, the people had rallied behind her. The Vincents offering protection. The Greens providing a way into the match race, putting themselves at risk of retaliation. All the officers on the police force volunteering their time to keep Chloe safe so Grace wouldn't worry. She loved her hometown as much as she loved Evan. Reality hit her full-force, and she desperately wanted to hear his voice.

Digging in her bag, she pulled her phone out. Still nothing.

Maybe the guard outside Chloe's room could contact Evan for her. Who was on duty today? It didn't matter. Whoever it was, she was sure they'd help her out.

Traffic started moving, and soon James was speeding, maneuvering the rental car through the morning rush hour traffic, Grace's heart soaring with each passing mile. Turning to face James, she said, "Thank you for taking me to Chloe."

"My pleasure." The smile that tugged the corners of his lips didn't match the storm in his eyes. "It's only fitting I get to tell her goodbye."

The way he said the word "goodbye" sent a shiver of apprehension up her spine that wrapped around her chest and squeezed her heart. In that instant, she knew without a doubt she'd messed up by going with him. A sickening thought settled in her stomach like a dose of bitter reality. James wasn't taking her to Chloe out of kindness or a sense of family loyalty.

Maybe she was wrong. After all she'd been through the past few days, could she simply be chasing shadows in the dark? *Stay calm.*

"Goodbye?" She turned to study his profile. "Are you moving?"

"No."

"Oh." Grace tried not to sound disappointed, though she hated the idea of her sister running into her ex-husband and his girlfriend or, someday, his second wife, in the grocery store.

"I plan to keep working as a vet. In Blackberry Falls." James pushed his sleeves up, revealing a tattoo. A wolf inside a triangle, midway up his forearm.

Her breath caught. He was taking her to Chloe to kill them both. Grace had no idea how he intended to get past the guard, but she had no doubt he had a plan in place. James had always been a very methodical person. There was no way he hadn't considered all the contingencies.

She casually picked up her cell phone and tried Evan's number again.

"Have you not given up on getting a call

through to your boyfriend, yet?" James laughed. "Did you know you could buy a device that jams cell phone frequencies?"

That was why she didn't have service. And why James had offered her the use of his phone. He knew she couldn't make a call.

"You and Chloe both have the most expressive faces, making it so easy to read what you're thinking. I see you're finally starting to understand the situation."

No use denying the truth. "I believe so."

The sneer evolved into full-blown manic laughter.

Grace fidgeted with her hands, clenching and unclenching her fists until his fit subsided.

"Why are you doing this?" she asked. "Is it because Chloe's divorcing you? Or because you're trying to cover up the fact you've been using the clinic to supply drugs to racehorses?"

He sobered and glared at her. "If it wasn't for me, Porter Animal Clinic wouldn't be the successful, thriving business it is today. Your father was a bleeding heart. I can't even begin to count the number of house calls he made without billing for the services. Or the number of ranch owners who had overdue accounts. And he never charged a late fee."

"I will not listen to you bad-mouth my father.

He was a good man who tried his best to live by the Golden Rule."

"That *good man* was ungrateful and condescending. I brought in a lot of new clients—ones who never came in with sob stories to get out of paying—and even though I was married to his daughter, he planned to boot me out of the business. Said I was a sorry excuse for a vet."

"I never knew any of this."

"Yeah. Because he died in the car accident before he could tell anyone he'd fired me."

"You don't mean you…" She couldn't make herself say the words.

"Orchestrated his death? No. I didn't have anything to do with the accident." James smirked. "I just didn't try to save him when I happened upon the scene."

Grace gasped, tears stinging her eyes. Her fingers brushed against the canister of Mace in her pocket. Dare she use it right now? No. It would be too dangerous. She'd have to wait until they arrived at the hospital. Then she'd use it at the first opportunity.

"You might as well take it out of your pocket and give it to me."

"What?" she asked. He couldn't know she had a weapon.

"The Mace." He nodded toward her lap.

She glanced down and saw her shirt had ridden up, revealing the outline of the cylinder in her pocket.

"Did you think I wouldn't know what it was? Seriously, it's too big to be a tube of lipstick." He laughed. "Now, hand it to me and don't try anything funny. If you do, at this speed, you're guaranteed to take yourself out, too."

She pulled the Mace out of her pocket and deposited it into his outstretched hand.

"Good job, Amazing Grace," he guffawed.

Biting the inside of her cheek, she focused on the road ahead. She would not give him the satisfaction of acknowledging his use of her nickname.

They were about ten minutes away from the hospital. She'd been praying the entire ride a police officer wouldn't pull them over for speeding, keeping her from reaching Chloe as quickly as possible. Now, her prayer had shifted to the opposite. *Please, Lord, send someone to save me.*

James pulled across two lanes of traffic, barely avoiding being rear-ended by an 18-wheeler, and took the exit ramp.

"Don't try anything foolish," he commanded as he pulled into the Denver Memorial parking deck. "Or the deaths of innocent people will be on your head."

FIFTEEN

A feeling of déjà vu washed over Grace, her muscles taut and ready to spring out of the vehicle when it stopped. Four nights ago, she'd been in Evan's vehicle in a similar state of anxiety. The only difference was that this time she wouldn't sit and wait to be escorted into the building. When James stopped the vehicle, she planned to jump out and run with all her might. There was no way she'd placidly walk into the hospital with him, leading him to her sister.

He circled the first level of the deck and then took the ramp up to the second level, inching along in search of a parking spot. This was her chance. He was going so slowly, it wouldn't hurt too much to jump out. Right?

She wrapped her hand around the handle and pulled with all her might while pushing her shoulder against the door, but the door didn't budge. She tried again, James roaring with laughter in the background.

"Child safety locks are a wonderful invention, don't you think?" he asked as he pulled into a parking space and shifted the vehicle into Park.

Cutting the engine, he pulled a syringe out of the door pocket on the driver's side and turned to her. "I thought you'd like to see your sister, but if you can't behave, I can kill you now."

His face showed no emotion, his eyes cold as steel. "Well, what's it going to be? Do you want to get this over with and die here? Or would you like a little more time and a chance to say goodbye to Chloe?"

Her throat tightened and no words would form, striking fear in her that he'd take her nonresponse as agreement. Grace shook her head, finally managing to whisper, "I want to see Chloe."

"All right, then." James kept his eyes on her, the syringe still in his hand, while using his free hand to open the center console and remove a gun. "Now, you stay seated until I come around to let you out. If you try anything funny—like trying to escape or alert security—I will not hesitate to shoot you or anyone else in the area. Got it?"

She nodded, and her mind whirled. How was she going to get out of this mess?

"Dr. Porter, I'm so glad you're here." Evan heard the greeting through his earpiece. He was positioned in Room 1124 on the eleventh floor, and the female security guard posing as a nurse had just greeted Grace and James. Her words signaled that they had entered the reception area outside the Neuro ICU on the fourth floor. "Your sister is awake."

A gasp came over the earpiece.

"Really?" Grace asked at the same time James exclaimed, "What?"

"We tried to call but couldn't reach you," the undercover nurse replied.

"I've had horrible cell service today. But, um, we can wait to see her if the doctor needs to do scans and tests. You know, to make sure she's okay." Hopefulness mingled with fear in Grace's voice, propelling Evan toward the door of the room where he waited.

Bridget put a hand on his arm and shook her head. "I know it's hard, but you can't go barreling into the situation. Trust the plan."

He bit back a retort, closed his eyes and let her words sink in. Rolling his shoulders, he took a deep breath and released it slowly, willing some of the tension to subside. Bridget was right. He needed his head in the game, not his heart. Evan would do more harm than good if he tried to storm the waiting area of the Neuro ICU.

He nodded and stepped back, forcing himself

to focus on the words coming through the ear-piece. What had he missed?

"So Chloe has made a full recovery?" James asked.

"Dr. Carson says she's going to be fine," the undercover nurse continued.

Though Dr. Carson had said these very words last night, Evan hated that Grace was being given false hope her sister had awoken and was headed for a complete recovery. He prayed, after everything was over, she would understand they had only lied to save her and Chloe.

"Well, let's go see her," James commanded as footsteps echoed over the earpiece.

"No, not that way," came the urgent reply. "Chloe has been moved out of Neuro ICU. Actually, you just missed her. We moved her into a regular room on the eleventh floor. I'll have an orderly show you the way."

"That won't be necessary," James said gruffly. "Just tell us the room number."

"No trouble. Oh, Mark, perfect timing. Can you take Dr. Porter and this gentleman to Chloe Osborne's room?"

"Sure, no problem."

"Mark is the orderly who transported your sister to her new room."

The orderly was actually one of Ryan's Protective Instincts employees. His job was to keep

James and Grace in his sights at all times, ensuring James didn't detour from the carefully mapped-out plan.

"Really, there's no need. I'm sure Mark here has other duties he needs to see to," James insisted.

"No trouble at all," Mark answered. "This way, please." There was a ding, like the sound of elevator doors opening, and then muffled voices.

Ryan's voice broke through Evan's earpiece. "Okay, everyone. They're on the elevator."

From his position in the security office, watching the surveillance cameras, Ryan added, "We knew we couldn't control every scenario. Three other people were already on the elevator, and Mark wasn't able to prevent James from boarding. The elevator will stop on the seventh and ninth floors, but we won't allow it to stop on any others. I'm sending security to prevent other people from boarding."

Evan was impressed with Ryan's ability to get things done in a short amount of time. He really *was* good at his job, conducting the sting like a well-choreographed play with himself as the producer. Maybe one day, once this was all over and behind them, Evan could get his friend to explain how he'd pulled off such a large undertaking in less than two hours.

First, they had to save Grace. And save her they would, because Evan did not intend to spend another fifteen years without her in his life, even if it meant uprooting his and Camden's life and taking a job with the Denver PD. Or maybe he could get Ryan to give him a job at Protective Instincts. He'd concentrate on that after they had taken James into custody.

"What does it look like in the elevator?" Evan had to know.

"James is standing in the back corner, holding Grace almost like a shield in front of him. I can't be sure, but I suspect he has a weapon of some sort in his pocket he's using to threaten her." Ryan continued, "Looks like the takedown will happen as planned."

The eleventh floor, part of a new addition to the hospital, was still under construction. On the surface it looked complete, with the hallways and common areas painted and the nurses' stations outfitted with filing cabinets and monitors. However, a look into one of the patient rooms, with its half-completed molding and no bed or wardrobe, would make it obvious the floor was not yet in use.

"Okay, folks, this is it," Ryan said over the earpiece. "All the other people are off the elevator. Next stop, eleventh floor."

"I guess they sent Officer Wilkes back home,

huh?" James's voice sounded across the earpiece.

Evan was on full alert.

"No, sir. He's upstairs outside the room," Mark replied truthfully.

Evan had wanted his officer in on the takedown, so they had put a bodyguard from Protective Instincts outside Chloe's real room in the Neuro ICU.

"Why would he still be here?" James sounded incredulous. "The person who attacked Chloe was killed last night."

"I wouldn't know, sir," Mark replied.

Evan's mind whirled. How did James know who was on guard duty today? Especially since Wilkes hadn't even been on the schedule.

The elevator stopped with a slight jolt, and a ding announced their arrival as the doors opened. Grace stood rooted to the spot, her heart thrashing against her rib cage.

The orderly waved his hand toward the opening. "After you."

"No, you lead the way," James insisted. "We'll follow."

The man hesitated then met her eyes and smiled before he stepped out into the hall. If he knew he was leading her to her death, would he try to intervene? She opened her mouth, the words *Save me* desperate to escape, but closed it again. Grace would not be the cause of an innocent person being injured or possibly losing their life.

"Remember, don't try anything," James whispered into her ear before nudging her forward, the gun in his jacket pocket poking her back.

Grace nodded, her mouth too dry to form words. She followed the orderly down the hall, past the nurses' station where a lone male nurse was talking on the phone.

The eleventh floor seemed eerily quiet and there was a strong odor of paint and turpentine.

The orderly turned down the hall to the left of the nurses' station. A sign on the wall identified the hall as Eleven West. A man sat in a chair outside a room at the end of the long hallway. Officer Wilkes. Her heart soared at the sight of the familiar face. *Please, Lord, let him stop James.*

"Thank you for your help, Mark. We're fine on our own from here." James stopped, turned his back to the wall and pulled her to stand in front of him.

The orderly smiled and told them to have a good day as he turned to walk away, oblivious to Grace's struggle. She looked down the hall. Officer Wilkes stared in their direction. Could she alert him to the danger? She tried to signal him with her eyes, cocking them upward and to the side toward James like they always did in the movies. But the officer didn't budge. Maybe Evan was right. She watched too many whodunits. But, seriously, how could these people not see James was using her as a human shield?

Once the orderly had disappeared, James jerked her arm and led her down the hall toward her doom. As they drew closer, Officer Wilkes jerked his head ever so slightly at the door to room 1124. Was he trying to signal her? Was help inside? Her heart leaped.

Ten feet from their destination, James pulled the gun out of his pocket and put the barrel against the side of her head. "This is a setup."

Wilkes's eyes widened, and he jumped up from the chair, knocking it over with a clang. "Don't do anything foolish."

"Too late for that." James laughed. Walking backward, he pulled her through the door leading to the stairwell, the gun digging into her temple. Once inside, he raced up the stairs, dragging her behind him, his fingers biting into her upper arm.

"James, stop. Don't do this. Don't make things worse than they already are," Grace pleaded, but he continued on his mission, ignoring her appeals.

They were headed upward and had rounded

the first landing when, below them, the door they had come through flew open.

Evan filled the doorway. "Stop, Osborne! Let Grace go!"

James's reply was a bullet fired in Evan's direction while still dragging her up the stairs. The bullet pinged off the metal railing and ricocheted, hitting the wall a few feet above Evan's head.

Grace screamed and stumbled, banging her shins against a step. James jerked her upward by her arm, and she cried out as a fiery-hot pain shot through her shoulder.

"No!" Evan yelled. "You could hit Grace."

Grace looked down and over the railing. Officer Wilkes and Bridget Vincent had followed Evan into the stairwell, and Wilkes had his gun pointed in their direction.

The trio raced up the steps behind them, and at each turn, James fired in their direction, slowing them down. Thankfully, he had terrible aim.

Please, Lord, don't let James hit anyone.

"Get down!" Evan shouted as a bullet whizzed past his ear. It was the fifth time James had fired at them as they followed him and Grace up the stairs. This time the bullet had come closer to its target. Even with his terrible aim, Evan knew, if he fired enough times, James was likely to hit somebody.

Without being close enough to identify the exact handgun James was using, Evan couldn't be sure how many bullets he had left.

"My men have arrived on the roof and are in position," Ryan said over the earpiece as Evan, Wilkes and Bridget rounded the last landing in time to see James drag Grace through the door.

"They just stepped out onto the roof. Tell your men to stay out of view," Evan commanded. "James has shot at us five times. I don't know how many bullets he has left, and I don't want him to use one on Grace if he feels pushed."

"Yeah, I was counting, too. I'll try to ID the gun when he steps into view of the security camera. Let's pray he didn't do his research and he only has six rounds."

"It's a Glock 42 with a seven-round capacity, if he put one in the chamber and had six in the magazine," Wilkes said from behind Evan. "But I'm guessing he probably didn't know to put one in the chamber and then add an extra to the magazine, so he should only have one bullet left."

"How would you know?" Evan asked his officer. The older man didn't reply, his face impassive.

Questions nagged at Evan's brain. Like how had Osborne known Wilkes was guarding

Chloe today? And why had James suspected a setup after seeing Wilkes? Was it possible one of his officers—one who had showed him the ropes when he'd first joined the force as a rookie and who was only a few months away from retirement—could be corrupt?

"You need to go wait in the lobby, Wilkes. I'll talk to you once I'm done here."

"I can't do that. You need help rescuing Grace, and I need to know she's okay. I won't let you down. And I'll explain everything once Grace is safe and James is in custody."

"See that you do." Evan didn't like his officer having secrets, but he read sincerity in the man's eyes. He'd save judgment for later. Saving Grace was the priority right now.

"Okay, guys, we have them in our sights," Ryan said. "Grace looks okay, but she's holding her arm funny."

"I'm not surprised. Her arm made a sickening popping sound when he jerked her up the stairs earlier," Bridget chimed in. "Have a medic on standby, big bro. My guess is Grace's shoulder is either broken or dislocated."

Evan's gut tightened at the memory. "The longer we stand here chitchatting, the greater the chance she will be hurt a lot worse. Now, let's move."

The trio charged up the last rise of stairs.

Bridget and Wilkes had their weapons at the ready, having had them out since entering the stairwell. Evan pulled his service revolver from its holster and slowly opened the door. They stepped out into a small semi-enclosed area with a block wall obstructing their view of the roof.

"Ryan, tell your men no one shoots unless I give the okay," he instructed. Turning to Wilkes and Bridget, he added, "Stay out of sight. We don't want to agitate him."

Evan stepped out from behind the wall.

James was walking backward, facing him, while holding Grace tightly like a shield, the gun pressed to her head. "Don't come any closer."

"What's your plan?" Evan asked. "Do you expect me to provide you with an escape? Maybe a helicopter to take you far away?"

James smiled. "You're good at this, chief. That's exactly what I want."

There was no way Evan was going to let Grace out of his sight. Instinct told him the other man only had one bullet left otherwise he would have fired at Evan when he stepped into view on the rooftop. His only hope was to redirect James's focus onto himself, and maybe get him to release the last bullet, so Ryan's team could take him without a gunfire exchange.

"Remember, stay back," he whispered to his

team as he took a tentative step forward, his eyes locked on James.

"I told you, don't come any closer." James pointed his gun at Evan, his hand visibly shaking.

Good, let him keep it pointed at me and not Grace.

Evan bent, placed his gun on the ground and then stood with both hands up, palms forward. "I only want to talk."

"If you want to talk to someone, get your phone out and call for the helicopter."

"I hate to say it, but I think you've been watching the same whodunit movies Grace has." Evan snickered.

"You think this is funny, Chief?" James tightened his grip on Grace and she winced, her arm dangling at her side. "Do you want me to kill your girlfriend in front of your eyes? Maybe seeing one woman you loved die wasn't enough for you."

Grace gasped, but Evan willed himself not to react and kept his focus on James. "You know, Osborne, you've always struck me as being very intelligent. There's no way you can think I'd send in a helicopter to whisk you away. But even if I did send one, do you really think I wouldn't have a trained law-enforcement officer on board to take you out?"

"Well then, I guess you signed her death warrant." James turned the gun back to Grace.

"You kill her, and you've signed yours." Evan forced himself to keep his tone even and matter-of-fact while he slowly inched forward.

James walked backward, getting closer to the edge. About four feet of rooftop and a three-foot-tall block wall was the only thing between Grace and the ground.

"Uh, Evan, we've got a problem," Ryan said in his earpiece. "There's an incoming medical transport helicopter that needs to land where you're standing. ETA four minutes. Or less."

He froze. James and Grace were standing on the edge of the landing pad, with Evan in the center. There was no way he was going to move back and put more distance between himself and Grace. But if he continued to move forward, James would keep moving closer to the edge.

Dear Lord, help me end this showdown without anyone getting hurt.

He forced air into his lungs and then puffed it out. "If someone has a clear shot, take it," he said under his breath, praying James couldn't hear but Ryan and his men could.

Grace continued to struggle against James's grip, fear etched on her face. Evan had to put a stop to this. Time was running out.

"James, turn yourself in. Don't make it

worse," Evan pleaded. "There's an air ambulance helicopter coming. It needs to land—" he pointed to the helipad where they stood "—here."

"Well then, I guess they're going to have to land on top of us, aren't they?" James smirked.

"James, no. Stop this. They're bringing a criti—" Grace gasped as James dragged her backward by her injured arm.

"Yeah, then let's end this," he said, backing closer to the edge.

Evan rushed forward, and James turned the gun in his direction. "Don't make me kill you, too."

The whirling rotor noise of a helicopter sounded in the distance. James turned toward the sound, loosening his grip on Grace.

Evan watched, as if in slow motion, as she bent her arm, raised it and brought her elbow down on the inside of James's outstretched arm. His hand jerked upward, and the gun went off, the bullet shattering a floodlight on the side of the building.

Then she lifted her leg and brought her heel down on the top of her captor's foot. Caught by surprise, James lost his grip on her, and she ran as fast as she could in Evan's direction.

James straightened, lifting his gun and pointing it toward Grace's back.

Evan yelled, "Get down," but she couldn't hear him over the roar of the helicopter drawing nearer.

He reached behind his back and pulled his backup revolver from his waistband. But before he could get off a shot, a bright red circle appeared on James's chest, and he slumped to the ground.

Grace barreled into Evan, burying her head in his chest, tears soaking his shirt as a flurry of activity exploded around them. He slipped his arms under her, lifted her to his chest and ran to the stairwell. The helicopter hovered nearby, waiting to land, as a medical team and hospital security rushed to take care of James.

SIXTEEN

An hour later, Evan and Wilkes sat in a small room outside the surgical unit waiting area. The room, no larger than a broom closet with two hard-backed chairs, was a place for doctors to inform families how their loved ones did during surgery and what to expect for their recovery. In this case, Evan and his officer were waiting to hear if James had come through surgery.

Grace was asleep in the ER, one floor below them. Her shoulder had been dislocated and the doctor had given her a sedative before popping it back into place. She'd fallen asleep soon afterward, most likely from a combination of an adrenaline crash and the sedative. He'd left Bridget sitting with her, with strict orders to call him when she woke up.

He hated to be away from Grace even for a moment, but was glad for the opportunity to grill Wilkes about his connection to James.

"Let me get this straight." Evan leaned forward, elbows on his knees, as he studied Wilkes. "You've been working part-time as a bodyguard for James Osborne?"

"Yes, sir." Wilkes sat stoically, hands clasped and head bowed.

"How long has this been going on, and why didn't you tell me before?"

"He approached me a month ago. Said he owed this guy, Antonio Torres, some money, and he was getting threats because he hadn't been able to repay it. He said he only needed me for a month or two. Once his divorce was settled and the property divided, he'd be able to pay off Torres, and wouldn't need me any longer." Wilkes looked up, anguish in his eyes. "I didn't tell you or the other officers because I didn't want you to know I was having financial trouble, what with Martha's medical bills and all."

Wilkes's wife had been diagnosed with the onset of dementia a year ago, and he'd hired a nurse to stay with her while he worked. Evan felt instant remorse. He had checked on his officer's emotional health numerous times since the diagnosis, but he hadn't realized Wilkes might be struggling financially, too. Still, if there was the slightest possibility Wilkes had helped James with his plan to kill Chloe and Grace, there would have to be an internal investigation.

"Did you know he planned to kill Chloe and Grace?"

Wilkes gasped as if the words had slapped him. "No! I would have come to you immediately. I would never want either one of those girls hurt. Their daddy was a dear friend."

Evan hated to push further, but he had to know to proceed. "You didn't know his plan, but did you help him in any way?"

"Inadvertently, yes. He called to ask me to escort him home from the clinic Saturday afternoon. I told him I couldn't because I was at Mountain View Ranch with Dr. Porter." The older man's shoulders slumped. "I'm pretty sure that's how Avery knew where to find Grace."

"Anything else I need to know?"

"He called around five this morning to ask my availability for today. I told him I was headed to the hospital to cover Officer Nolan's shift because his vehicle wouldn't start."

"Which we now know was due to tampering. Johnson told me a few minutes ago someone had removed the fuel pump fuse from Nolan's car."

"Probably Osborne. He knew my work schedule, so he would have known I was off and would volunteer to come to the hospital in Nolan's place, especially since Martha is still in Albuquerque."

Wilkes met his gaze. "I'm sorry, sir. I only

put two and two together when you came in this morning talking about Osborne bringing Grace to the hospital. I should have told you then, but I was afraid he would know it was a setup if he didn't see me."

"About that. How do you think he knew it was a setup?" Evan could not figure out where they'd gone wrong. He was eternally grateful that Grace was alive, but the scenario should have had a better ending.

"Well, sir. When you look at the video footage, you'll see Grace trying to signal me with her eyes—"

"I've told that woman she watches too many whodunits." Evan sighed.

Wilkes smiled for the first time since they'd taken off chasing James and Grace up the stairwell. "It took all my willpower not to burst out laughing, but I felt sorry for her, so I tilted my head and offered what I hoped was an encouraging smile." He sobered. "Only, Osborne looked at me and our eyes met and…" He bowed his head.

It pained Evan's heart to see his officer, and one-time mentor, looking so old and defeated. "I have to place you on administrative leave until an internal investigation has been conducted to make sure you didn't break any ethics rules."

"I know…and after the investigation is over, I'll retire."

"You don't have to do that."

"Yes, I do. It'll be for the best. I can be home to take care of Martha and spend time with her before she forgets who I am."

Evan's cell phone rang, and Agent Ingalls's number displayed on the screen. "Bradshaw here."

"I thought you'd like to know, we found Avery's phone in the wreckage. Antonio Torres tipped him off that when you left the diner, you turned in the opposite direction of the interstate."

"That's how he was able to find us. Avery had to have known I'd take that route back to Blackberry Falls." Evan sat up straighter. "Does this mean Torres is involved in the attacks on Chloe and Grace?"

"No. According to the text, the information was given as a means to clear up a debt Torres owed Avery. You don't have to worry about Torres any longer. The other reason I called was to let you know he's disappeared."

"What? When did this happen?"

"We've not been able to locate him since you and Grace saw him at the diner. The house where he was staying has been cleaned out." A heavy sigh sounded across the line. "Unfortunately, this is his standard MO. When he feels like the authorities are getting close, he closes up shop and goes into hiding. In a few months, he'll find a new location and start his operation up again. When he does, I'll be there."

"I'm sure you'll get him next time." There was a knock at the door. "Sorry, I've gotta go. Let me know if you ever need my help again."

Evan disconnected the call as Ryan entered the room, a somber expression on his face. "James Osborne died on the operating table."

The next morning, fumbling with the roll of masking tape, Grace slipped her thumbnail under the cut end, inched it along until she'd loosened a piece about three inches in length, and then used her teeth to tear the tan-colored tape. Success. Sliding the roll of adhesive into the sling supporting her right arm, she pulled the note announcing the clinic's temporary closure from under her arm and one-handedly taped it to the glass door at the entrance of the clinic. The note was hung crookedly, but it would do.

"Come on, Barkley," she called to the Great Dane lying on the floor in front of the receptionist desk as she headed for the stairs to the apartment.

She'd only taken a few steps when someone knocked on the glass door. Couldn't people read?

Grace turned. "I'm sorry, we're—"

Camden stood on the other side of the door grinning at her. "Grace, let me in."

Evan stood behind his son, a matching grin on his face and a picnic basket in his hand.

Unlocking the door, she stepped aside to let them enter. "What are you guys doing here so early?"

"We brought you breakfast. And flowers," Camden said, pulling a bunch of wildflowers triumphantly from behind his back. "Dad said you got a boo-boo and we needed to make you feel better." The child stared up at her with a hopeful expression on his face. "Did we?"

She smiled and knelt beside him, his eyes melting her heart. "Yes, you did."

He threw his arms around Grace's neck and she grimaced.

"Careful there, buddy. You don't want to hurt Grace's arm." Evan put his hand on his son's shoulder and pulled him back a little.

"I'm sorry. Did I hurt you?" Concern etched Camden's face.

"No." Grace shook her head. "I tell you what. Why don't you see if Barkley will follow you up to the apartment, and I'll let you feed him? Then we'll have breakfast."

"Oh, boy! Come on, Barkley, I'll race you!" The child took off running, laughter floating behind him as the Great Dane followed close behind.

Trying to stand, Grace wobbled and tilted backward. Evan dropped the basket onto the floor and rescued her, helping to steady her.

"Thank you."

"My pleasure," he murmured, his face so close she could smell the faint scent of his shaving cream.

Her eyes widened. "You shaved."

"If I recall, you once said you preferred me clean-shaved." He winked, turned and headed toward the stairs.

Her heart raced, and she fanned herself with her free hand. She had said that—when they were sixteen. He'd grown a mustache, and it had tickled when he kissed her.

"Are you coming?" he asked, smiling at her from the foot of the stairs.

If he continued to look at her like that, she'd follow him anywhere.

Thirty minutes later, Grace had eaten her fill of chocolate-chip muffins, fruit, and a ham-and-cheese quiche. "My dear Chief, I didn't realize you were such a superb chef."

Camden giggled. "Dad didn't cook. Grammy did."

"Hey, buddy, you're not supposed to tell your

old man's secrets." Evan smiled and playfully tickled him while he squealed with delight.

A horn sounded outside. "Who could that be?" Grace asked, getting up to look out the window.

"Grammy's here!" Camden hugged Barkley. "Gotta go, boy. It's field trip day!"

She met Evan's laughing eyes as Camden gave her a side hug, being mindful of her arm in the sling, and bounded to the door leading to the outside stairs.

"I guess that answers your question. I'll walk Cam out then I'll be right back."

Evan opened the door and followed his son down the steps as she watched from the window.

After Evan retrieved Camden's backpack from his vehicle, he checked that his son was fastened into his booster seat. Then he kissed his mom's cheek, turned and headed back in Grace's direction. Pausing on the bottom step, he looked up at her with a smile and winked. He'd caught her staring.

Grace turned and busied herself clearing the breakfast dishes, a difficult task with her heart racing and one arm in a sling. Other than the ride back to Blackberry Falls, she and Evan hadn't been alone since she cried in his arms after escaping James. And she'd slept most of the way home after taking a pain pill the doctor had prescribed.

The door opened, and Evan came over to her, taking the plate out of her hand.

"I'll get this. You go rest on the couch."

Before she could protest, he turned and began loading the dishes into the dishwasher, whistling a tune as he worked.

Grace did as he suggested and settled on the couch. Tucking her feet under her, she pulled a lightweight floral-print throw across her lap, leaned her head against the cushion and closed her eyes. Her mind hummed with a myriad of thoughts. She had so much she needed to say to Evan. Could she string the words together into coherent thoughts? Was this how he'd felt on graduation day when he'd come to her, offering her his heart forever?

"Penny for them."

"What?" She opened her eyes to see him walking toward her.

"When I was younger, any time I looked deep in thought, Grandma Bradshaw would offer me a penny for my thoughts." He sat beside her on the couch, his smile reaching all the way to his eyes. "I always thought it was the funniest thing to say. But just now, seeing your brow furrowed, I suddenly realized I'd give much more than a penny to know what you're thinking."

"I was thinking how blessed I am. Yesterday, I didn't think I'd live to see today." She shrugged. "But here I am. I'm not going to take that for granted."

He took her hand in his. "Grace—"

Her cell phone rang, cutting off his words. Bridget Vincent's number flashed on the screen. Reaching for it, she slid her finger across the screen and hit the speaker button.

"She's awake, Grace! Chloe is awake!"

"What?" Grace looked at Evan. "I thought Dr. Carson wasn't going to try to bring her out of the coma for another day or two."

"I don't know what happened. Or why he changed his mind. All I know is I stopped by to visit, you know it kind of became a habit, seeing her every day, and…"

"Bridget, you're rambling," Evan interjected. "Does Chloe seem to be okay?"

"I'm sorry. Yes, she seems perfectly okay, other than a headache, but I guess that's normal. I mean she did sustain a bump on her head."

"Bridget, you're doing it again." Grace laughed, having a hard time rallying anger at the talkative girl. "Can you stay with Chloe until I get there?"

"Yes. Of course."

"Great, see you soon." She disconnected before Bridget could start rambling again. Then reality hit. "Oh. You weren't planning to drive me back to Denver until this afternoon. If you need to work this morn—"

"Nope. I'll take you as promised." He looked around. "Are your bags packed?"

"By the door." She nodded at the small overnight case she'd put there earlier.

He frowned. "What about the rest of your bags? I assumed you wouldn't be coming back for a while."

"Why would you think that?"

"Isn't that why you closed the clinic?"

"I closed the clinic because the doctor said I needed to wear this sling for three or four days. But also so I could go back to Denver to oversee my apartment being packed up."

"You're moving?"

"Yes. Back to Blackberry Falls."

His eyes widened, and she rushed on, needing to explain her change of heart. "The past five days have taught me this is where I belong. With people who love me enough to want to know everything going on in my life, so they know I'm okay. And when I'm not, I know they'll be there to pick me up and cheer me on."

"Are you sure you're okay with the *gossips* knowing all of your business?" he teased.

"I have lived in my apartment for ten years. Not one person in my building has a clue about the struggles I've been through. And if they did, they wouldn't care. They would think it wasn't their business." She nodded toward the basket on the table. "Your mom made me breakfast. Officer Wilkes has offered to mow Chloe's lawn, and Lieutenant Johnson is driving my vehicle to Denver so I'll have it to bring Chloe home. Oh, and Valerie is coming over in a little while to get Barkley so he can stay with her until Chloe and I get back."

"Have you forgiven Valerie?"

She recalled her friend's tearful phone call a few hours earlier. "Nothing to forgive. James manipulated her, like he did everyone else. He's the one who set her up with Avery Hebert, and he's also the one who told her I saw Avery's face when he attacked Chloe." Grace smiled. "Valerie is a friend, and I appreciate her desire to help me during this time."

"It's nice having people there for you. Helping you out and showing support."

She nodded. "Yes, that is nice. It's also nice being near the ones you love."

She bit her lower lip. Time to tell him. If he rejected her, she'd be okay, but she would never forgive herself if she didn't tell him what was in her heart.

She took his hand in hers, her eyes never leaving his. "I'm sorry I hurt you. That it took me fifteen years to realize how rare our love was."

"What are you saying?"

"I hope, now I'm moving home, you'll give me a second chance. And…" She took a deep breath.

"And?" His eyes twinkled.

"I know we can't rush things. I mean Camden has to get to know me. But I hope someday we can be more than friends again."

"Are you asking me to marry you?" He wasn't cutting her any slack, but she didn't care.

"Maybe someday I will."

"Why wait?"

"You don't even know anything about my life these last fifteen years."

"I know enough about who you are now to know I still love you. Nothing that happened will change that."

Her hands shook, and he squeezed them. "Evan Curtis Bradshaw, I love you, and I do not want to spend another minute of my life without you and Camden in it. Will you marry me?"

"I thought you'd never ask." He lowered his head and claimed her lips, and she knew she was finally home.

EPILOGUE

Five months later

"I can't do this!" Evan threw his hands up and stared at his reflection in the mirror. "Why did I let the salesman talk me into getting a self-tie bow tie?"

"Because, my friend, pre-tied bow ties look cheap and lack the elegance of a self-tie. And on your wedding day, it's important to look refined." Ryan laughed and turned Evan to face him, his fingers working quickly to complete the task at hand. "You're nervous, that's all."

"Nervous? I'm not nervous. I am ecstatic. This is the day I've dreamed of for half of my life." Evan caught a glimpse of Lisa's mom in the doorway, a sad smile on her face. He turned to her. "I'm sorry, Mom. I didn't mean that the way it sounded."

She smiled, tears glistening in her eyes. "I know."

Ryan quietly slipped out of the room, leaving them alone.

"Lisa loved you, and I know you loved her, too."

"I miss her," he acknowledged. "I will always miss her."

Sally Miller gave him a hug and then pulled back. "She would want you to be happy. So do her dad and I. We can't bring her back, but promise me, you will keep her memory alive for Camden."

"Of course! And, since Grace's parents are deceased, both of us hope you and Dean will be grandparents to any brothers or sisters Cam might have one day."

A smile lit her face, and she placed a hand on his cheek. "We'd be honored." Wiping her eyes, she added, "I was afraid you'd get busy with your new family and forget us."

"You can't get rid of me that easy." Evan bent and kissed his mother-in-law's cheek. "I love you, Mom."

"It's time." Ryan entered the room, Camden and Barkley at his heels. The latter wore a special doggie bow tie that matched the ones the wedding party wore.

"I'll leave you guys and get to my seat," Sally said, bending to kiss Camden on the top of his head.

"Okay, guys, let's do this." Evan led the way out of the room to where the preacher waited.

The small group went down the hall and entered the front of the auditorium through a side door.

The decorations were simple and elegant. Candles flickered on the windowsills, and the pews were adorned with sprays of white flowers and greenery.

In spite of an early season snowstorm that deposited an unexpected eight inches of snow overnight, the small church where Evan and Grace's families had always worshiped was packed with friends, neighbors and loved ones.

The music began and Evan, with Ryan, Camden and Barkley at his side, turned to face the double doors his bride would walk through. The doors opened and Chloe, wearing a long navy blue gown, entered.

When she reached the stage, his soon-to-be sister-in-law smiled and whispered, "Wait until you see your bride."

A moment later, Evan's breath caught as Grace glided down the aisle toward him. She was wearing her mother's wedding dress, a flowing white gown with a beaded-lace bodice, her hair gathered into a low bun. Her face was beaming.

He met her at the foot of the stage, unable to take his eyes off her. "You. Look. Gorgeous."

She laughed. "What? This old thing?"

"I love you," they said in unison.

The preacher cleared his throat. "Would you two care to join me on the stage, so we can proceed with the ceremony?"

The audience laughed, and Evan offered his arm to Grace as they took the steps to their happily-ever-after.

* * * * *

*Uncover the truth in thrilling stories
of faith in the
face of crime from Love Inspired Suspense.*

*Look for six new releases every month,
available wherever
Love Inspired Suspense books
and ebooks are sold.*

Find more great reads at
www.LoveInspired.com

Dear Reader,

Thank you for reading my first Love Inspired Suspense. I hope you liked Grace and Evan's story. When we are faced with loss and difficult times, it's easy to lose faith and turn from God, like Evan did. Often, it takes another life-altering event to lead us back to God for the strength that only He can provide.

As I was writing this story, I knew Grace had to be a strong woman who had moments of vulnerability but would ultimately face danger with strength and, well, grace. I also knew Evan had to be a man of action who loved his family and his hometown, but who, being a widower, guarded his heart and didn't believe he deserved a happily-ever-after.

I would love to hear from you. Please connect with me at www.rhondastarnes.com or find me on Facebook @AuthorRhondaStarnes.

All my best,
Rhonda Starnes